Social History

General Editor Jeremy Black

Social History in Perspective is a series of in-depth studies of the
many topics in social, cultural and religious history for students. They
also give the student clear surveys of the subject and present
the most recent research in an accessible way.

PUBLISHED

FORTHCOMING

Titles continued overleaf

Please note that a sister series, *British History in Perspective*, is available which covers all the key topics in British political history.

EDUCATION IN
EARLY MODERN ENGLAND

Helen M. Jewell
Senior Lecturer in History
University of Liverpool

First published in Great Britain 1998 by
MACMILLAN PRESS LTD
Houndmills, Basingstoke, Hampshire RG21 6XS and London
Companies and representatives throughout the world

A catalogue record for this book is available from the British Library.

ISBN 0–333–63642–2 hardcover
ISBN 0–333–63643–0 paperback

First published in the United States of America 1998 by
ST. MARTIN'S PRESS, INC.,
Scholarly and Reference Division,
175 Fifth Avenue, New York, N.Y. 10010

ISBN 0–312–21747–1

Library of Congress Cataloging-in-Publication Data
Jewell, Helen M.
Education in early modern England / Helen M. Jewell.
    p.   cm. — (Social history in perspective)
Includes bibliographical references (p.   ) and index.
ISBN 0–312–21747–1 (cloth)
1. Education—England—History.   I. Title.   II. Series.
LA631.5.J49   1998
370'.942—dc21   98–7577
                                                                        CIP

This book is printed on paper suitable for recycling and made from fully managed and
sustained forest sources.

10   9   8   7   6   5   4   3   2   1
07   06   05   04   03   02   01   00   99   98

Printed in Hong Kong

CONTENTS

The well Educating of their Children is so much the Duty and Concern of Parents, and the Welfare and Prosperity of the Nation so much depends on it, that I would have every one lay it seriously to Heart.

John Locke, *Some thoughts concerning Education*, prefatory letter to Edward Clarke of Chipley, 7 March 1690

PREFACE

Everyone has ideas about education. Adults reminisce about subjects they liked or disliked at school, and popular or hated teachers, generally thinking less about the nature and ethos of the institutional side. Across the generations arguments range over falling or different standards, selective and comprehensive teaching, single-sex and mixed schools. Subtle and not so subtle changes pushed by governments nudging students towards, or driving them from, particular subjects in what is deemed national interest are acknowledged. Everyone who has been through the education process, and continues to have involvement in it as a parent, teacher or ratepayer, feels to have something to say about it. So education is controversial: socially, politically and religiously.

In its history, it proves equally full of controversy, though distance soothes. The nature of the subject requires care to avoid giving unintentional offence. Contemporaries made comments about the educational practices of classes, sects and races, meaning to be offensive in some cases, being well-intentioned in others, but often being equally ill-informed; it is not easy now to handle these justly, yet misleading to ignore them. Discrimination against women was so essentially part of the mindset of the times that it would do violence to the atmosphere to fudge this; equally anachronism may be committed in using a term such as 'feminist', bearing all its modern connotations, of a woman such as Mary Astell. In researching this book I found the diversity of viewpoints taken by individuals writing for different purposes in times of different educational fashions stimulating, but in writing it I found this variety a problem. It is clearly impossible to write a history of early modern education fair to all reasonable cases and causes yet short enough not to exhaust its readers' patience. At the same time an overall consensus interpretation would be bland to the point of boredom. I therefore present what follows as my unashamedly selective analysis of education in early modern England.

One of my convictions is that a survey of education is only valuable if it embraces all levels of educational activity going on at the time. I do not wish to concentrate on the academic elite, about whom much has been written already. I personally find the opening-up of literacy to ever more of the population a particularly interesting subject, but I confess I may err on the side of optimism in inclining to credit halting readers of this period with the motivation, time and opportunities to improve their skill. However I am not so naive as to suppose this would have been easy for them. Still, the pedlars carrying the cheap printed word into the northern fells impress me. I am unapologetic for attempting to raise the subject of women's education in all walks of life in this period, because I believe this is not just a fashionable focus now, but a worthwhile one given the available evidence. A surprisingly wide range of individual women demonstrated that they had been educated, if untypically. We need to know the typical but need not be restricted to it. My view of educational development is not an institution-led history. I believe the history of education is much more than the history of schools, and I believe that this is particularly true of periods before the advent of state-controlled education which was in England a feature of the nineteenth century.

The bibliographies indicate my indebtedness to over a century of writers on different aspects of the subject. Earlier works are no help if they cannot be obtained, and I am pleased to acknowledge here my appreciation of the unfailing efforts of the staff of the Sydney Jones Library, University of Liverpool, to facilitate my researches on this, as on earlier, projects. Michael Collinson, Gordon Forster, Barrie Dobson and Cecil Clough encouraged my earlier forays into writing on aspects of education in late medieval and early eighteenth-century England, and so gave me the confidence to accept Jeremy Black's invitation to write this book. I am pleased to record here my appreciation of all this help.

HELEN M. JEWELL

1

INTRODUCTION

What constitutes education is a matter of diverse opinion. In the history of education, emphases on its purpose, method and content have always fluctuated with social changes. All communities train their young to behave in conformity with certain social expectations. Communication skills begin to be taught early, first aurally and orally, by talking to the baby or stimulating (or soothing) it with music or other noises, which it is encouraged to repeat, and later to re-create, purposefully, as it begins to understand a meaning to individual words. Philosophers recommended ways of teaching the young as far back as Plato and there has been no lack of theories from his day to ours.

By watching and copying and becoming involved in helping older relatives, children learn, as they always have, socially useful skills such as fetching and carrying, minding a younger baby, doing allocated chores in home and garden, and making any suitable contribution to the parents' trade or craft. Informally, by such unstructured learning, children who were going to support themselves by agricultural or domestic labour could learn at home the 'transferable skills' which would eventually render them employable when they became able to sell their labour. In early modern England children's labour apparently began to be saleable at about the age of seven. Some employments, however, have always been more demanding: technical crafts require formal apprenticeship, and intellectually demanding careers, which arose first in the church and the law, require education of the type generally termed 'academic'; here the practitioners are hardly fully qualified by their mid-twenties.

Learning is a continuous process, not confined to childhood, and it has many media. Not all of this learning process is considered formal education. In England today, for example, children become literally 'house-trained' in infancy. They may learn plastic modelling at playgroup, under supervision. They learn not to grasp nettles by painful experience in field or garden. Early formal schooling inculcates the basic intellectual skills of the 'three R's', reading, writing and arithmetic; later the children advance to more complex development of these subjects, including such studies as foreign languages and science. They are taught games with rules such as football or tennis. Outside formal education, which the state insists upon, they may voluntarily attend riding school or dancing class, or learn snooker at a youth club or canoeing on an Outward Bound course. They may have educationally beneficial access to television and home computers. Some visit art galleries, museums and stately homes with their families, or are taken on such visits, at home or abroad, by schools. As young adults they may enter some form of youth training, or the more academic pass into higher education, a sector vastly expanded in recent years. Some stay at university beyond graduation, even into postdoctoral research, while the Open University continues to attract adults whose formal education often ended years earlier with their potential unfulfilled. What parts of all this are education, what parts training, what parts hobbies, what parts recreation? Are they separable, in fact? A programme of social rehabilitation, in some eyes, may seem to others a tearaway's holiday at the taxpayers' expense. The pattern today is more complex than in earlier times, and the options are wider, but the mature adult is and always has been a product of many experiences.

To some extent all learning and training processes can be considered as education. But when people are described as 'educated' it is usually meant that they have advanced beyond assimilating the basics of acceptable behaviour, and beyond bare literacy and numeracy. This more selective definition of education involves the exposure of the pupil to a recognisable curriculum far exceeding the basic requirements for practical social participation. It embraces a core of subjects which, though adapted to successive generations' needs, have a long history as pedagogic requisites, incorporating values from more than two thousand years of civilisation.

Taking early modern times in broad terms as the period between the Reformation and the Industrial Revolution, from around 1530 to around 1760, it can be seen as an extraordinarily unsettled yet formative era in English educational history. The evolved educational ideas of the later Middle Ages were shaken up in rapid succession by the ideological influences of humanism, the Reformation and the Counter-Reformation, and subsequently influenced, more gradually, by the sustained struggle between orthodox Anglicanism and nonconformity, both Catholic recusancy and Protestant dissent. Chapter 2 will begin with a description of education on the eve of the Reformation, to show that the changes ushered in during the 1530s were not sudden jolts to a long fossilised system. As early as 1488 the University of Cambridge had amended its Arts curriculum to begin with two years of humane letters before a third year of logic and a fourth of philosophy, increasing the weighting of humane learning in the prescribed studies. Already on the eve of the Reformation the grammar schools in England were reflecting the spread of humanist ideas. John Colet's foundation at St Paul's was begun in 1509, and in 1512 placed under the management of the Mercers' Company, and under the tuition of a married master, William Lily. Active teachers were producing useful textbooks, updating earlier works. To John Stanbridge, successively master at Magdalen's grammar school and master of St John's hospital at Banbury, are credited an unoriginal *Accidence* (on parts of speech), two short English tracts on adjectives and irregular verbs, an updated *Parvula* (a short tract on elementary syntax), a *Vocabularia* (vocabulary of Latin words) and a *Vulgaria* (collection of English sentences with model Latin translation). His works were soon in use at Eton, St Paul's and Winchester, and 'Stanbridge grammar' was prescribed in the 1525 statutes of the grammar school at Manchester. Stanbridge's usher at Magdalen, John Holt, wrote the elementary grammar book *Lac Puerorum* (*c*.1497). Stanbridge's pupil, Lily, first high-master of St Paul's, was a grammarian, and it was largely his work which emerged as the prescribed King's Grammar in 1540 (*Institutio compendiaria totius grammaticae*). This remained the standard Latin grammar until transformed into the Eton Latin Grammar of 1758. On the eve of the Reformation the English grammar schools, and indeed the universities, were already responding to the new humanist emphases on elegant instead of functional Latin, and on the Greek language, and were beginning to build out with man-centred history and the self-improving potentiality of a liberal education in poetry, history, philosophy and oratory.

Although the medieval grammar schools had ecclesiastical origin, by the late fifteenth century there were already secular influences and requirements being acknowledged, and the archiepiscopal founder of

Jesus College Rotherham (1483), recognising that many able youths did not all aspire to the priesthood, established for them within the foundation facilities for the teaching and learning of writing and accounts, to fit them better for 'mechanical arts and worldly business'. By the early sixteenth century much business, and pleasure, was communicated in writing in the vernacular, which meant that there was more motivation to learn to read in English. The reading schools were already, before the Reformation, catering for an enlarged demand for vernacular literacy, and using the new products of the printing presses to teach it. Meanwhile printing also encouraged more people to want to learn to read.

Just as it needs emphasising that change itself was not totally new, it also needs acknowledging that some quite fundamental changes trailed familiar trappings. After the Reformation education was little more free from church control than before. The institutional system inherited from the Middle Ages, which had developed initially within the church to train clergy and clerical auxiliaries, remained within the purview of the church, but began to feel the pressure of state intervention as the post-Reformation Anglican church became virtually the religious arm of the state. Control took a variety of forms: standardisation of teaching material (by way of the authorised Latin grammar, and a succession of Latin, and later English, primers and catechisms), proscription of subjects (canon law was ejected from the university syllabus), the licensing of schoolmasters (rather more comprehensively than that exercised by cathedral chancellors in the Middle Ages) and their binding by oath to church and state orthodoxy. The new wave of inspection and licensing began under Mary; then from 1563 schoolmasters had to subscribe to the Thirty-nine Articles and to the Royal Supremacy. The bishops had the licensing of Latin schoolmasters, who by the 1571 canons were to teach only the grammar the queen commanded to be read in schools, and the 1570 Latin catechism, with the English translation for young children ignorant of Latin. The abolition of the bishops in 1646 removed this licensing machinery, but major-generals and commissioners granted licences to teach, and after the Restoration the grip of orthodox Anglicanism on education tightened at law. By the Act of Uniformity (1662) schoolmasters, along with clergymen, had to swear the illegality of taking arms against the king, declare their conformity to the Church of England as by law established, and deny the binding force of the oath 'commonly called the Solemn League and Covenant'. Both Catholic recusants and Protestant nonconformists were targeted in these regulations, which were part of the Clarendon Code, but for both religious extremes the education of the young in what their parents so fervently believed, despite all the disadvantages such dissent entailed, was not easily suppressed. There is evidence of clandestine Catholic schooling remaining available in England, and in addition Catholic children of both sexes were sent abroad for education, despite the penalties this could court. Nonconformists set up schools and dissenting academies which also offered a higher education, since nonconformists were barred from the two universities.

In the century after the Reformation the state increased its control over education without taking corresponding responsibility for the costs. The basic funding of educational facilities was only exceptionally, in the 1650s, a state concern. Normally educational provision depended on existing endowments, new benefactions and current fees. An early shake-up here occurred through the dissolution of the chantries, whereby teaching facilities which were part of a chantry foundation ceased to be funded from the chantry's landed endowment and were supported instead, where the commissioners recommended continuation, by fixed-rate funding from the court of augmentations. It was soon apparent that this did not work well, and some schools were fortunate to regain endowment with ex-chantry lands. Where they did not, they were unlucky, as the fixed funding usually took the form of provision of the master's salary as at the date of dissolution, so inflation eroded its purchasing power. Intentionally or otherwise the educational provision was devalued, and schools either foundered or relied on new private or municipal endowment, or increased fees. The extraordinary period of the Interregnum boldly tackled the issue of state-funded education more directly, and an annual grant of money was voted for educational purposes in 1649. This was paid out of the confiscated lands of deans and chapters, to which the revenues returned after the Restoration. It was, like the parliamentary constituency reforms of the period, a brave and forward-looking brief experiment which suffered suffocation after 1660 for over a century and a half.

Exciting though experiments with state funding of education were, other changes crowded round them. The seventeenth century was particularly one of new ideas in terms of syllabus and methodology and change in the types of teacher and pupil, and numbers of participants. Some very interesting proposals for educational change survive from the period, from such men as Samuel Harmar, John Dury, Samuel Hartlib and John Comenius, covering all ranges of opinion from extending to restricting educational opportunity. It was almost always agreed that it was desirable to produce dutiful children, industrious servants and discreet masters. Fear that opening up education more democratically would lead to disruptive social discontent was obviously widespread enough to need counteracting by those who were radical in promoting education but still envisaging basically the preservation of the social status quo. In the next century the Charity School movement harnessed these sympathies with the avowed aim of making children tractable and submissive.

An educational revolution, located between 1560 and 1640, has been challenged as only intermittent, and largely confined to higher education (see Chapter 2). Certainly this period was not one of steady overall progress in terms of scholarship or even of basic literacy. There were surges forward, and lapses back, not all happening at the same time in different places, and some affecting only particular sectors of the population. J. H. Gleason's *The Justices of the Peace in England 1558 to 1640* (1969) shows the educational advance made by the magistracy in five counties and just one of the Yorkshire ridings, the North, over the period. In the North Riding, the early Elizabethan bench – with relatively few inns of court or university men, and little overlap with members of parliament – became a Caroline bench of men, with much the same experience of the inns of court and universities as their counterparts in other counties. This tells us something about the more ambitious cultural horizons of the early Stuart North Riding gentry, but very little about the level of education locally in the Riding.

One of the problems for historians of education is attempting to balance qualitative and quantitative approaches. Extraordinary geniuses such as William Shakespeare, John Milton, John Locke and Isaac Newton demonstrate what individuals could achieve, but they remain utterly exceptional and are hardly products of anything we can call an educational 'system', still less judge as one. Even more strikingly is this the case with the few exceptionally well educated women. Archival sources setting out in detail the prescribed course of study in different classes of a grammar school, such as that dating from 1574 quoted in Claire Cross's *The Free Grammar School of Leicester* (1953), give some idea of the intended quality of the educational content, but not of the actual effectiveness of the classroom teaching. The surge in output from the printing press implies a greater reading public, but there is no way of quantifying this satisfactorily. David Cressy's use of signatures (collected as part of the associations and oaths of loyal male subjects in the seventeenth century) as a basic test of literacy is acceptable on his terms, but leaves much to be desired qualitatively. It tells us absolutely nothing about the active literacy (if any) of the signatories in any other context, and worse, leaves out of account, as Margaret Spufford has argued, all those who could read but could not write; furthermore there is no similar 'test' for numeracy at all.[1]

There are three facets to the history of education in any period, be it a time of change or stagnation, and these form the main investigations of this book. The first, which will be treated in Chapter 3, is what education was trying to do. Who was being taught, and what was being taught, and to what end? There is no single simple answer to each of these questions. One very striking feature of late medieval and early modern formal education is that it was dominated by social class, and almost exclusively male. Its aims were quite radically affected by the impact of humanism, which emphasised the drawing-out or development of character, and supplanted the medieval tendency to regard the educational process as the cramming-in of the approved rulings of unquestioned authorities. Essentially applied to the education of the governing classes, humanism revised the curriculum of the universities and grammar schools, establishing the classical syllabus thereafter approved for centuries, and prescribing a standard Latin grammar textbook. On this syllabus aristocratic and gentry boys and sons of town merchants at boarding schools such as Eton, and a less aristocratic clientele at large town grammar schools such as Manchester, were prepared for university entrance in eloquent Latin, with perhaps some Greek, and in places even Hebrew, classical literature, history, plays and poetry, with the purpose of fitting them to be courtiers, magistrates and leaders of society. Small-town schools such as Halifax followed suit. The grammar schools were intentionally elitist, and in later centuries they fossilised with this curriculum, partly by choice, but partly because of the constraints of their founding statutes, which laid down their syllabus and made no provision for change. Arithmetic, if taught at all in grammar schools, was paid for as an 'extra'. Advances in science and mathematics passed these schools by, causing a few practically minded men to set up self-proclaimed technical schools, especially in places where the need was most pressing, for example Sir Joseph Williamson's Mathematical School in Rochester (1701), to equip boys for service at sea.

At the start of the period young aristocrats were largely educated at home with household tutors, but already a few were going to boarding schools, then to the universities and/or inns of court, and already on to the Grand Tour which was to remain a characteristic module in their careers in the seventeenth and eighteenth centuries. Overlapping with them were sons of the gentry, though others of this class merely made use of the local grammar schools. An upper middle class, of squires and commercial families, probably ceased education at the grammar-school level, but might then buy entry into prestigious apprenticeship. Edward Hughes wrote of the placing of younger sons from the North-East in the early eighteenth century in mercantile and banking careers, showing that London merchants were asking an apprentice premium of £500 to £1000, while Liverpool or York merchants would take an apprentice for £130.[2] Lower middle-class education would most often stop with the local grammar school, or even a more petty elementary school, and might include lower-status apprenticeship. For the ranks of the urban artisans and rural labouring poor there was no regular provision until charitable organisations took a hand, though individuals had become upwardly mobile through limited institutional benefactions or with individual sponsors' encouragement.

One school of thought throughout wished to keep labourers in their place. Cranmer's ambitions for the lower orders met with criticism:

> it was meet for the ploughman's son to go to the plough, and the artificer's son to apply the trade of his parents' vocation and the gentleman's children are meet to have the knowledge of government and rule in the commonwealth. For we have as much need of ploughmen as any other state and all sorts of men may not go to school.[3]

James Howell, in a letter to the earl of Dorset (d. 1652), wrote of artisans' ambitions and sacrifices for education:

> every Man strains his Fortunes to keep his Children at School: the Cobler [sic] will clout it till Midnight, the Porter will carry Burdens till his Bones crack again, the Plough-man will pinch both Back and Belly to give his son Learning

but obviously the school fees, and the maintenance of the otherwise unproductive scholar, would be beyond many. Spufford believes more children learned to read than to write because reading was learned by the age of seven, before the child could be put to paid labour, but writing was taught after this age, when many children had been put to lucrative employment and were thus unavailable for schooling.[4]

Exceptionally, there were social engineering attempts built into school statutes. Archbishop Holgate provided foundation scholarships at his school at Hemsworth (1548) for six poor children, defined as sons of husbandmen or men of occupations. Hemsworth was a grammar school, offering Latin, Greek and Hebrew, so this was a proposal to offer grammar schooling to boys whose parents certainly had not been educated to any such level. Realistically, maintenance grants of £1 13s 4d per annum were included in the provision, not just payment of fees. A century later Howell's comments suggest, disparagingly, 'working men' struggling to maintain and raise fees for their children, and later in the passage he refers to ambition, so obviously he saw these parents as wishing to raise their children above their own attainment. But one should be wary of classing all labourers as visionless roughnecks. Before the Welfare State, the urgency of earning a living pulled many a part-educated child away from school if, for example, a parent died. Spufford cites the case of the Quaker convert Josiah Langdale, who had begun Latin at eight when his father died, was then put to harrowing, ploughing and cattle keeping, and at fifteen became an in-servant in husbandry. He gave up his attempts to keep up Latin, but managed to keep his English, and read his Bible. He became friends with a blind thresher who had lost his sight at ten, and so had been taught no further than the psalter. Spufford believes there must have been a steady trickle of semi-literate people into agricultural labour for reasons of illness, parental loss and such like.[5]

The aims of the charity schools in the early eighteenth century were not upwardly mobile. Subscriptions were solicited to establish schools to teach reading, religion and things 'suitable to their condition and capacity' to poor children, submissiveness and obedience prevailing. It remains obvious that class very much controlled opportunity, and that people did not often cross ranks. The situation was self-perpetuating: brought up at a level with one set of expectations, a person would live by them and demand much the same of the next generation. So it needed extraordinary circumstances to make the patterns change, to include a higher proportion of an age cohort, or draw in a different level of participants, or indeed to exclude a group, or to further a different, say more technical, curriculum. The extraordinary factors could be ideological or economic, and rapid or slow in their expression, and more marked in some circumstances than others, as will be unfolded below.

The second facet to the history of education will be the subject of Chapter 4, and is the provision of facilities to effect the identified aims.

This area embraces buildings, teachers and textbooks in identifiable schools of all levels, universities, dissenting academies and inns of court, the less institutional facilities of apprenticeships, and the even less formal educative opportunities afforded by discussion groups and libraries. It would be far too narrow to write the history of early modern education concentrating on the grammar schools and universities. People who did not aspire to these academic heights were by no means uneducated in the early modern period, and it is intended here to call the fullest possible attention to schooling in the vernacular, the teaching of modern practical subjects for careers such as surveying and naval occupations, apprenticeships for boys and girls, and evening classes for established mechanics. Thus education is being interpreted as including practical training and not as being restricted to academic learning.

The facilities for education were obviously affected by booms and slumps in the economy. In hard times, parents may have been unable to pay school fees, or to support children in the luxury of being at school, and indeed may have had to put them to paid employment at the earliest opportunity. In such periods, current philanthropic subventions of education, though acutely necessary, may also decline. In good times, the reverse may apply. Individual families may be able to spare their children's labour, and support them at school, while benefactors may be able to afford to be more generous. From the institutional standpoint, *ad hoc* subventions from gifts are one-off boons and cannot be relied upon; landed endowment secures a less volatile income but one tending to decrease in real value in inflationary times, as do fixed fundings from the treasury or a local corporate body. Developments take time to work through, so a surge in educational activity may take place the decade after a peak of investment. On the other hand, some conditions change and revert quickly, such that voluntary reading scholars might materialise at slack seasons of the agricultural year and disappear at busy ones.

The third facet, which will be the subject of Chapter 5, is what can be seen to have been achieved, in terms of individual attainment and basic literacy. The period continually throws up a cultured elite of writers, dramatists, historians, genealogists, diarists and commentators, and men of science and observation in medicine, astronomy, architecture and mathematics, and shows an entrenched enlightened elite in the local magistracy and in parliament, and this circle includes many women. But the attainments of this elite are the product of many factors, certainly embracing more influences than simply individuals' formal education. As for the ebb and flow of basic literacy over time and across classes, this is a fascinating subject but difficult to probe with satisfaction for lack of comparable evidence from different groupings and places.

Throughout the period girls were educationally disadvantaged. Basically, they were simply not admitted to the universities, inns of court, or grammar schools, whatever their social class. It has been argued that girls were allowed in grammar schools at their elementary level, but not permitted to stay on to the Latin course. This is supported by the ruling at Banbury Grammar School in 1594 that girls should not be included above the age of nine, or when they could read English. It does not really counter the general rule, since as the girls are generally agreed to have been excluded from the core curriculum grammar teaching, the essential *raison d'être* of the grammar school, they were not receiving grammar-school education, even if a few could be found in virtually the preparatory departments of such schools. Before the Reformation there was no institutional provision for educating girls except in convents and elementary schools. In late medieval convents it appears the level of educational attainment by the nuns was low, so any education provided for secular boarders was presumably no better. Household – and, from the early seventeenth century, private-school – education was the pattern for the upper-class girls, and individuals reached remarkable levels of achievement. The Tudor queens, Mary and Elizabeth, were a class apart. Elizabeth in particular, though it was doubtless politic to flatter her scholarship in later years, benefited from a classical education (her teacher was Roger Ascham) and rose to the challenge of trouncing the Polish ambassador in *extempore* Latin in 1597. Lady Jane Grey's educational achievements, and those of Thomas More's daughter Margaret, and her daughter Mary Bassett, who made an English translation of her grandfather's *De tristitia Christi*, show that individual girls in Renaissance families could take advantage of a similar education to that of the boys when they could get access to it. A century later similar, but never systematic, opportunities were still producing girls educated well above most of their sex, though with less emphasis on the classical academic standards reached by the Tudor prodigies. Lucy Hutchinson, née Apsley, born in 1620, had learned to read by the age of four, and grew up bilingual in English and French through the benefit of having a French nurse. Her father had her taught Latin by the family chaplain, and she fared better than her brothers who were at school. A few years later John Thornton entered the earl of Bedford's household as a tutor to the earl's sons, but their sisters Diana and Margaret also benefited from his instruction, though not apparently in Latin.

More will be said about girls' education below: the point which has to be made about the high achievers among girls is that they came from unusual circumstances and usually prove to have been encouraged by a brother, father or uncle and not to owe their education to any formal provision which was also available to others of their sex. Institutionally, the first clearly identifiable private boarding school for upper-class girls was the establishment at Deptford which entertained Anne of Denmark with a masque in 1617. Many small private schools for girls are known from the 1620s and 1630s: one run by the Perwich family in Hackney is known to have had over 100 pupils at one time. Though the capital and its environs had a certain social cachet for finishing young ladies, there were similar schools in the provinces: Mrs Amye's school in Manchester flourished for at least thirty-five years, 1638–73. Herein is one of the clear differences between boys' and girls' schools. Thirty-five years is considered a noteworthy life for a girls' school, whereas the leading boys' schools had continuous existence for centuries. The difference is that girls' schools were not established institutional foundations but individual enterprises rarely outlasting the working life of the proprietor/proprietress (as indeed were some, also short-lived, general schools for boys). But a more serious difference was in the purposes and standards: girls' boarding schools generally were teaching accomplishments rather than academic subjects. This was fully realised by the few women advocates of better education for their sex. Mary Astell believed that the cause of the defects women laboured under owed much to the mistakes of their education. She urged her readers to rescue themselves from the 'woful incogitancy' they had slipped into, to awaken their sleeping powers and make good use of their God-given reason.[6] Astell wrote for an upper-class readership able to contemplate sparing £500 for a daughter, but she did practical work for the less fortunate, founding the charity school for the daughters of Chelsea pensioners in 1709. The elementary reading schools were open to girls from the Middle Ages onwards, but we have little idea of the numbers benefiting from them. Certainly more of the elementary teachers seem to have been women as time went by, as is reflected in the very term 'dame school'. The charity schools (the Society for Promoting Christian Knowledge, or SPCK, was founded in 1698) were willing to teach girls, but their level was largely confined to the degree of literacy needed for pious reading, and there was much time devoted to teaching girls useful crafts such as knitting, sewing and spinning, whereas the boys from the same social class were more likely to be treated to some elementary arithmetic.

Because of the complexity of the changes, a brief chronological outline of the educational developments in England $c.1530–c.1760$ will be given in Chapter 2 as a background to the analytical chapters which follow. Chapter 6 will extend the analysis to compare briefly Scottish, Welsh and Irish education in the same period, and to draw attention to the developments in certain Western European countries and North America. The conclusions will briefly highlight the key trends and features in the development of early modern English education.

2

OUTLINE OF DEVELOPMENTS

Education on the Eve of the Reformation

The curriculum of academic education, along with the Roman alphabet and the Latin language, was first brought to Britain during the Roman occupation. Originally a pagan education for administrative and cultural (including religious) purposes, Roman secular education, in the provinces as at Rome itself, was an elevating, civilising experience aimed at producing a cultured citizen elite capable of participating in the state's affairs, for example, as magistrates. When the Roman occupation ended, the Latin language survived in Britain in the Christian priesthood, and it received a new lease of life with the sending of the Gregorian mission to the Anglo-Saxons in 597. Anglo-Saxon recruits to the priesthood learned Latin, the language of the Rome-based church, and the art of metre, astronomy and ecclesiastical computation. According to Bede some knew Latin and Greek as well as their native tongue. Thus the two classical Mediterranean civilisations of Greece and Rome and their ancient tongues entered the curriculum of scholarly education in the European offshore islands of Britain. However, though Bede was well educated for the seventh century, he viewed education as cramming in approved learning ('pouring streams of wholesome learning' into minds) rather than drawing out the pupil's potential. The minds were passive receptacles and the desirable education was precensored so that 'wholesome' knowledge was selected for the drip feed.

Thus it was in the ecclesiastical context that classical education was re-established in England, and for nearly a millennium it was principally for ecclesiastical purposes that any child was taught Latin. The lowest level of Latin literacy was mere reading ability, acquired in order to sing Latin hymns in a church choir. The next level was reading Latin with any real understanding, necessary for 'professional' churchmen for reading the Bible, Church Fathers and theological works, and for the accurate scribal copying of texts. The final level was the ability to compose Latin, and contribute in it to the communications circulated in Latin between scholars throughout the Christian world. Though predominantly an education for males, this level of learning was achieved by a few Anglo-Saxon nuns, whose Latin correspondence has survived to prove the point. This education was never, however, exclusively Christian, and classical pagan literature was passed down with the teaching of language. A tension between the sacred and the secular resulted, and was never fully resolved. Colet's 1518 statutes for his school at St Paul's wanted good literature in Latin and Greek but especially Christian authors, though Wolsey's foundation at Ipswich (1528) used exclusively pagan reading. After the Reformation, the 1571 canons, repeated in 1604, in pursuit of the 'fullness and fineness of the Latin and Greek tongue', wanted the books used to be 'those especially which profit to the knowledge of Christ and godliness'.[1] Latin remained the language of international research communication until the eighteenth century.

Two periods in the Middle Ages were particularly progressive educationally, the twelfth-century renaissance and the better known renaissance beginning in the fifteenth century. The first, through communication with the Arabs in southern Spain and the eastern Mediterranean, opened up mathematics and science and much more Greek learning, and led to the challenge (for Christians) of reconciling Christianity and Aristotelian thought. Cathedral schools became educational centres, and the Lateran Councils of 1179 and 1215 ordered every cathedral to provide a schoolmaster to teach clerks and poor scholars free of charge. The institutional origins of the English universities can be traced back to the twelfth century. University members were all tonsured males, under the discipline of their diocesan bishop, respectively Lincoln at Oxford and Ely at Cambridge. Already the secular cathedrals had chancellors in charge of education, who licensed schoolmasters; where the cathedral was monastic the bishop appointed them. It was no great stretch of nomenclature for the bishop to appoint a chancellor to be locally in charge of each of the two universities, and the chancellors later became independent of their diocesans.

The fifteenth-century Renaissance, which developed first in Italy, rediscovered more texts of Latin classical writers and selected different authors to emulate, for example enhancing the evaluation of Cicero. At this period too, the educational writings of Quintilian were influential. The term 'humanist' is used of these developments, which turned away from the medieval God-centred view of the universe, where everything was seen as God's unfolding plan, and centred much more on man himself, allowing him motivation, purpose and personal character. The humanist education of the sixteenth century, which placed rhetoric before logic, and literary studies before scholasticism, is quite recognisably the forerunner of the grammar-school tradition which prevailed, selectively, in England until after the Second World War.

The grammar schools in England in the early sixteenth century taught Latin grammar, not English. Greek was largely confined to the universities; the first English schoolmaster to teach it is believed to have been William Horman of Eton (1485–94) and Winchester (1494–1502). The emphasis was on literary culture, not practical skills, and the intended product was the 'whole man' fit for local magistracy. These well-educated citizens, supremely illustrated by Thomas More and his circle, were taught to have self-control before governing others. They enjoyed reading plays and poetry in Latin, French or English, at leisure, and translated and indeed composed original works for their own and their friends' entertainment. This was a courtly, liberal education for leadership, and was by definition elitist. The foundations were laid in grammar schools all over the country. Most towns had one grammar school, in some places endowed as part of a chantry, in others existing on the fees pupils paid. Far more boys must have passed through the town grammar schools than could have proceeded to be accommodated at the two universities, so obviously boys were not sent to grammar schools purely to prepare for university. Writing of Hull Grammar School, John Lawson suggests the well-written orderly Latin records of the medieval corporation reflected 'long and careful schooling', probably in the town.[2] Latin literacy was needed to create such archives, but not several years of study at university. So one must assume the town grammar school leavened the local learning level, producing men whose educational experience was similar to Shakespeare's, only lacking his dramatic genius. The grammar schools of England around 1530 went on to develop in very different ways. Winchester and Eton are public schools, Jesus College Rotherham, now Thomas Rotherham College, has become a sixth-form college.

The grammar schools in the sixteenth century recruited mostly boys who had already learned to read. School statutes, for example Manchester's, generally assumed reading ability in those admitted, but to ensure that the master's time was not distracted by having to teach inadequately prepared entrants, provided for older pupils in the school to teach elementary reading when required. Writing was seen as a separate skill: 'scrivener craft' was Robert Stillington's term for it when he founded the school at Acaster Selby (1483) with its technical and academic streams, and it was sometimes taught as an extra at additional cost.

Reading had originally been taught in ABC or song schools. The latter title explains the situation: choirboys needed to be able to read, so had to be taught. Whatever the purpose in teaching a boy to read, once he could do it, he could find other uses for it, and the same alphabet was used for Latin and English. So literacy taught for one end was adaptable to many. For girls it was more obviously useful to learn to read in English than in Latin. A statute of 1406 allowed parents to send both boys and girls to school, but for the girls only the elementary reading school seems to have been envisaged, since there was never grammar-school provision for them. In the higher social classes girls might learn to read English and French in the household, but rarely Latin. That extraordinarily educationally minded benefactress Henry VII's mother, Margaret Beaufort, knew French well enough to translate from it, but regretted her inability to understand Latin.

Grammar schooling requires more institutional continuity than does teaching children to read. A grammar school needs a teacher or two competent in the language(s) taught, textbooks, and a cohort of pupils prepared to spend several years of advancing difficulty on the subject. Teaching reading is a shorter-term task, needing less equipment, first a hornbook, then a primer, and the teacher has a less exclusive skill, as is clear from the appearance in medieval records, though rarely, of women teachers at this level. Teaching children to read could be done with rather less formality, and reading schools are clearly much less completely recorded, and probably many were much less continuous in their existence than grammar schools were. Evidence of literacy tells us such schools must have existed, but many escaped record. Even grammar teaching was sometimes carried on in private houses by rectors and vicars taking up to half a dozen or so boys; how much more often must reading have been taught, even part-time, in small gatherings with no perpetuity?

On the testimony of Sir Thomas More, who as a conservative in religion feared an outbreak of English bible reading, it is estimated that some 60 per cent of the population was literate in the south of England in his day, but this appears exaggerative. It would obviously have included those who were only basically literate for pragmatic purposes. By 1478 the Goldsmiths' Company in London required apprentices to be able to read and write, and such literacy for secular advancement was obviously a coming thing. The proportion who could read Latin would be much smaller, and the proportion going on to study at university level, for which Latin was requisite, smaller still.

On the eve of the Reformation the two universities were still part of the ecclesiastical establishment, but were no longer exclusively institutions of tonsured clerks. (They remained exclusively male preserves until the late 1870s.) Sons of the comfortably placed were already attending them without necessarily being committed to entering the church as a career. Already some grammar schools had been founded as feeder schools for university colleges, for example Winchester (1382) for New College, and Eton (1440) for King's. Other colleges possessed integral grammar schools, for example Magdalen, which had a school by 1480. In the early sixteenth century there was a burst of school foundations over the country, linked, despite remoteness, to university colleges. Manchester Grammar School, founded in 1515 (the statutes date from 1525), was linked to Corpus Christi College Oxford, whose president had the nomination of the high master and usher. Sedbergh School (founded 1525/8) was linked to St John's College Cambridge which received £1000 from the founder, Roger Lupton, for fellowships and scholarships, eight scholarships to be for boys from the school.

The two English universities of Oxford and Cambridge can be traced to origins respectively in the twelfth and thirteenth centuries. The term derived from *universitas*, the community of (male) masters and scholars, and the origins were informal, not institutional. As Oxford and Cambridge developed, the informality gave way to greater structure. Colleges began to be founded in the thirteenth century, and were pious foundations for graduate fellows to pursue learning mainly in the higher faculties of theology or civil and canon law. Undergraduates on the foundation, or in attendance as commoners of the college, were a later development, much stabilised by the foundations of New College (1379) and King's (1441). The undergraduate population in the Middle

Ages had not generally been affiliated to colleges, but matriculated to the university, assigned to a tutor who was himself a Master of Arts. At Oxford the foundation of Magdalen in 1458 proved significant in the development towards a collegiate structure acknowledging the importance of undergraduates and their academic tuition. Magdalen's founder, William Waynflete, envisaged admitting up to twenty undergraduate commoners, sons of noble or distinguished persons, and providing teaching not only in the college but, via lectureships in natural and moral philosophy and theology, to the university at large. Brasenose, founded in 1512, foresaw the expansion of undergraduates and by 1552 about 40 per cent of the college's members were undergraduate commoners, tutored by the principal or one of the fellows. Corpus Christi, chartered in 1517, provided for twenty fellows and as many undergraduate 'disciples' intended to succeed their seniors. Here too three public lecturers were appointed, to teach humanity, Greek and theology, and the undergraduates were taught by one or two of the fellows. These foundations mark the beginning of the shift at Oxford towards a university dominated by its collegiate structure, with the colleges increasingly concerned with teaching Arts undergraduates. Meanwhile in Cambridge two influential colleges were Christ's (1506), a refoundation of Godshouse, starting with twelve fellows and forty-seven pupil scholars mainly studying in the Arts faculty, six pursuing the master of grammar degree, and St John's, which initially had thirty Arts undergraduates, with seven senior fellows, two deans and twenty-eight foundation fellows already Bachelors of Arts in holy orders. College teaching in addition to university instruction was provided at both colleges, which also had pensioners. To show these two colleges' numerical importance, Daniel Leader cites the tax census of 1522 listing 500 to 550 members of the university, about 100 at Christ's and ninety-five at St John's, most of them undergraduates.[3]

The Faculty of Arts provided the foundation courses, studied for four years before one could 'determine' as a Bachelor of Arts. Bachelors could 'incept' as Masters of Arts after a further three years of study and disputation. In the Middle Ages they were then required to lecture as regent masters for one or two years, but this died out in the early sixteenth century. Masters of Arts could proceed to the higher faculties of theology or canon or civil law. Medicine was also a postgraduate faculty. The arts of the basic Arts degree consisted originally of the seven liberal arts (or sciences) of the classical curriculum, subdivided into the trivium: grammar, logic (or dialectic) and rhetoric, and the quadrivium: arithmetic, geometry, astronomy and music, and Oxford retained this syllabus longer than Cambridge. But in practice subtle changes had taken place, bringing logic and philosophy to the fore. A degree of master of grammar is noted in the fifteenth century, and was last conferred at Cambridge in 1548.

Only during the fifteenth century did the universities, as distinct from the colleges, begin to acquire their own buildings, both, for example, building libraries. They seem to have gained a firmer hold on the career structure within the church in the fifteenth century, when a larger proportion of higher clergy were graduates than before, and the episcopal bench was almost entirely graduate. At the same time there is increasing evidence that students were entering the universities without thereby feeling committed to any career within the church, though it is important not to exaggerate the amount of secularisation. The drop-out rate was high, and many of the socially superior students probably never intended to embark on the long course of study, attending for a few terms almost as a finishing school. By the eve of the Reformation the universities had already responded to some winds of change. Benefactors sent them manuscripts from Italy with the avowed intent of improving the students' Latin style. Standards were changing, and rising, and there was a pursuit of the perfect in the linguistic study. Grocyn may have taught Greek at Oxford in the 1490s, but Erasmus's in Cambridge in 1511 is the first recorded Greek class at either university. Richard Croke became Reader in Greek at Cambridge in 1518, the year Wolsey's humanity lecturer in Oxford, John Clement, took up tenure, 'almost certainly teaching Greek at least in part'.[4]

The English government was centred at Westminster, and the top common law courts, King's Bench and Common Pleas, and the equitable jurisdiction of Chancery, were based there. For this reason the common law training, exclusively for men, was housed in London, not at the universities. Much of the law was laid down in Latin or law French, as were the court records; proceedings since the late fourteenth century were conducted in French or English. Lawyers needed linguistic skills as well as an understanding of the law's technicalities, including its writs. Their studies were based on the study of texts and precedents and practice runs in moots. The institutions which had come to provide this instruction were the inns of chancery and inns of court. In the late fifteenth century Sir John Fortescue, Chief Justice of the King's Bench, wrote about the studies at the inns of court and their duration and the sort of people who attended in his Latin tract *De Laudibus Legum Angliae*

(1468). It was so long and costly a training that only people of quality attempted it. Even then the inns, like the universities, were being used as finishing schools, and by the same social classes. It did not worry Fortescue that these young people spent some of their time learning dancing and other social accomplishments. A smattering of the law might well be useful to a future landowner in a litigious age, so there was some purpose to these studies even when they were not embarked on with the intention of pursuing a legal career.

Pre-Reformation England had educational institutions well spread geographically and diverse in purpose to cope with society's needs. This education had been for 800 years principally for religious purposes. Saving souls was the first aim of education, hence responsible persons, clergy, teachers and parents, were enjoined to teach the Lord's Prayer and Ten Commandments and other rudiments of the faith to children. This could be taught without literacy at all. Teaching to read was the next stage, originally with the purpose of producing choirboys, but capable of totally secular application. Those who had mastered their letters, and were able and encouraged to train more intellectually, went on to Latin at grammar school. From there some were creamed off into the legal inns and universities. None of this was the responsibility of the state. Certain professions needed a graduate intake or qualification of an equivalent sort, so appropriate training had to be available, and the people who wanted it had either to pay or take advantage of charitable subvention. This applied at both university and grammar-school level. Many careers, however, needed less highly educated entrants, and there were few contemporary complaints that the balance of supply and demand was other than fairly satisfactory, though provision was undoubtedly of easier access in some circumstances than in others, and must have been uneven in quality.

The tenor of recent educational research has been greatly to increase the estimate of schools available by the early sixteenth century.[5] Some of these schools were sufficiently endowed to support free teaching for all the pupils, some for only a selective intake, of founder's kin, or local children, or deserving poor. In the former case all the children would attend without fees being paid, in the latter foundation scholars would sit alongside fee-payers. Most of the original medieval endowment had come from religious motivation: the late medieval grammar and reading schools were often part of chantry foundations and the scholars were expected to pray for the soul of the donor and his relatives or nominees, in their gratitude. By the end of the fifteenth century, however, the motivation was already becoming more practical and secular. Basic literacy was in growing demand and was apparently informally as well as formally provided. If education is studied down to basic literacy levels there is no problem in integrating it with more technical and practical training since, as previously noted, some trading and craft organisations, especially in London, demanded or expected literacy of members and apprentices.

Thus, at the end of the Middle Ages people in England's class-divided society generally received the training or education then seen as appropriate to their status. As fees had to be paid, unless charitable support was secured, people bought no more than they needed. The state had no responsibility in the provision of education, nor was any attendance compulsory. There were, however, both private and institutional benefactors who thought educating children (almost exclusively the boys) good both for society and for the children's souls and careers, and there was already some provision for education as a means of mobilising boys upwards socially. The education provided, moreover, was itself changing, as can be seen from its absorption of humanism. Changes outside education, notably the invention and spread of the printing press, had repercussions within it, affecting the availability of teaching material and the incentive to learn. Suddenly, standard editions replaced handcopied texts at a fraction of the price. Readers could now take advantage of everything from elegant translations down to broadsheets. Thus the late medieval educational world was not as backward as might be supposed, and was already showing itself positively responsive to change.

The Impact of the Reformation on Education, c.1530–1560

With the Reformation, state intervention in education began and the ecclesiastical hold over education diminished, most obviously in institutional terms, though pious purpose and dominant orthodoxy remained important factors throughout our period. The English Reformation destroyed the monasteries between 1536 and 1540, which meant that all the internal education within the monastic system, in the monasteries for young monks, and in the universities in the support of monk students at monastic colleges, disappeared at a stroke, and the monks' external educational activity in their almonry schools, and where monastic houses were trustees of endowments or appointers and paymasters of schoolmasters, suffered disruption if not extinction. In educational terms it cannot be argued that the dissolution of the nunneries was as noticeable. There were far fewer nuns than monks, their houses and libraries were poorer, and their educational standards were much less ambitious and of course did not include facilities at the universities. The number of lay girls being educated in convents seems to have been smaller than was once imagined. The abolition of the friaries in 1538 was a further blow to total educational provision, since their orders had been more active in education than the monasteries in their last centuries, and had internal educational provision in their various divisions, at convent, custody, limit, province and university level.

The dissolution of colleges of priests, chantries and religious guilds in 1548 has been the subject of much debate in educational history. For some 350 years Edward VI had a good reputation as a patron of education, reinforced by the existence of individual schools titled Edward VI Grammar School: for example the Free Grammar School of King Edward VI at Retford (1551), which was grafted on to the stock of an earlier school.[6] The historian A. F. Leach was the first to launch a serious assault on this perspective, arguing that Edward VI and his council were despoilers rather than creators of educational institutions. Clearly it was appreciated at the time that many chantries and collegiate churches, and even guilds, offered schooling by terms of their foundation charters, and that this aspect, being separable from the superstitious religious activities frowned on by the government, should be preserved. The surviving chantry certificates indicate many instances where educational activity enjoined in the foundation statutes was ordered to be continued. But not all was as it appeared. There were chantries which had been intended to provide education where it had lapsed, and others which had acquired the role despite silence in their charters. Grammar schooling on such foundations was more likely to be identifiable and to survive than elementary teaching was. The permitted survival, however, involved considerable upheaval in funding. The dissolution of the chantries led to the disposal by the Crown of their landed endowment. Initially schools received income from the government, not by endowment, and the teachers' salaries were funded at a fixed level based on the net income of the old endowment at the date of suppression. This had the unintended effect of freezing salaries, and as times were inflationary this devalued the rewards for the career, and eventually forced supplementation of salaries from local resources. In some cases the refounded schools were soon allocated ex-chantry lands:

the grammar school at Retford received former chantries worth £15 5*s* 3¼ *d* in clear rents.

The real argument, however, is not about the unforeseen long-term consequences of the Chantries Act but about its short-term implementation. Leach estimated that some 300 grammar schools were destroyed or damaged, but the problem here is that numbers both 'before' and 'after' are uncertain. Leach was inclined to assume unproven continuity, and so to credit impermanent schools with long survival. Though Leach's assumptions of continuity should be viewed critically, interrupted opportunities should not be disregarded either. Too many early modern historians, having no clear interest in the medieval situation, attribute individual schools to sixteenth-century foundation when it is absolutely clear that at least some type of formal schooling was institutionalised in the place earlier, though not necessarily continuously. Historians in the 1960s accused Leach of exaggerating the pre-Reformation provision, but more recent research on the diocese of York, a believed educationally backward area, while criticising Leach's neglect of elementary schools, testifies to the plentiful number of schools in later medieval England, thus vindicating him 'on the statistical level'.[7] Certainly contemporaries expressed public disquiet about the fate of grammar schools in particular, within two and three years of the Act, and in 1563 the Commons Speaker, Thomas Williams, told the queen, 'I dare say a hundred schools want in England which afore this time hath been.'[8] Furthermore, activities in the 1550s testify to the entrenched value of education in society even where disruption had occurred. The Commissioners ordered some teaching stipends where there was no mention of schooling in the foundation deed, and they seemed generally willing to allow competent teaching to continue. Many towns petitioned for the refoundation of the local school under municipal trusteeship. Cressy suggests that the real significance of the Edwardian reforms was administrative, and in fact beneficial, as irregular and poorly administered establishments subordinated to priestly purposes became securely endowed, carefully governed, and orientated to preparing boys for university entrance or apprenticeship.[9]

The dissolution dislocated schooling but did not close schools wholesale. At the universities, there was a withdrawal of the monastic and mendicant presence, and of canon law from the curriculum. But Henry VIII used some of the dissolved religious lands to found the re-endowed Christ Church (formerly Wolsey's Cardinal College) and Trinity at Cambridge, and the five regius professorships of theology/

divinity, medicine, civil law, Greek and Hebrew at both universities (1540/6). From here Greek and Hebrew (studied primarily for scriptural purposes) passed down into grammar schools. Greek was well established in school curricula by the 1560s: grammar masters at the schools of the cathedrals of new foundation (1541) were to be learned in Latin and Greek; Greek was required at Witton in 1558, Merchant Taylors' in 1561, Rivington in 1566, St Bees and Hawkshead in 1583 and 1588, Harrow in 1590, Durham in 1593 and Heath (Halifax) around 1600. Some schools were beginning to teach Hebrew: the first reference to this in school statutes is claimed to be at Archbishop Holgate's School at York in 1547.[10] The monastic colleges and friary sites at Oxford and Cambridge largely passed to secular colleges, so all was not lost there, though their purpose was changed. There was a horrendous dispersal and destruction of books in monastic, university and college libraries. Commissioners were sent to both universities in 1535 to destroy works of scholastic theology, and in 1550 greater damage was inflicted on the two university libraries, and selectively on college ones. Duke Humphrey's library above the Oxford Divinity School was completely dispersed, and in 1556 Convocation ordered the sale of the desks and book presses, since they were no longer needed. A catalogue of Cambridge's books shows the library had shrunk to 175 volumes in 1556, and Oxford's needed refoundation by Sir Thomas Bodley in 1602. The universities, with Winchester and Eton, were exempt from the collegiate dissolutions of 1548.

One unwelcome development from the more innovative humanist teaching at the universities had been a spread of heretical opinions among scholars and students. Lutheranism was active at Cambridge by 1520, and ironically some of the scholars there transferred the heresy to Wolsey's Cardinal College in the mid-1520s. At the Reformation the universities were forced to yield to royal supremacy and to become powerhouses of the approved religion, controlled by oath-taking and royal visitation and injunctions. Thomas Cromwell was the first Visitor, in 1535, and there were further visitations in 1549 and 1556 and 1559. During this period, the universities made further progress towards the pattern of a collegiate university, with a greatly increased importance for undergraduate commoners and their teaching and examination, and became further cowed under state control. Orthodoxy became more critical in schoolteaching too. In May 1555 the Catholic Mary enacted that all schoolmasters had to be examined and licensed by bishops or other senior officials of the church, and this practice was retained by

Elizabeth and continued in the seventeenth century, only broken by the disestablishment period 1646–60.

Thus the state increased its interference in education and took a more pushful role in the direction the established church developed. Henry VIII's break with Rome led to the oath of supremacy. Edward's reign pushed education in a more Protestant direction: there was a new Latin catechism in 1552, translated into English in 1553 for 'schoolmasters and teachers of youth'. Peter Martyr at Oxford and Martin Bucer at Cambridge, respectively regius professors of theology from 1548 and 1549, tried to bring the more radical reformed doctrine of Cranmer and his allies into favour. Henceforth religious predilection polarised, with the result that families to the Puritan left or the Catholic right of the state church educated their children very differently. Cressy dismisses Mary's reign as too short, and Protestant resistance too strong, for her Catholicising educational policies to be nationally effective, but persistent Catholics were left with an educational problem as Elizabeth's policies began to bite. Meanwhile in the mainstream the importance of the Bible in Protestant theology enhanced biblical study, and biblical translation opened it up to a vastly increased circle of those literate in the vernacular.

One should not of course assume that all post-Reformation developments were due to the Reformation. There was an ongoing population increase which enlarged the numbers of children and young people, and the desirability of at least pragmatic literacy for earning a living became ever more noticeable. The output of the printing presses continued to grow, both feeding and stimulating demand. The imposition of uniformity achieved by state intervention in prescribing a standard Latin grammar was only possible because of printing, a craft only half a century old. A textbook market was now a reality, and an assistance to formal schooling; however the same technology also turned out self-instructional manuals of surprising diversity.

The Educational Revolution, 1560–1640

Humanist reforms in the first half of the sixteenth century had fixed the pattern of the grammar-school classical curriculum and the Reformation had eradicated some superstitious connections previously held by some educational institutions. Advances in state control had prescribed texts and proscribed the disapproved. Mary had set up the machinery for constant control by licensing schoolmasters. All these things continued under Elizabeth and the early Stuarts.

The statutes and orders for the Free Grammar School at Leicester in 1574 illustrate the curriculum, prescribing Calvin's or Nowell's Catechism in English, English reading and parts of speech, and writing, for the earliest form; English concords and elementary Latin for the second; more Latin, Catechism and Cato or Aesop for the third; more Catechism and Latin with Castellion's Latin dialogues or Cicero's epistles for the fourth; and a heavy Ciceronian diet followed in the fifth and sixth forms, varied with Erasmus, Terence, Ovid or Horace, and the introduction of Greek. Cicero dominated the seventh year too, where the pupils also tackled the Greek testament or Calvin's Catechism in Greek.[11] The 1571 canons, repeated in 1604, underlined episcopal supervision of licensing, restricted the teaching to the royally approved grammar text, and prescribed the 1570 Latin catechism with the English translation for children ignorant of Latin. Scholars had to be taken to sermons 'as often as any sermon shall be', and on return to school were to be individually tested on what they had learned from it. (There were, of course, at this date, penalties for non-attendance at church on Sundays.) It all looks like a stabilisation of the developments of the previous half-century. Where then, was there a revolution?

In an article in 1969[12] Lawrence Stone set himself to consider the scale of growth, and the shifts in the social distribution of education in England between 1560 and 1640. In five-and-a-half pages devoted to schools, he wrote of 'the teaching of basic literacy to the bulk of the population' in petty schools, and while dismissing More's estimate of over half the population being able to read the Bible in English in 1533 as alarmist, thought the proportion 'may have been approaching this figure in certain favoured areas' a century later. Forty-seven per cent of 204 men sentenced to death by Middlesex justices in 1612–14 were saved by benefit of clergy, saving themselves, that is, by sufficient literacy to read the 'neck verse', and 'even among the poor some women were now able to read'. Passing to the 'grammar school proper' through an eight-line paragraph on practical schooling in English, mathematics and account-keeping, Stone eventually concluded that the growth in secondary education was far greater than the increase of places at endowed grammar schools would suggest. (The number of new foundations impresses, however: 136 added to the existing endowed grammar schools between 1558 and 1603, eighty-three in James I's reign, and fifty-nine in Charles I's.[13]) Stone's thesis really took off in relation to higher education, arguing that numbers rose to a far higher level than previously believed. He postulated a wave of expansion in admissions in the 1560s, peaking around 1583, falling off until around 1604 and then soaring up to the outbreak of the Civil War, when entrants were at a level not reached again before the 1860s. Taking the inns of court into account, he estimated that in the peak decade of the 1630s not less than 1240 young men were entering higher education every year, about 2.5 per cent of the male age cohort. He believed 80 per cent of the inns of court entrants came from the landed classes, while at Oxford he estimated 37–40 per cent were of country gentry origin, 51–54 per cent lower, lower middle and middle-class. Stone thought 'perhaps the most surprising feature of the age was the continued presence in the universities of men in relatively humble circumstances'. In higher education 'everyone was included except the very poor (who probably embraced the majority of the population)'.

Even Stone did not always mean precisely what he wrote, as is clear from contradictions within the article, and where he did, others have found fault with him. Stone made no attempt to substantiate a case for 'the bulk of the population' learning literacy at petty schools. When he talked of a figure approaching half of the population being literate in English he qualified it with 'in favoured places', and later in the article, more accurately, implied he was actually only considering the *male* population, despite his earlier paragraph referring to even poor women able to read. His conclusion began

> if it is accepted that over half the male population of London was literate, that a high proportion of the one third of adult males who could sign their names in the home counties could read, and that 2.5 per cent of the male seventeen-year-old age group was going on each year to higher education, then the English in 1640 were infinitely better educated than they were before,

and he thought literacy may have been more democratically distributed among the English than it was again until the end of the eighteenth century. But as Cressy wrote, this educational revolution passed most people by. 'Not even at the peak of the educational revolution did every parish have a school or schoolmaster, but most places could find a licensed teacher within a few miles.' Stone's enthusiasm for expanded basic literacy, and his belief that this may have been more democratically distributed among the English at this period than again for two centuries cannot conceal the fact that 'England was massively illiterate despite an epoch of educational expansion and a barrage of sermons.'[14] More than two-thirds of men and nine-tenths of women could not write their own names as late as the Civil War. Stone dismissed education for apprenticeship in eight lines; it deserves more attention (see below, 'Precursors of Industrial Training'). Most of Stone's article is devoted to the 2.5 per cent of males entering higher education. In 1964, when Stone was writing, he could cite male entry to university as recently as 1931 as 2.3 per cent of the male age group, so the 1630s figure looked quite 'modern'; set against the 1990s participation targets across the sexes in what is now called higher education, it looks worlds apart.

Not all was as novel as it seemed, or as accessible. Stone's reference to the inns of court providing a general education for the gentry at large only confirms Sir John Fortescue's comments relating to a century earlier. Stone criticised W. K. Jordan's attempts to quantify educational expansion as exaggerating the accessibility to the poor, conflating grammar with lesser schools, and ignoring private schooling. (A more fundamental criticism came from Bittle and Lane, who rightly show that Jordan's deliberate disregard of inflation undermined his claim to be able to quantify increased generosity to educational causes.[15]) Jordan reckoned there was a school for every 4400 of the population, and every 12 miles, by the mid-seventeenth century. But though this sounds 'accessible' today, twelve miles meant great inaccessibility in this period. With schooldays starting as early as five, six and seven in the morning according to summer and winter conditions, no child could attend a school ten miles away and live at home, and if he had to be boarded, this would put a rather different complexion on the family's commitment to education. The chantry commissioners recognised this situation, surely, when they moved Thomasine Percival's school at remote Week St Mary to slightly more populous and accessible Launceston, seven miles away.

Historians' tendency to underestimate pre-Reformation schools numerically made post-Reformation developments seem more revolutionary, but many schools claimed as new were in places which had something probably similar earlier. Moreover, medieval education had never lacked patronage for the poor boy of aptitude, and the universities' benefactors had long expressed deliberate preference for backward areas which needed leavening up. Even Stone referred to the 'continued presence' of relatively humble boys in higher education, thus admitting they were there at the start. Maybe early social engineering was slight and patronising, but we must set against it the suspicion that later prospering middle classes secured endowments originally intended for the deserving poor.

Often what is most revolutionary about the educational scene in this period, certainly when compared with earlier times, is the amount of evidence available. The documentation of licensing and visitations, though often defective, provides information on individuals and types of schooling. Published works begin to abound on teaching methods and objectives, and the status of masters. Stone's claim that parsons, curates and unbeneficed schoolmasters were teaching a handful of boys up to university level in this period can be substantiated by matriculation records, but something similar earlier may have gone largely unrecorded. [16] Stone's phenomenon effected all that he said but it is arguable it was not as much of a change as he thought, and more importantly it is clear that it affected so small a percentage of the population that, important as it was, it should not be allowed to colour the period overmuch. In one respect, however, it may be an understatement. One of Stone's assumptions was that 'a high proportion' of the third of the male population able to sign in Surrey in 1642 could read. In fact, as reading was taught before writing, it is probable that 'reading literacy' was more widespread than 'signing literacy'. For those who could read, there was some scope for self-teaching. Edmund Coote's *The English Schoolmaster* (1596) went through forty-eight editions in a century and has been called a 'teach-yourself' text. It cheerfully acknowledged that craftsmen such as tailors could use the book to teach others (ideally while doing their 'proper' job at the same time!).[17] In this period, literacy was seen as a tool for godliness rather than as a career asset.

To criticise aspects of Stone's argument for an overall educational revolution does not belittle the educational achievements of the few who were really well educated in Elizabethan and early Stuart England, and indeed more widespread basic literacy may be defended on sounder arguments than Stone's. In this period, Shakespeare was educated at Stratford-upon-Avon grammar school, and absorbed a vast treasury of classical and historical lore, with a strong input of philosophy and politics. A huge range of reading material came from the presses, despite episcopal censorship. Output included bibles, catechisms, thousands of sermons, school textbooks, legal and medical works for experts, practical books on surveying and measurement, navigation aids, maps, histories and literature in Elizabeth's reign, joined by dictionaries in the early seventeenth century, home-care medical works 'for the poorer sort', even *Arithmetique made easie* (1630). The Authorised Version of the Bible, published in 1611, became one of the most popular and influential books of all time. Patently there was plenty of self-improvement going on, in addition to formal education at schools and universities.

One educational development of these years which deserves more attention than it has generally received is the establishment of Gresham College in London, founded under the will of Sir Thomas Gresham (d. 1579). The mayor and commonalty of London were made responsible for the professors of divinity/theology, astronomy, music and geometry, and the Mercers' Company for those of civil law, rhetoric and physic at the establishment in Gresham's home in Bishopgate Street, after his widow's death (1596). The first appointees were Anthony Wootton (divinity), Matthew Gwynne (physic), Henry Mountlow (civil law), John Bull (music), Edward Brerewood (astronomy), Henry Briggs (geometry) and Caleb Williams (rhetoric). The lectures were to take place daily in term-time, Sundays excepted, and were read in Latin between nine and ten in the morning, and in English between two and three in the afternoon, but Dr Bull was dispensed to read his music lecture only in English on Thursday and Saturday afternoons between three and four. The lectures in Latin were for the benefit of foreigners. The lectures were free, and followed by discussion. Gresham College provided free adult education of the most up-to-date kind. The lecturers had to break away from the university tradition of commenting on set texts, and had to expound their subjects practically: thus the astronomer had to demonstrate nautical instruments for mariners, and the law lectures had to be on common practicalities such as wills, trusts and contracts. Gresham bridged the old universities and the new experimental science in a remarkable way. Six of the seven professors initially appointed (after consultation with the universities of Oxford and Cambridge) were Oxbridge men, and some eventually left to take up Oxbridge chairs. It was a remarkable vision, amply fulfilled in the rest of our period, and still flourishing.

The higher educational echelons did of course influence the lower. At Oxford and Cambridge, where statutes of 1636 and 1570 formed the basic regulations for the rest of our period, control over the universities' members increased. In McConica's phrase, 'the protestant undergraduate collegiate university was now an accomplished fact'.[18] Oxford's 1581 matriculation statute required students to subscribe to the Thirty-nine Articles and the Royal Supremacy, and undergraduates were given organised college teaching. These developments took place against an expansionist background in financially inflationary times. The colleges wanted to attract fee-paying undergraduates, and expanded accommodation for them. Consequently more graduates emerged for employment, and more teachers had degrees. In this period all the headmasters of the Leicester Free Grammar School after 1594 were BAs or MAs, with the exception of one.[19] Twenty-seven per cent of the licensed schoolmasters in the diocese of London were graduates in the 1580s; 59 per cent in the 1630s. In Cambridgeshire, Spufford found the quality of the schoolmasters active between 1574 and 1604 'extra-ordinarily high', two-thirds of those licensed to teach grammar being graduates, and a third of those licensed to teach reading, writing and the casting of accounts.[20] The graduate clergyman was increasingly common: in 1603 there were 3804 licensed preachers with degrees in England's 9244 parishes. Clergymen and schoolteachers were professionally associated, and many had experience of both professions.

Government was increasingly by the educated: 219 of 460 members of parliament in 1584 (48 per cent) had been at university or inns of court, 386 of 552 (70 per cent) of the members of parliament of 1640–42. At least eighty of the 108 justices of the peace, lieutenants and sheriffs of Somerset between 1625 and 1640 had been similarly educated.[21] If academic education has any enlightening value this should have counted for something. It cannot, however, be said that the education of girls of this class generally advanced in quality or quantity. As will be seen below, the well-educated exceptions were not reared in as much classical literature as their Tudor predecessors, and the new seventeenth-century boarding schools for girls were more social finishing schools than intellectual stimuli.

Something which was new in this period was the provision of teaching outside, and in criticism of, the Church of England, despite its best efforts to stifle such education. The 1571 canons limiting teaching to the licensed applied to teaching 'openly in the schools' and 'privately, in any man's house'. Enforcement was slack until Elizabeth's excommunication, but hunts for papists began in the 1570s, and Cardinal Allen founded Douai as a seminary for priests for the English mission in 1568; lay students were soon admitted. A. C. Beales calls the country 'infested with Catholic tutors in houses of the rich and . . . illicit Catholic schools in the villages and even towns', despite episcopal crusades, fines, and the execution of twenty-three Catholic schoolmasters as traitors between 1570 and 1610.[22] Attested Catholic schools were most numerous in Yorkshire, Lancashire and London. James I's reign intensified the struggle, though toleration increased under Charles I between 1629 and 1640. The Catholic émigré Mary Ward (born in 1585) founded a boarding school for English girls at St Omer, but ran into criticism for too optimistic or ambitious a view of girls' potential. The Puritans, on the other extreme, were better able, in this period, to influence schooling within the law. Cross comments: 'the county of Leicester was being efficiently indoctrinated with the Elizabethan religious settlement in its most radical form' under the influence of the Puritan earl of Huntingdon.[23] The Puritans were not particularly progressive educationally at this time, but their ascendancy was to be dominant in the next period. Puritans wanted to deflect revenues of deans and chapters to finance a preaching ministry in every parish, to establish schools and endow poor relief, and supplementary lectureships were set up which were under less episcopal control than ministers with cure of souls, but Laud waged war on these. Some ideas and experiments seem significant, with hindsight. Emmanuel College Cambridge, Sir Walter Mildmay's Puritan foundation of 1584, designed to prepare men for the preaching ministry, grew to over 200 undergraduates by 1617, and held to its mission well, being the leading contributor of ministers and teachers to New England in the years before 1645. Richard Mulcaster, head of Merchant Taylors' and later of St Paul's, recommended a teacher-training college. He was also favourably disposed towards the education of girls, though only as an accessory to that of boys. Clergymen and teachers who attended local conferences, prophesyings and exercises could gain a form of in-service training to enhance their professional competence.

The Effect of the Puritan Revolution, 1640–1660

The educational experiments of the Puritan revolution look exciting and progressive today, because they contained so many foreshadowings of later educational theory and practice. Puritanism gradually diverged more widely from the established Church of England in Elizabeth's reign, on the critical left of the religious spectrum. The division widened under the early Stuarts, as Laudian–Arminian (anti-Calvinist) influence pressed the Church of England to the right. In educational terms the Puritans were wary of non-scriptural learning, and the mental ambitions and vanities associated with it. They had a high view of the calling of a minister, who was likely to be the most learned person in any rural parish, and whose view of a just society required him to catechise and give sermons, preaching obedience to the lower orders and just rule to those in power. Puritan magistrates expected preaching to be exerted to keep the people biddable. This ministry had to be educated, and by the revolution almost all ministers were graduates.

In Puritan families the household was itself a centre of godly instruction, and children were brought up in a god-fearing atmosphere stressing the virtues of duty, humility, sobriety and self-denial. Children's sinful will had to be crushed, and idleness was an evil. Servants had to be saved as well as children, and the Puritan household was able to turn in on itself when Puritanism in public pulpit, school and college fell into state disfavour. English bibles became more commonplace, and for some access to scripture was the whole point of education. However, the dominant patriarchal views of society continued, so though there were women teaching in elementary schools, 'there was a social structural and economic bias against full literacy for both women and members of the lower orders'.[24]

If the Puritans had not been noticeably progressive in England in the period before 1640, the next twenty years were more encouraging to innovation. Censorship was lifted in the 1640s, and religious toleration encouraged. Cheap newspapers flourished: there were 722 in 1645. Universal education for both sexes was fiercely argued. Samuel Harmar's *Vox Populi or Glostershere's Desire* (1642) contained a cry for general schooling over the land, and John Dury in *The Reformed School* (1649) gave a mix of religious and economic justifications for education including girls. While theorists were able to publish innovatory suggestions they were inconsistent (to twentieth-century eyes) in espousing mixtures of radical and conservative policies. Thus the radical Polish-born reformer Samuel Hartlib (d. 1690) in *Considerations tending to the happy accomplishment of England's Reformation* (1647) preserved the class system in his scheme:

> the schools should be of four several kinds or degrees. The first for the vulgar, whose life is mechanical. The second for the gentry and nobles, who are to bear charges in the commonwealth. The third for scholars who are to teach others humane arts and sciences. And the fourth for the sons of the prophets, who are a seminary of the ministry.[25]

The 'vulgar' were the substance of Howell's complaint about cobblers' children and the like at school, but John Amos Comenius's *The Great Didactic* (1657) took a more optimistic view:

If any ask, 'What will be the result if artisans, rustics, porters and even women become lettered?' I answer, If this universal instruction of youth be brought about by the proper means, none of these will lack the material for thinking, choosing following and doing good things... all will regale themselves, even in the midst of their toil, by meditation on the words and works of God, and, by the constant reading of the Bible and other good books, will avoid that idleness which is so dangerous to flesh and blood.[26]

At the universities, providing on the one hand for the ministry and on the other for gentlemen, science began to take root. After the parliamentary commission of 1648 translated to Oxford John Wilkins, John Wallis and Jonathan Goddard, men of the Gresham circle later to be founders of the Royal Society, the university found itself becoming a leading centre of scientific activity, where Wren, Boyle and Locke were educated. As warden of Wadham College 1648–59, Wilkins made it a centre of scientific learning and wrote religious, mathematical and astronomical works. Wallis became Savilian professor of geometry at Oxford in 1649 and survived the Restoration. Goddard was warden of Merton College 1651–60 and was appointed Professor of Physic at Gresham College in 1655. Thomas Spratt, author of the approved history of the Royal Society, referring to the Wadham meetings which were antecedents of the Society, spoke of the university having 'many members of its own who had begun a free way of reasoning'.[27]

In this period, education was much embroiled with politics. The 1640 'Root and Branch Petition' referred to 'the discouragement of many from bringing up their children in learning' and the 'gross and lamentable ignorance almost everywhere among the people'. The Grand Remonstrance (1641) proposed reforming and purging the universities. In 1644 Parliament set up committees to investigate ministers and schoolmasters and eject and replace unfit ones. However the licensing of schoolmasters by bishops collapsed with the abolition of the episcopate, and many just moved. Commissions for the propagation of the Gospel in Wales and the North Parts (1650) stressed religious rather than educational purposes, but the two were to some extent inseparable, and it was the Commonwealth and Protectorate's desire to impose English Puritanism on Wales which led to the first state grant to education in the British Isles in 1649. Money from the sale of dean and chapter lands (1649) was used to augment the stipends of ministers and schoolmasters: the commissioners for the propagation of the

Gospel in the four northern counties augmented schoolmasters' pay by £20 at Durham, Darlington and Bishop Auckland. After the Restoration the funds were restored to deans and chapters. In this period too, England's third university made a tentative start at Durham.

Reformers pressed for greater state intervention. Hartlib tried to get the first Protectorate Parliament to reform education by changing Latin teaching. Harrington urged attendance from nine to fifteen, gratis for the poor, in *Oceana* (1656). The ejection of scandalous schoolmasters continued and in the Protectorate major-generals and commissioners granted licences to teach, looking into political affiliation and fitness. From the Long Parliament through the Protectorate free schools and colleges benefited from regular rate exemption.

Many of the lines which were subsequently followed in English educational funding and practice saw the light of day in this period. Dawns were false, for few survived the Restoration. It must also be acknowledged that for many educated people the reformers' dreams were nightmares, threatening to bring about the rise of a dangerously educated, dissatisfied underclass. Study of the local situation suggests one should be cynical about reformers' schemes and acts of parliament alike. Like the Vicar of Bray, the schoolmaster might be expected to be flexible in politically turbulent times.

Not all change was constructive. In the civil war situation education suffered setbacks from disturbance. Institutional rents became uncollectable, towns were besieged, and soldiers did damage. Oxford in particular was vastly disrupted by the Royalist removal there, and then by parliamentary visitation. Determiners declined from over 200 in 1641 to thirty-one in 1645, and inceptors fell from 131 in 1642 to twenty-five in 1644. Parliamentary visitors expelled 233 fellows, though forty-three of these were expelled but remained. Further visitations followed in the Cromwellian regime, and the university was subjected to religious indoctrination.[28] The two decades offered legacies to totalitarian regimes as well as some moves to liberalise education.

Conformity and Exclusion, 1660–1700

The Restoration restored more than the monarchy and the House of Lords. The somewhat anarchic freedoms of the Interregnum were reined in. Censorship was re-established by the Licensing Acts

(1662–95). By a series of acts known collectively as the Clarendon Code (the Corporation Act, 1661; Act of Uniformity, 1662; Conventicle Act, 1664 and Five Mile Act, 1665) nonconformists were excluded from all local government and from the universities. The Act of Uniformity, embracing ecclesiastics from cathedral deans to curates and 'every other person in holy orders', extended to 'every schoolmaster keeping any public or private school, and every person instructing or teaching youth in any house or private family as a tutor or schoolmaster' on 1 May 1662 or any time thereafter. They all had to subscribe to a declaration that it was not lawful to take up arms against the king, and that they would conform to the liturgy of the Church of England, and would hold no obligation extending from the oath to the Solemn League and Covenant. Any teacher instructing youth before being licensed by his archbishop or bishop and before making the subscription, should suffer three months of imprisonment for the first offence, and three months plus £5 fine for any subsequent offence. The wording of the Act provides a contemporary summary of the educational alternatives of public and private schools and home tutoring. Subscriptions from this date offer valuable information as to who was teaching where, but by the end of the period licensing was only held to be necessary for grammar schools. Some 1760 ministers and 150 dons and schoolmasters were ejected as dissenters. Despite promises of religious toleration made at Breda, and Charles II's declarations of indulgence in 1662 and 1672/3, Parliament tried to impose exclusive Anglican orthodoxy by the Test Act of 1673. This Act was repealed in 1828, but non-Anglicans were discriminated against at the universities until the University Tests Act of 1871. For the dissenters alternative higher educational institutions had to be established.

In 1687 and 1688 James II issued declarations of indulgence suspending the Test Act and granting freedom to worship publicly to dissenters. His personal predilection was for Catholicism, and he particularly wanted to foster it at the universities. The resistance at Oxford is well known. James was forced from his kingdom by the Revolution of 1688 and in 1689 the Toleration Act finally abandoned the ideal of one single state church, of which all were members, without, however, granting full civil equality to those who opted out of it.

For education, the Clarendon Code meant conformity or exclusion; however in practice situations seem to have been much less clear-cut. The 'stop-go' vacillations between periods of law enforcement and its suspension under various declarations of indulgence did nothing for constructive development. Both Charles II and James II were Catholic

sympathisers and their declarations of indulgence were largely to alle-
viate Catholics' disadvantages, only accidentally relieving also Protestant
dissenters. Generally speaking, however, the full severity of the restrict-
ive laws was only applied selectively, against Catholics on the one
extreme and Quakers on the other. The general assumption has been
that all this created a period of educational stagnation, when the universities and grammar schools were controlled by and restricted to
Anglicans, dissenters were driven to set up their own academies, and
the grammar schools were left languishing in a decline accentuated by
their fossilised classical curriculum.

Joan Simon's study of Leicestershire schools in the period 1660–1700
suggests that this is too much of a simplification. The picture Simon
unfolds of Leicestershire education is of village schools teaching English
to the age of nine or ten, and Latin grammar schools concentrated in
towns. Protestant dissenters sent their children to Anglican schools, the
dissenting academies being rather alternatives to the exclusively Anglican universities. Outside places covered by the Corporation Act, dissenters were still active in mainstream education, even acting as school
governors and benefactors. The education of the poor, including girls,
made some quiet progress. At Loughborough in 1683 Bartholomew
Hickling left £4 for the stipend of a schoolmistress, and £6 to equip
twenty girls with books, gowns, shoes and stockings; at Rothley he left
£8 for fifteen poor boys learning Latin or English. At Ashby-de-la-Zouch
in 1695 William Langley established a school for twelve poor boys or
girls to be taught for three years, the master having 1½ d per week per
pupil. Barrow school, founded in 1691, accepted boys from Woodhouse,
Barrow and Quorndon able to read the Bible on entry. They learned
English, Latin, writing and arithmetic. Michael Matthews, a Presbyterian, was the master from 1695 to 1705.[29]

In 1676 the percentage of nonconformists recorded in the Compton
Census was low, at 4–5 per cent, with less than a further one per cent
Catholic. Clearly dissent was a greater phenomenon than this, partly
difficult to quantify because there were elements of conformity, or at any
rate occasional conformity, within it. After 1689 Protestant dissenters
were allowed registered places of worship, preachers and teachers.
Openly sectarian schools could now run freely. In 1702 the clerk of
the Leicester Quaker Quarterly Meeting was appointed also schoolmaster and at least one Baptist was keeping a school in Leicester in 1718.
Dissent's most striking contribution to the English educational spectrum
was, however, the higher educational dissenting academy, discussed

below in Chapter 4. For the Catholics, Beales found in Charles II's reign twenty-one attested schools.[30] James II's reign was disastrous to Catholic missionary and educational enterprise, because reaction was quick and severe and the Toleration Act did not help papists. Catholic schools were still not tolerated here, and from 1700 sending a child abroad for a 'Romish' education attracted a fine of £100, in addition to the penalties suffered by the children themselves, who were already disinherited for such activity. Thus religion still laid a heavy hand on educational opportunity. Its missionary side, however, was about to launch new development. In 1608 the SPCK was founded, which, like the commissions for the propagation of the Gospel in Wales and the north in the commonwealth period, promoted education in promoting religion.

Compared with the preceding twenty years, this period has many sterile characteristics. The struggle between conformity and dissent has been given centre stage, with too little attention being paid to what facilities actually existed for the youth of the day in urban and rural England. As in the 1560–1640 period, the focus on the universities and grammar schools after 1660, where a picture of decline and stagnation may be painted, has been allowed to obscure the good progress made at less lofty levels. But the stagnation may be exaggerated. Simon's picture of Leicestershire's economic and social changes affecting educational supply and demand may well prove valid in other areas too. Stagnation was not the characteristic there: a variety of new schools can be traced, and changing roles for existing ones. Indeed, enough was being done to improve the education of the poor in seventeenth-century Leicestershire to cast doubts on the claims to significance of the later Charity School movement. What matter, at this level, if Leicestershire entrants to the universities dropped off after 1680? Cressy believes the period 1660–80 saw one of the surges against illiteracy. The illiteracy rate of London tradesmen and craftsmen was down to 13 per cent in the 1690s, while women's illiteracy in the capital declined from 78 per cent in the 1670s to 64 per cent in the 1680s and 52 per cent in the 1690s. 'By the end of the Stuart period the English had achieved a level of literacy unknown in the past and unmatched elsewhere in early modern Europe.'[31] Between basic literacy and the old grammar-school tradition came experiments with modern subjects directly relevant to employment. Even university stagnation may be exaggerated: Oxford's Ashmolean Museum opened in 1683, providing an institutional home for chemistry, natural history and antiquarian studies. The dissenting academies espoused a more modern curriculum. Christopher Hill disparaged them in claiming they provided the best training for the lower grades of the civil service, for their alumni reached up to the politicians Harley and Bolingbroke, the writer Defoe, and more surprisingly, Thomas Secker, archbishop of Canterbury. If a social wedge widened the gap between the shrinking, traditionally upper-class universities and the multiplying middle-class dissenting academies, a similar wedge divided the prestigious but dilettante Royal Society from the practical innovations of the day. Progress was being made, but it was not always identifiable with institutions.

For girls, Mrs Bathsua Makin, née Pell, born in 1612, a rector's daughter precociously credited with Latin, Greek, Hebrew, French and Italian at the age of nine, due to the influence of her prodigiously gifted brother, despised 'meerly to teach Gentlewomen to Frisk and Dance, to paint their Faces, to curl their Hair'.[32] One-time governess to Charles I's sister Elizabeth, Mrs Makin made a plea in an essay in 1673 'to Revive the Ancient education of Gentlewomen' in religion, manners, arts and tongues, but the school she established around this time at Tottenham compromised more demanding academic study with the more practical and decorative accomplishments parents prepared to pay fees of £20 per annum might expect: a variety of languages could be exchanged for 'experimental philosophy' as one half of a syllabus whose other half was dancing, music, singing, writing, and keeping accounts. Such a school, for such a clientele, was unconventional indeed. Girls educated at home or in schools were commonly engrossed in fancy crafts taught by governesses and accomplishments taught by specialist visiting masters.

Recession in the Early Eighteenth Century

The conventional picture of education in England in the period 1700–60 is dismal, especially when the focus is on the higher, traditional echelons, the universities, the 'public' schools and the grammar schools. The clergy and gentry, whose essentially traditional and orthodox education the universities had become dedicated to supplying, were declining in numbers and importance, and the universities continued their own decline. George I established regius professorships in history in 1724, expressly to train public servants, but at Oxford only the first two were energetic. Cambridge overall was perhaps the less lethargic, and beginning to specialise in mathematics. University students varied from poor scholars and humble servitors or sizars to the idle gentlemen or fellow commoners who were not seriously studying at all. Students were coming up on tied awards from provincial grammar schools of varied quality. The major public schools, Eton, Winchester and Westminster, were providing old-fashioned Latin and Greek education, with perfunctory French, mathematics and geography taught on holidays. Some of the town grammar schools were doing better: Cross reckoned that the Free School at Leicester reached a peak of success under Garrard Andrewes, MA (1739–62), a Balliol man, under whom about thirty boarders were attracted.[33] The girls' boarding schools remained a very mixed bag, but demand for them increased as commercial prosperity gave birth to upwardly mobile social aspirations. Girls' schools were still very much the private ventures of proprietors, and short-lived compared with schools for boys.

Religious tests kept dissenters out of the universities and (perhaps less rigorously) the grammar schools. After the Toleration Act dissenting academies flourished and these institutions have been seen as far more vigorous than the traditional establishments. Classics, French, Italian, history and political theory, English literature, inductive logic and science competed for space in the curricula of these academies. Distinguished ones included Stoke Newington (where Defoe was educated), Northampton, and Warrington (where Joseph Priestley was a lecturer). The academies served as universities as well as senior schools, since the dissenting students could not enter Oxford or Cambridge, but after the Act of Union of 1707 the way was open for them to enter Scottish universities such as Edinburgh or Glasgow, and some students went abroad to Utrecht or Leiden. Originally the academies were set up to train dissenting ministers, but they expanded to take in general students; Warrington provided a shorter course for students intending to enter business and commerce.

Lower down the social scale this period is popularly seen as the age of the Charity School, about which there is some controversy. The SPCK certainly promoted the establishment of charity schools for the poor. It provided guidelines for doing it, from soliciting initial subscriptions to maintaining the school, running it, and supervising the subjects taught. By 1723 it is claimed 1329 charity schools had been set up, and 1419 by 1729. They varied from small schools providing only the most elementary education to schools which also clothed the pupils and attempted to launch them into suitable apprenticeships. All were firmly confined to teaching religious instruction, reading and writing, with some basic arithmetic for boys and needlework, especially knitting, for girls. The idea was to increase the piety and industriousness of the poor, not to help them upwards socially. 'The charity school movement', as it has been identified, has been credited as changing the course of educational development and carrying all before it, but based on the Leicestershire evidence, Joan Simon questioned whether there was any such movement, and certainly its supposed continuance throughout the eighteenth century. She argued that the charity school proper should be distinguished from other specifically charitable schooling as an institution to rescue unemployed poor children aged seven to twelve from idleness and irreligion, and to redirect them to a useful working life. The SPCK's own reports indicate Leicestershire was the star example outside London, with thirty-five schools in the county, but Simon discovered some were over fifty years old already, and she cut the valid claims down to twenty-two. Outside London in the first quarter of the century Simon sees little evidence of a 'movement'.[34]

In London and Westminster there were fifty-four charity schools teaching 2000 pupils, and the numbers rose to 132 teaching 5225 by 1729. By 1799 179 schools were teaching 7108.[35] In Bristol and Newcastle there was some success, but in general Simon's case that the charity schools have been overrated seems attractive. Concern for teaching the poor neither began nor ended with charity schooling. On the other hand, tens of thousands of children did pass through the schools, and even if they were indoctrinated in Anglican Tory principles, many must have managed to achieve a literacy they would not have acquired otherwise. Whatever was causing it, the illiteracy rate was falling, with interruptions, in many areas. Using Northern Assize Circuit depositions, Houston postulated a decline of illiteracy from 65 per cent among males in the 1640s to 41 per cent in the 1690s, a rise of one per cent by the 1720s, falling to 27 per cent in the 1730s, rising to 30 per cent in the 1740s. For women at the same dates the rates were 93 per cent, 86 per cent, 74 per cent and 68 per cent. Higher levels of literacy were found in cities, such as Newcastle, Durham and Carlisle.[36]

Precursors of Industrial Training

By the later eighteenth century, industrial employment beckoned large numbers of the population, from an early age. For them, training rather than education was what society required. Machinery to provide this had been set up centuries earlier, but the history of its operation is a melancholy story of declining standards and increasing opportunities for abuse.

The Poor Law of 1536 empowered parish authorities to apprentice healthy, idle, begging children between the ages of five and fourteen to masters in husbandry or other crafts, to train them to earn a living. The Act of 1547 rendered such children liable to slavery on recapture if they ran away, and the age for 'graduating' from the service entered was set at twenty for women and twenty-four for men. In 1549 this law was ameliorated and service shortened to the ages of fifteen (or marriage) for girls and eighteen for boys. From the Statute of Artificers of 1563, reinforced by the Poor Laws of 1597 and 1601, basically operative until 1834, apprenticeship can be seen as an intentionally socially stratified system. Overseas traders, mercers, drapers, goldsmiths, embroiderers and outputting clothiers were to accept into these high-class opportunities only apprentices whose parents had £3 per annum freehold. Children of landless parents were only acceptable into lesser crafts such as those of smiths, wheelwrights, carpenters, bricklayers, thatchers, domestic weavers and fullers. These apprenticeships were supposed to be for seven years, and guilds were able to add their own traditional monopolistic interpretations to the execution of the law, limiting the numbers of apprentices a master might take and thus controlling entry into the craft, and generally maintaining regulation over apprenticeship conditions. An inferior form of apprenticeship enforced under the 1597 and 1601 Poor Laws combined boarding out with learning a livelihood, for paupers, orphans and children whose parents could not support them. These parish apprentices were bound not by their own parents but by the local authorities, the churchwardens and overseers of the poor, with the supervision of the justices of the peace, and were often bound to masters to learn husbandry or handicraft. This end of the spectrum soon degenerated into 'a system of boarding out at minimum cost to the rates',[37] exploiting young boys in husbandry and young girls as domestics. The system was widely abused after the 1662 Act of Settlement complicated the local calculations by making the serving of an apprenticeship within a parish a way of gaining settlement. Parish apprentices were more open to abuse than the apprentices protected by the old guild systems, but the guild authority was in decline from the early eighteenth century. Much of the most effective industrial training belonged to particular towns which took their obligations more seriously than most. Norwich set up a scheme in 1571 whereby selected women were paid 20s per annum to take up to a dozen women and children and supervise their work in the cloth industry; for some years this worked well (in expansionist times) and the city claimed to have 900 children in work. Bristol in 1589 set up a school to teach children to knit worsted hose, and its efforts to put out boys appropriately to masters 'of ability and honesty also of some sort of employment or faculty' after legislation in 1696, earned the approval of Pinchbeck and Hewitt.[38] Good practice in this field was not commonplace, and it seems the Tudor foundations of industrial training supported an unworthy edifice by the eve of mass industrialisation.

3

THE AIMS OF EDUCATION

The Medieval Legacy

Late medieval society did not invest in education as such, which in itself casts light on the aims of what educational provision there was. The chief institutional interest in education came from the church, not the state. The church saw basic training in the rudiments of the faith as essential for the souls of Christian individuals, but this did not necessarily extend to literacy, and could remain compartmentalised, so that an individual learned very little from religion to apply to other aspects of experience. By English provincial legislation parish clergy were required to instruct their parishioners four times a year in the Creed, the Ten Commandments, and the seven sacraments, virtues, deadly sins and works of mercy. Education in literacy, from the church's point of view, meant progression in Latin, which was vocationally requisite for all professional clergymen, and so much their monopoly that a reading test in it (the passage set was so commonly the first verse of the fifty-first psalm that this became known as the 'neck verse') was given to test those claiming the privilege of clerical status (benefit of clergy) at law, which might save a man from hanging. The purpose of the secular clergy's education was to produce men who could perform the eight services of the divine office, and those in priests' orders had to celebrate daily mass and perform other sacraments, such as baptism, as required. The liturgy was in Latin, and clergymen were encouraged also to read the Bible in Latin, and required knowledge of plainsong. This at any rate was the ideal, but there is considerable evidence of late medieval clerical short-comings. The purpose of education for monks and friars was equally Latinate, the friars in particular placing a high value on education to combat heresy and indifference.

With Latin grammar seen as 'the foundation, gate and source of all the other liberal arts', to quote William of Wykeham's foundation deed for Winchester College (1382), an expression typical of his own day and the following centuries, it was the essential qualification for any deeper academic study at university level. Arts degrees, and higher degrees in theology and civil and canon law, were levels of attainment which provided the church with its leading administrators and most disciplined thinkers. Towards providing a framework of educational facilities the Lateran Council of 1179 made cathedral churches responsible for supporting a master to teach 'the clerks of the same church and poor scholars freely', a provision extended by the next Lateran Council in 1215. These educational provisions had, by the end of the Middle Ages, been widened at the local level by an extension of schooling in reading and grammar. The great age of chantry foundation was the fourteenth and fifteenth centuries, and chantry priests were sometimes required to teach local children as part of their obligations, and in other places did this in hours not occupied by chantry duties. Chantry teaching ranged from being specifically offered as free to all, to being provided for a mixture of free and fee-paying pupils, or indeed only for fee-paying pupils (chantry stipends were rarely an adequate living unsupplemented). An injunction of the Convocation of Canterbury in 1530 ordered all rectors, vicars and chantry priests to employ themselves, when not engaged in divine service, in study, prayer, preaching or instructing boys in the alphabet, reading, song or grammar.

At the apex of English educational provision at the end of the Middle Ages stood the two universities of Oxford and Cambridge. Each had achieved recognition as a *studium generale*, respectively in the late twelfth and thirteenth centuries; the term signified a school of advanced study drawing students from beyond the immediate region. Each offered instruction in all four faculties: arts, law (civil and canon), theology and medicine. The Arts faculty provided the foundation course leading to the degrees of bachelor of arts and, if pursued further, master of arts. The other faculties were what we would term postgraduate. The earliest college foundations, from the second half of the thirteenth century, were essentially to further postgraduate study, undergraduates on the foundation being first found at the King's Hall at Cambridge (which also had the first undergraduate commoners) and New College at Oxford. The universities were vocational and utilitarian, 'buttressing the fabric of England's political, administrative, legal and ecclesiastical structures'.[1] Seven of the ten colleges founded between 1350 and 1450 concentrated on training men for the secular clergy: Trinity Hall, Corpus Christi, King's and Queens' at Cambridge, New College, Lincoln, and All Souls at Oxford. Godshouse at Cambridge was specifically founded to train schoolmasters. Originally communities of clerics, the universities were by the late fifteenth century beginning to attract students who were not committed to, or indeed not even contemplating, a career in the church. It was, however, the universities' ecclesiastical character which largely secured their funding in various ways, from the attracting of institutional endowment, to the subsidising of individual students by means of an income from benefices wherein they were not resident because of their studies.

With the church's encouragement, educational charities had indeed become an object of piety right through the educational spectrum. Motives may be questioned in some areas. Though it was a good deed, and in the case of Balliol College even a penance, to found a college or school, and doubtless the pre-Reformation benefactors placed some store on the prayers of the beneficiaries to be amassed in future generations, one suspects there may have been an element of self-gratification in having the resultant school or college bear one's own or family name. Pembroke College at Cambridge, founded in 1347 by Marie de St Pol, widow of Aymer de Valence earl of Pembroke, was originally titled the hall of Valence-Mary, linking the family name with the Blessed Virgin of the dedication. Open to no such suspicions of dynastic aggrandisement were the altruistic small gifts of lesser persons towards the founding or maintenance of less ambitious schools in their localities, for example the tanner Edmund Peresone's bequest at Beetham (Westmorland) in 1542. Edmund left goods of unspecified value for 'a stokke at my . . . parishe church towarde the fyndynge off a preste for to teche a free scole and to praye for my sawle and all cristen sawles'.[2]

Church recommendation and piety combined to make the teaching of Latin and the academic subjects desirable because these were adjuncts of the faith. In extending such educational facilities one was furthering the church's work. The same could not be said about providing practical education for craft or trade purposes, nor even about providing the rather more academic education needed for a career in the common law. It is clear from the comparative lack of institutional or personal sponsorship in these latter fields that it was the religious, rather than the educational, motive which was the stronger force in the endowment of medieval schools and colleges. No one created scholarships to subsidise the learning of conveyancing, or keeping accounts, or to forward promising boys from the grammar school to the inns of court. Intending common lawyers and scribes, or their parents or personal patrons, had to pay for their education as an investment for the future. The first signs of supporting practical education as in itself a deserving cause came in Archbishop Rotherham's statutes for Jesus College Rotherham in 1483, providing, as well as the masters of grammar and song, a teacher of writing and accounts for able boys to fit them for mechanical arts and worldly business.

After the church, the most prestigious career was in the common law, initially learned by attendance at the courts. By the late thirteenth century the main development of the common law system in England had occurred, creating a network of central and local courts, requiring a supply of practitioners to work them. Common law as a profession for laymen emerged in the second half of the thirteenth century, and laymen had taken over almost completely by 1340. The language of the law was predominantly Latin until the early fourteenth century, then law French; English became the language of pleading by statute in 1362, but the records remained in Latin and French until 1733, excepting the Commonwealth period. A career in common law required as great a linguistic skill as a church career, and perhaps indeed greater flexibility between the three languages. It also required a textual familiarity with writs, statute law and study of precedent. It was a highly literate career, recruiting largely from the knightly and gentry classes. From the grounding of grammar schooling, the late medieval law student would proceed to London, to the inns of chancery, the obvious training ground for familiarity with writs, and then to the superior inns of court, which developed their educational aspects in the fifteenth century. Fortescue in *De Laudibus Legum Angliae* referred to over ten lesser inns or inns of chancery, and four greater inns or inns of court, forming a public academy more suitable to the law training than any university. It was an expensive progression, so only the well-born managed it. Two generations of Pastons illustrate the enhancing of the training as the family moved upwards socially in the fifteenth century: William Paston went from grammar school to London, rising to become a sergeant-at-law and eventually a justice of the court of common pleas. He sent three sons to Cambridge University, whence the eldest went on to the

Inner Temple, a pattern which became common in the later sixteenth century. Sir John Fortescue in the eighth chapter of *De Laudibus* assured the prince that he should be able to acquire a working knowledge of the principles of the law in a year, instead of the twenty taken by judges, who had to know the precise points.

Below fully-fledged lawyers there were administrators of varied skills. An Oxford University statute of 1432 was devised to control students we might recognise as 'university extension students', studying *ars dictandi*, the art of writing (composition, that is, not calligraphy), French, composition of deeds, and procedural routine in the English courts. This 'business training' in Oxford seems to have existed in some form from the early thirteenth to the mid-fifteenth century, when it died away, probably in the face of the development of the London inns. Much administration was carried out by people who had the clerkly education of the universities, but who had chosen to move away from an ecclesiastical career, and in some cases had married. William of Worcestre, Sir John Fastolf's secretary, was one. However, John Vale became the London draper Thomas Cook's factor, 'an indispensable general clerk, accountant, administrator and day to day legal advisor' apparently on the strength of his education in Bury St Edmunds and then training in the Cook household, where he may or may not have been formally apprenticed.[3] Stewards and bailiffs who needed to receive and send written communications and keep records may well have had this type of education: an elementary or more advanced introduction to letters, followed by experience on the job, and perhaps aided by some quite technical manuals which were circulating in manuscript from the late thirteenth century onwards, for example Walter of Henley's *Husbandry* (in Anglo-Norman).

Mechanical arts had their own training methods. Medieval apprenticeship was an enviable opportunity since, if all worked out well, it held out prospects of well-founded betterment. Most of the characteristics of early modern apprenticeship were already in place by the end of the Middle Ages. An adolescent would be apprenticed to a master usually at fifteen or sixteen in London by the end of the fourteenth century, and even eighteen in the fifteenth century, which Barbara Hanawalt, in *Growing up in Medieval London* (1993) attributes to the fact that the elite guilds, such as the mercers, goldsmiths and ironmongers, required apprentices to be educated before entering into their contract. In the provinces, the age of entry was lower. The apprenticeship was a well-defined agreement, binding the adolescent to a master by a contract to which the apprentice's family or other sponsor was party. Fees were paid to the regulating guilds, and premiums to the master. There were regulations on the length of apprenticeship and the numbers a master could have at one time. During the term, which varied in length from about seven to about ten years, the apprentice progressed from being little more than an errand-boy to being a fully-fledged craftsman. This was both technical training and regulated practice, and absolutely vocational, since an apprenticeship in one trade was no qualification in another.

Some apprenticeship agreements stipulated that the boy would be released for schooling, and pragmatic literacy, in English, was expected of the apprentices in the more demanding trades; either they had to have it when they started, or they had to gain it while they trained. Apprenticeship included girls, but in limited fields. The best researched area of female apprenticeship is London silkworking, which lacked a guild structure, but did have seven-year apprenticeships. Silkworking was almost entirely in women's hands, but in other crafts, including ones which would hardly appear to be suitable for women, such as bell-founding, the wives and daughters of a master craftsman were expected to gain some familiarity with his trade, and guild regulations permitted them to help him, and to carry on running the business, sometimes under certain specified conditions, after his death. How they learned the necessary skills is not clear, but presumably it came of long familiarity in the house and shop.

Agricultural labour must have been similarly learned by experience, in a domestic farm setting. Many young people went through a period of servanthood in the household of a social superior, in both town and country in the late Middle Ages and early modern times. It was an educative experience, but is not part of the formally recognised educational structure.

To no group in the Middle Ages was there assured educational opportunity tailored to aptitude. Aptitude is mentioned, as a necessary consideration in selecting beneficiaries for limited resources: the six scholar choristers at Rotherham who were to be maintained to the age of eighteen were to be chosen by the college Provost from 'the poorer boys of the area most fit and apt for learning and virtue'.[4] These conditions combined the merit of benefiting 'the poor' while limiting the expenditure to 'the apt' among them. Much educational opportunity was offered as a matter of chance, to pupils who happened to live in a favoured area. When Edmund Shaa founded the grammar school at

Stockport (1488) it was to set up a master 'to keep a school continually... without asking wages or salary... and teach all manner of persons children as well of the town as of other towns thereabout'. Thus was the locality and its hinterland advantaged. The grammar school at Macclesfield, established in 1503, was a free grammar school for 'gentlemen's sons and other goodmen's children of that town and country thereabouts', a similar opportunity for those happy enough to live in the catchment zone.[5]

To some groups, from medieval and early modern into comparatively recent times, educational advantages were assured ahead of open competition. John Crosse, Lancashire-born rector of a London church, endowed a chantry priest at St Katherine's image in the chapel of St Mary del Kay at Liverpool, in his will of 1515, requiring him to keep a grammar school, taking fees, but teaching freely 'all children whose names be Crosse and poor children'.[6] Wykeham's Winchester and New College gave outright priority in entering to the founder's kin. Attempt was made to limit the number of beneficiaries in 1586, but in 1651 the quota was raised to twenty at each college, adversely affecting the quality of intake over the next two centuries. It is scarcely surprising that, believing in the advantages of education, and sacrificing (from their immediate relatives' point of view) dynastic wealth by granting away land or capital, benefactors could not bring themselves to bar their own kin from having prior claim on the facilities which were being set up. The tendency also ran comfortably alongside the element of dynastic aggrandisement in having a school, college or scholarship as one's memorial. Maybe such educational foundations should be viewed from a different perspective – instead of hailing them as altruistic foundations imperfected by the closed scholarships to favoured blood, perhaps they should be seen as an aspect of far-sighted provision for one's family in the broadest sense, usefully and practically laid open to others when places were unfilled, and generously providing for these extra beneficiaries.

Some of the guaranteed places were reserved, as just shown, to favour not kin but locality, and this indicates the founders' next circle of identity: after kin and clan comes native heath, or the place where one had made one's fortune, or, in a mobile career in church or commerce, where one had spent memorable times, or empathised with the people. Archbishop Rotherham was one of the first benefactors to record in writing his memory of his childhood experience in Rotherham, and his desire to establish educational benefits there for the people of the town and its surrounding district. London merchants who prospered were particularly disposed towards their birthplaces, many founding schools, almshouses or hospitals there, as was the case with Shaa of Stockport and Percival of Macclesfield, who both became lord mayors of London. After the death of Sir John Perceval, who had been involved in the foundation of the grammar school at Macclesfield, his widow Thomasine, a native of Cornwall, set up a similar establishment at Week St Mary. In the Macclesfield enterprise, Percival had been assisted by Sir Richard Sutton, a lawyer and Privy Councillor, who in turn was associated with the Lancashire-born bishop William Smith in the foundation of Brasenose College at Oxford, where the original foundation, and benefactions made before the middle of the sixteenth century, established fellowships and scholarships for Lancashire and Cheshire men. When Roger Lupton founded the school at Sedbergh and affiliated it to St John's College Cambridge, St John's referred to the area as a rough people and a wild country where there was no school within forty to fifty miles. Again, taking advantage of these opportunities was largely a matter of luck. Some endowments piled up the facilities in a favoured area; some deliberately claimed to right the balance in more barren soil. Whatever the intentions of the benefactors, it is not clear how strictly they were administered.

The medieval legacy was thus a formative bequest. It had established the essentially utilitarian purpose of education, defining it by evolved custom for particular social purposes. None of it was automatically available, or subsidised. Though the well-placed could afford the fees, and the lucky find some sort of charitable sponsorship, nobody had money to waste on buying more education than was necessary. Though humanism was having some impact on the universities and grammar schools, it had not effected any major extension of traditional educational horizons. Education for its own sake was too luxurious to contemplate; however, this came nearest to achievement in the Tudor and Stuart education for governors.

Education for Governors: Nobility and Gentry

The literature of chivalry, epitomised in the European Arthurian canon, reflects a practical but civilising education, centred in the households of the nobility. After the end of infancy, about the age of seven, the young noble was removed from the 'child care' of women, and subjected to male-orientated training, often in the household of a social superior. The placing of the boy reflected the clientship of his parents and their patron, and this pattern was reproduced at different social levels. *The Black Book of the Household of Edward IV* tells us that the king had half a dozen noble children at court, under a Master of the Henchmen, who was required

> to show the schools of urbanity and nurture of England, to learn them to ride cleanly and surely; to draw them also to jousts; to learn them wear their harness; to have all courtesy in words, deeds and degrees; diligently to keep them in rules of goings and sittings after they be of honour

and teach sundry languages and other virtuous learning and social accomplishments.[7] The purpose of this traditional chivalric education was not academic, but vocational, in a military, feudal, landholding society. The training inculcated physical hardiness and generosity of spirit. Practically, the boys learned horsemanship and appropriate skills in arms. Emotionally, they learned self-control and the dignity of service: due deference to superiors, magnanimity in good fortune and bad. The noble households had their own chapels and attendant clergy, so the religious requirements of the age would be well provided. On the cultural side this education might include languages (more likely French, the tongue of polite communication, than Latin), instrumental music, and pastimes such as chess. While some noble children became young henchmen at the royal court, gentry children were sent up to ducal households, and lower-gentry children to higher-gentry families. Girls, too, could be treated in this way. In these households the experience was a form of social apprenticeship: the boys served as pages and valets, the girls as damsels and companions, an honourable 'above stairs' service while gaining social graces. All through the Middle Ages, besides these secular household 'schools of urbanity and nurture', there were similar opportunities for boys in the households of bishops, opportunities which one suspects would be slightly less military and slightly more academic and/or religious in emphasis. Among his educational experiences, Sir Thomas More spent a couple of years in the household of John Morton, Archbishop of Canterbury and later Cardinal, around 1490–92.

This in-house type of education continued through the sixteenth century, as is shown in Ben Jonson's description of 'nurseries of nobility'.[8] Sir Thomas Elyot's *The Governour* (1531) reveals how far formal academic education was pushing into this regime in the early sixteenth century. Elyot required the young governor to start learning Greek and Latin at seven, and although he appreciated the recent advances in teaching aids for both these studies, he played down the actual grammar study, 'for a gentle wit is therewith soon fatigate'. His youngsters were to read Aesop's *Fables*, the *Select Dialogues* of Lucian, the comedies of Aristophanes, Homer, Virgil, Silius, Lucanus and Hesiodus, all before they were twelve. Later they studied Xenophon, Aristotle and Plato. For Elyot, moral philosophy was the highest of humanistic disciplines. He was himself the compiler of a Latin dictionary, first printed by Berthelet in 1538.

The Governor's emphasis on Greek and Latin shows us how the old chivalric educational system in the household was capable of adaptation to a much more specifically academic focus. The career of Roger Ascham illustrates this to the full. Ascham was reared in the household manner, in the house of Sir Anthony Wingfield. His book *The Scholemaster*, posthumously published in 1570, 'specially purposed for the private bringing up of youth in gentlemen's and noblemen's houses', set high scholarly demands. Ascham's method was the double translation – translation into English was written out by the pupil into a paper book; later, a retranslation back into Latin was written in another, and was then compared with the original. In a third paper book the pupil had to write down collected phrases, constructions and grammatical notes. The teaching was essentially close and personal supervision, achievable in the household framework, but less easy when the master had responsibility for a whole school.

Further reinforcement of the noble education pattern came from abroad. Between 1513 and 1527 Baldassare Castiglione, looking back to his time at the sophisticated Italian ducal court of Urbino, wrote his *Il Cortigiano*. This was translated by Sir Thomas Hoby and published in 1561 as *The Courtier*; Hoby had begun the project by translating Book III of the work (a gender debate) for the wife of his patron, William Parr, marquis of Northampton. The courtier's training was to make everything look natural. He had to be skilled in martial arts on foot and horse, well-spoken and accomplished in languages, able to dance, sing and play on the lute or viol. The secret was being, and putting others, at ease. The courtier appeared to be gifted and effortlessly superior. It should be noted that another Englishman, Bartholomew Clerke, published a translation of the Italian original into Latin in 1571, and that the Latin version ran through at least four editions by 1603, while Hoby produced a text in Italian, French and English in 1588. These translations demonstrate a market of cultivated readers who did not seek to read their texts necessarily, or exclusively, in their mother tongue. Such readers included women: Lady Brilliana Harley, asking her son to provide her with a book in 1638, asked for it in French, 'for I would rather read that tongue than English'.[9]

Throughout the sixteenth century the governing classes patronised both the private household and 'public' school education, and whether it was better for the young gentleman to be taught privately or in a public school remained an open question through the seventeenth century; Locke preferred the private tutor in his *Thoughts concerning Education*, published in five editions between 1693 and 1705. (By this time, it is estimated that 4–5 per cent of the population classed as gentry or above.) Discussing Elyot and Ascham, Foster Watson wrote: 'the fact seems to be that the education of the nobles was mainly outside of the Grammar School and the University'.[10] Each stream, however, contributed to the other. Sir Philip Sidney has long enjoyed the reputation of being the perfect Renaissance patron, soldier, lover and courtier. He appears to be the embodiment of all that Elyot and Ascham valued, but his education was at Shrewsbury School, followed by Christ Church Oxford, with travel on the Continent between 1572 and 1575, studying astronomy and mathematics at Padua. 'Years of comparative idleness', states the *Oxford Companion to English Literature*, 'enabled him to write and revise the *Arcadia*, and to complete *The Defence of Poetry* (influenced by Ascham's *Scholemaster*), *The Lady of May*, and *Astrophel and Stella*', all published after his death in 1586 from injuries received in the attack at Zutphen. Here is the arch example of education for self-fulfilment, enabling a man to occupy 'years of comparative idleness' with literary activity which he was in no hurry to publish.

Cultivation of the courtier's easy grace survived the transition from household education to the environment of the public school and grammar school, and students initially reared either way passed on through university and/or inns of court (especially before the Civil War) and on to the Grand Tour. J. T. Cliffe, writing of the Yorkshire gentry from the Reformation to the Civil War, pointed out that it was rare for them to send sons to Eton or Winchester (the two schools of greatest cachet), but many of their sons were sent to Pocklington School. Going on to university or inns of court was not uncommon among the Yorkshire gentry. Of 679 heads of such families in 1642, 172, 25 per

cent, had been at an English university, though many did not graduate
or complete legal studies, and between 1558 and 1642 over a hundred
Yorkshire gentry sons had been on foreign tour, more particularly after
1604 when peace with Spain was made. Among them was Thomas
Wentworth, later first earl of Strafford. Thomas was educated at first
with the Dean of Ripon who took a few pupils at his house at Well, then
at St John's College Cambridge, and the Inner Temple. His first wife
was Margaret Clifford, daughter of the earl of Cumberland, and it was
after this marriage that Thomas, still only eighteen, went abroad, without his wife, on a Grand Tour which lasted fourteen months. Charles
Howard, third earl of Carlisle, who married Lady Anne Capel in 1688,
when she was thirteen, offers a later example of the post-marital Grand
Tour.

In the eighteenth century a clear social hierarchy of educational
opportunity can also be illustrated best from the provinces. William
Cotesworth, the Newcastle coal magnate, was the son of a yeoman.
Hughes showed how his sons were initially at school locally, at the
Royal Grammar School, Newcastle, but in 1716 he moved them, aged
fifteen and fourteen, to Sedbergh; from there the elder proceeded to
Trinity College Cambridge and the younger was at a writing master's
school in London in 1718. The boys' sisters were sent to London 'to
bring them home marriageable'. One of the girls married into the
Ellison family, and her sons, Cotesworth's grandsons, were sent to
Eton between 1745 and 1753. In 1789 two young Ellisons, both under
nine, were sent to a preparatory school in High Wycombe, and one of
the aims of their parent was to improve their elocution by ridding them
of their north-country cadence. (After four terms he was complaining
they still spoke with the northern rise on the last syllable.) Another
northerner, Admiral Collingwood, sent his daughters to London 'to
correct their language'. Local County Durham schools still satisfied
the local gentry of less ambition. In the North-West, Hughes illustrates
a similar pattern of social climbing. Boys in the Senhouse family were
sent to school at Cockermouth mid-century; the next generation
attended Hawkshead and then St Bees, whence Humphrey III Senhouse went on to Christ's, and became a fellow of Pembroke College
Cambridge, but Humphrey IV went to Eton, moving thence in 1791 to
Pembroke.[11] Upward social mobility was causing families once content
with the services of the local grammar school to send later generations to
board at superior schools, dominated by Eton and Winchester. The class
which, at the start of the period, was most commonly educated by

private tutor, became before the end the class most commonly sent away to boarding schools, schools' boarding houses, or approved town lodgings.

The late Tudor and early Stuart passion for learning among the elite declined by the end of the seventeenth century, leaving the universities commonly seen as mainly training grounds for clergymen and schoolmasters, neither of which were careers entertained by aristocrats and landed gentry for their successors, though a younger son might have to make do with it. A more utilitarian education was coming into vogue and university admissions declined as a consequence. The aristocratic education was purchased for pupils who ranged from the eager to the resentful via the indifferent. Often it was a smattering of everything, sampled but not thoroughly pursued. Surviving correspondence throws light on the educational experiences of the young fourth Viscount Irwin, Edward Ingram, at the start of the eighteenth century. He left Eton at sixteen, in the summer of 1702, within a few months of his father's death. His trustees appointed a German-born tutor, John Haccius, who accompanied him to Christ's College Cambridge, and reported his progress, asserting 'my intention is, my lord should be pretty well versed in Logic, Morals, History, Geography, true settled notions about government and some parts of Mathematics, which having got, a man is fit for everything'.[12] After much wrangling over expenditure, the pair left Cambridge and commenced the Grand Tour together in May 1704. Edward claimed to be 'wholly taken up in learning French' at Delft, and Haccius sent him to Leiden to study Latin. But events turned awry: the tutor was dismissed by the trustees after his charge had been involved in a duel; pupil and tutor fled together to Düsseldorf, and were still together in Cologne and Augsburg in April 1705. Edward was alone in Venice the next month, and went on to Siena and Rome, lamenting in the spring of 1706 that he could not afford to cut the figure he should in Roman society. He had left a trail of debts behind him and still owed 1033 guilders to a tailor in The Hague! This particular Grand Tour seems to have ceased to be an educational experience and to have become a social adventure. Perhaps it should be argued that this was an education in itself.

W. R. Prest refers to the inns of court as the environment where 'the young men who would eventually inherit the natural magistracy of the nation' came together.[13] Most of the young men admitted to the inns of court in their educational heyday came for an elementary knowledge of law, not to be called to the Bar. Socially superior to many Oxbridge students, they were attracted to the prospects of being based in glitter-ing London, in the company of their peers, and under the wing of institutions which disciplined them only minimally, left them to study or not as they felt inclined, and provided a backcloth of masques and revels. It is tempting to polarise wasteful coxcombs and serious students, but dangerous. Known careers prove that many were, as Clarendon's uncle put it, 'students yet revellers', and while a little knowledge of the law could be a dangerous thing, those who did not get as far as the Bar were by no means failures or wasteful of opportunity. Eric Ives argues that the useful books of surveying and husbandry attributed to 'Master Fitzherbert', published in 1523, were compiled by John Fitzherbert rather than by his younger brother Anthony, the justice; John had spent four years in London learning law, and became 'an active farmer with a legal education', owned some law books, and became a justice of the peace.[14] His education made him a useful magistrate, though never a barrister.

In purely vocational terms the governing class had become over-educated: it had access to more education than was strictly necessary to run its agricultural estates, and to a different kind of education than that which was requisite for investing in the West Indies sugar trade or developing mineral exploitation. Here, in this class alone, can be found education for leisure: the cultivation of the niceties of life, art and literature. The education of successive generations of aristocrats and gentry went alongside the building and furnishing of stately homes (showing often the Grand Tour influence), the acquisition of libraries, subscription to county histories and music recitals, and patronage of writers and dramatists. Many of these classes sat on the commissions of the peace governing their localities, and sat in both Houses of Parlia-ment, where the standard of debate throughout these centuries was high. The Long Parliament elected in 1640 was, in terms of graduate attendance, the best educated in English history, and over half the Commons members belonged to the inns of court. The governing class held together well because it spoke with one voice derived from its common (and exclusive) education. It understood Latin and Greek quotations and classical allusions, it rode and hunted, and shared a cultural tradition confident of the correctness of one governing class being rightfully so occupied, and considered that it was properly trained separately from those merely destined to be governed.

It was among this class that the earliest outstanding examples of educated women spring. Only here could the luxury of non-vocational education for leisure extend to daughters. Private tutors taught Sir Thomas More's daughters at home, with their brother: they included Dr John Clement, William Gunnell and Richard Hyrde. Margaret More (later Roper) wrote Latin and Greek fluently, and had some acquaintance with philosophy, astronomy, physics, arithmetic, logic, rhetoric and music. Humanist education for women in early sixteenth-century England was not designed to develop them fully for their own sakes, but to make them learned wives, intellectual companions to their husbands and wise teachers of their children, enriching the home with music and conversation. Lady Jane Grey, born in 1537, daughter of the Marquis of Dorset, studied with John Aylmer, the family chaplain and tutor. She acquired fluency in Latin and Greek, and was credited with French, Italian, Hebrew, Arabic and Chaldee. Elizabeth I shared her early studies with her younger brother, but later passed to her own tutor, first William Grindal, then Roger Ascham. Ascham wrote of her when she was sixteen: 'she talks French and Italian as well as she does English, and has often talked to me readily and well in Latin, moderately in Greek'. She read 'almost all Cicero' with Ascham, and a great part of Livy, and in Greek read the New Testament, Isocrates, Sophocles and Demosthenes.[15]

In the later part of the century women of the governing class continued to outstrip all others educationally. Sir Philip Sidney's sister Mary Countess of Pembroke wrote translations, as did Elizabeth née Tanfield, Lady Falkland. Significantly, women's intellectual achievements were assessed in terms of the dominant male culture. So Ascham praised Elizabeth as follows: 'her mind has no womanly weakness, her perseverance is equal to that of a man', while Lettice née Morison, Vicountess Falkland was accredited by Clarendon with 'a most masculine understanding'.[16]

High classical learning was very unusual in a woman, but English works were read by aristocratic women. Lady Anne Clifford's diary for 26 April 1617 reports for the evening 'going down to my lord's closet where I sat and read much Turkish history and Chaucer'. At this period of her life, at Knole, Lady Anne often had works read to her, including a history of the Netherlands, Montaigne's essays, *The Faerie Queene*, *Arcadia*, Ovid's Metamorphoses, and the Bible and other religious works, for example, 'a book of the preparation to the sacrament' on Good Friday 1617. Wives in this class of society were generally required to be benevolent to their households and tenants, and their education prepared them for this. They were expected to catechise the maids, as is recorded of Mary Countess of Warwick, and to relieve the poor with food, like the exemplary Mrs Elizabeth Walker, wife of a minister. They were resorted to in medical emergencies: Elizabeth Talbot, Countess of Kent, wrote *A manuall of Rare and Select secrets in Physick and Chirurgery*, which was published after her death in 1651; she claimed to have tried the remedies successfully. Lady Margaret Hoby, the first known English female diarist, recorded attending a childbirth – 'in the morning at six o'clock I prayed privately; that done I went to a wife in travail of a child, about whom I was busy till one o'clock, about which time, she being delivered and I having praised God, returned home and betook myself to private prayer'. Prudence Potter, wife of the rector of Newton St Petroc, Devon, according to her tombstone had spent her life in the successful practice of physic, surgery and midwifery.[17]

Education for the Professions

The three traditional professions were the church, law and medicine, and the education designed to train entrants to these professions is the main concern of this section. The practitioners of certain other callings have at times succeeded in attracting professional status to themselves, and in the book *The Professions in Early Modern England* (1987), edited by Wilfrid Prest, schoolteachers, army and navy officers and estate stewards are included. Of these additional professionals, only teachers will be specifically considered here, because of their centrality to the subject. The early modern professions straddled several social strata, and recruitment and training varied considerably. They lacked the self-regulation and monopoly of practice which are characteristic of professions today. There was much less standardised training, very little 'paper qualification', and members of one profession not infrequently dabbled in another.

The Church

The English educational system had largely developed for training clergy. The song and grammar schools and the universities came into existence to provide boy choristers, Latinate ordinands and qualified holders of degrees in theology/divinity and canon and civil law for higher office in the church. Considering that the system had evolved for professional purposes, it must be admitted that it was showing weaknesses in achieving these ends by the early modern period. The size of the profession is known. A clerical estate of some 35 000 in a population of approximately 2.5 million in the early 1500s was transformed by the Reformation into a profession of 15 000 in a population of 3.5 million by 1545, and only about 300 vacancies a year needed filling in approximately 10 000 benefices in the established church in normal times. The violent changes under Edward VI and Mary, and deaths from the influenza epidemic rampant in the years 1557–59, left a higher proportion of benefices vacant in 1558 (estimates vary from 10–15 per cent to nearly 22 per cent), resulting in mass ordinations which recruited some unsatisfactory candidates at the start of Elizabeth's reign, and John Pruett describes bishops 'feverishly' ordaining more than enough clerical candidates to make up for the losses after ejections at the Restoration, but not generally at the expense of educational attainment.[18]

The educational qualifications and vocational aptitude of parochial clergy in the sixteenth century left much to be desired. In the diocese of York, Archbishop Grindal's 1575 investigations revealed fifty-four of 138 clergy in Bulmer, Cleveland, Craven and Buckrose below a respectable standard in Latin: eighteen had none, thirteen were bad, twenty-three moderate to poor. There was no established institutional remedy for such failings among instituted clergy. Clergy could be directed to study, and ordered to report to more experienced fellow clergy, but there was little machinery for encouraging or enforcing improvements. In this period of conscious effort to improve standards, exercises were set by the archdeacons for the clergy, and clerical gatherings took place at which these were tested, in some places becoming regular meetings: at Shrewsbury fortnightly on Thursdays according to Bishop Bentham's report to Grindal in 1576. 'Prophesyings' consisted of gatherings at which several sermons were preached consecutively on the same text, and summed up by a moderator to the assembled company of clergy, sometimes afforced by an audience of lay people. Afterwards, discipline was administered by clergy to clergy in private conference. Some of these prophesyings grew out of the exercises outlined above. The emphasis was very much on improving the scriptural learning of the clergy, which presumably was widely thought to be insufficient. While he was archbishop of the northern province, Edmund Grindal approved exercises and prophesyings as 'in-service' training, but when he was translated to Canterbury, Elizabeth ordered him to suppress such gatherings: they were forbidden in 1577. Clandestine conferences and occasional prophesyings or fasts, at which laity attended as audiences, survived where there was local zeal, but there was no official replacement and the vocational element in priests' training was left ill provided.

One obvious way of quantifying clerical learning is to analyse the proportion of graduate clergy in a place or period. Using this as a measure of clerical training, an undeniable improvement in quality appears. In 1576, 15 per cent of Leicestershire's clergymen were university graduates, by 1585, 31 per cent, by 1642, 90 per cent, in 1750, 95 per cent. Moreover, the majority of Leicestershire's clerical graduates were more than BAs: the MA became almost standard.[19] Undoubtedly educational standards among the clergy can be seen to have varied regionally, with the remoter areas the more backward. The London diocese had achieved a graduate clerical profession by the 1620s and this spread fairly rapidly to remoter areas. By the 1630s the clerical profession was basically graduate.

But what does this imply? It means certainly that the intending cleric had to pass through grammar schooling, or equivalent private tuition, and then complete at least the BA course at university. Cambridge's statutes, laid down in 1570, specified the study of rhetoric for the first year of the BA; logic for years two and three, and philosophy for the fourth. The intending clergyman, as an undergraduate, was not at a specialist training school. Oxford's John Eachard, writing in 1670, was critical of ill-prepared students going up to the universities, and of the outmoded curriculum they were exposed to there, which in his view emphasised Latin and Greek at the expense of English oratory (the delivery of sermons was a premium activity in the church in the late sixteenth and throughout the seventeenth century) and was insufficiently grounded in Protestant theology. If the bachelor went on to the MA (Oxford in the 1620s and 1630s was producing about 140 MAs per annum), he studied logic, Greek, natural and moral philosophy, metaphysics, history, geometry, astronomy, Hebrew, and at Oxford there was Arabic. These curricula were probably more suitable for intending clergy than they look, for in Kearney's words, 'the arts curriculum was arranged by divines with a view to the further study of divinity'.[20] Sermons and services abounded, and biblical textual study was undertaken, so the universities' output, especially from the more Puritan colleges, was potentially godly laymen along with clergy, rather than worldly clergy influenced by study alongside lay associates. Theology or divinity of course remained a higher faculty, dominating the activities of the college fellows, but not of the undergraduates. Oxford's output of BDs in the 1620s and 1630s was higher than ever again until the nineteenth century.

For clerical personnel a change was taking place which resulted in institutions designed for one purpose serving a slightly altered one, perhaps not to their full comfort. The medieval universities sent their graduate output into the church with higher degrees to fill the top positions there, not with BAs and MAs to staff the parish priesthood. By the early seventeenth century an Arts degree, especially the MA, was becoming the qualification for parish clergy. Thus degrees which had never been particularly pastorally orientated were being used to qualify men many of whom were never going to rise in the church above parish ministry. The disputative elements in the MA which were a good foundation for those who were entering canon law (abolished in 1540) or civil law (reduced in relevance after the Reformation) were less relevant for the pastoral clergy of the seventeenth and eighteenth centuries. So degrees which had not been designed as a package for parish clergy became necessary qualifications, without necessarily being adapted sufficiently to suit this situation. Clergy were by the 1620s required to be better qualified to set foot on the ladder, but may have been both over-educated intellectually and vocationally underprepared.

There was very little specifically vocational training for clergy. The new graduate hardly emerged equipped to be an effective clergyman, and indeed few were instituted immediately on graduation. A constructive period between graduation and ministry was a valuable experience, but it was provided only informally and by chance. Archbishop Whitgift provided vocational training in his household, and some Puritan lay households became informal academies, but these did not constitute lasting, institutionalised training provision. So unsystematic was entry into and establishment in the clerical profession that there was an element of role reversal in the relationships between college tutors and their pupils: the tutors might hope to gain clerical preferment from their pupils' parents. Many college fellowships were held on to by men waiting for benefices, who would eventually move out into them. Many livings were in the gift of colleges, which provided successive incumbents to them. When Henry VIII founded Trinity College Cambridge in 1546 he conferred forty advowsons on it, mostly from dissolved religious houses. New College had twenty-six clerical livings in its presentation by 1642, and Penry Williams argues that the eighteenth-century fellow used the college as a base 'from which he could hold curacies, and as a source of patronage which would ultimately supply him with a permanent living'.[21] Other men in the queue for preferment filled the gap between college and a living by acting as a tutor in a private household, or teaching in a school. Of all the professions, the church and teaching show the most interchangeability and overlap. Indeed, Orpen termed the schoolhouse 'a form of outdoor relief for the underpaid or aspiring cleric'.[22] Men commonly intercalated a few years of teaching in a clerical career, or combined the two activities. The 1604 canons gave the local curate first claim to the post of parish school-master, and some school foundations required the master to be an Anglican clergyman, for example Westminster School's 1560 statutes. An unbroken succession of clerical schoolmasters stretched from 1551 to 1903 at Great Yarmouth.[23] This all underlines the fact that the basic university Arts degrees qualified a man for either career, in an unspecialised way.

What was uniquely necessary to the advancing clergyman was the taking of holy orders, but this did not involve any preparatory instruction, though it did involve the examination of ordinands, and could be undertaken at very different stages in a career. The canons of 1571 and 1604 provided rules for ordination which generally prevailed, excluding the Puritan revolutionary period. Candidates for the diaconate had to be at least twenty-three, for priesthood twenty-four. (This made the MA a useful time-filler for the BA graduating at twenty-one or twenty-two, but ordination could be much later in life.) Both orders should not be received together (though commonly were in Elizabeth's reign), and ideally at least a year should be served in the diaconate. Candidates for ordination had to have testimonials from their colleges or parish ministers testifying to their soundness in doctrine, learning and morals, and bishops or their nominees were required to examine their fitness. How effective this was in screening out the deficient depended on the conscientiousness of the diocesan. Secker in the mid-eighteenth century was still critical of the preparation of ordinands in the universities.[24] Deacons and even laymen could be presented and even instituted to a cure of souls, but had to take priests' orders within a year of institution: in 1663 priestly orders had to be taken before institution, and deprivation could follow failure to comply.

The clerical profession was comparatively open to talents in the sixteenth and seventeenth centuries and the universities attracted

some students from fairly humble backgrounds who were usually aiming at a career in the church or teaching. Ralph Josselin, whose career
embraced both, was the son of a yeoman. The two universities gained
about 500 new scholarships for the tuition and maintenance of poor
boys between 1560 and 1640, and another route to a degree for poor
students was the servitorship or sizarship, a means of working one's way
through college, performing services and living frugally. Pruett estimates that two-thirds of late Stuart Leicestershire parsons had been servitors or sizars.[25] Expansion in the universities before 1640 led to a sated
clerical market for qualified men, and Mark Curtis argued that a class of
alienated intellectuals, under-employed and discontented, emerged at
this time. University entry was falling before the disruption of the Civil
War, and decline was marked after the 1670s. Stone estimates Oxford's
BA output as 230 per annum in the 1620s (which he thinks should be
multiplied by four or five to allow for under-registration), 150 per
annum from 1660 to the 1720s and 100 per annum from 1750 to the
1770s. The smaller numbers reflect that the universities were seen as
principally training for the church and/or teaching, but whether they
were doing this particularly appropriately was questioned. His university's institutional and social backing was perhaps more instrumental
than the actual curriculum in the clergyman's professional career. There
was the hope of appointment to the college's own livings, and through
collegiate networks both students and fellows acquired influential
patrons in 'Old Boy' bishops and lay holders of advowsons.

To some extent, the lack of practical vocational apprenticeship after
the failure of exercises and prophesyings may have been compensated
for by the familiarity with parsonage life already experienced by the
growing proportion of university students who were clergy sons: 5 per
cent of Oxford's entrants in 1600, 15 per cent in 1637, 21 per cent in
1661, 29 per cent in 1810. Pruett estimated 31 per cent of Leicestershire
incumbents in 1670 sent sons into the church, and 27 per cent of them
in 1714.[26] A famous eighteenth-century clergyman, the diarist James
Woodforde, was a rector's son. A New College man, he was ordained
deacon on 29 May 1763, three days before gaining his BA degree, and
began his clerical career by the following October as curate of Thurlox-
ton in his home county of Somerset. He was ordained to the priesthood
at Wells in 1764, and was eventually presented to New College's rectory
of Weston Longueville, Norfolk, taking up residence in 1776. Woodforde illustrates another not uncommon characteristic of clerical careers
in that his first curacy was in his home county. While graduates were

demonstrably attracted to London, clergy were predominantly locally recruited, though Pruett reckons late Stuart clergy were among the most geographically mobile of their day. Morgan, in *Godly Learning*, makes the point that regional dialects were still spoken by the learned in the early seventeenth century and that this occasioned so little difficulty probably because so many graduates returned to their home counties. This local familiarity could have lessened the need for training in presentational and communication skills at the start of a career, but it would not much narrow the gap between the graduate and rural parishioners, especially in remote areas. Committed, energetic clergy could survive and make a success of radical transplantation, however: Dr John Favour, minister of the sprawling West Riding parish of Halifax for thirty years from 1593, was one of the earl of Huntingdon's chaplains, and a Puritan sympathiser, and had been educated at Winchester and was an Oxford DCL, who originally came from Southampton.

Thus far only the training of the clergy of the established church has been considered, but each side of the via media there were men of the cloth whose training was very different. To the right of the Anglican church were the Catholics. Catholic education, as such, was proscribed in England from the late sixteenth century right through our period. Clandestine, usually small, schools struggled to teach the children of Catholic recusants in England, but Catholics could not graduate from the universities because graduands were required to subscribe to the Thirty-nine Articles of the Church of England. Clearly the training of Catholic clergy for missionary activity and secret ministry in this country could not take place in such conditions. Consequently a whole network of schools, colleges and seminaries was founded abroad to remedy the default. Douai was founded in 1568 as a seminary for priests for the English mission: it soon accepted Catholic lay students as well, and with an enforced stay in Reims from 1578 to 1593, remained operational throughout our period. There were also colleges for English Catholic priests in Rome, Valladolid, Seville, Madrid and Lisbon. The Jesuit college at St Omer, which also taught Catholic laymen, as did the schools of St Gregory's at Douai (the origin of Downside) and St Lawrence's of Dieulouard (the origin of Ampleforth), was a feeder for these seminaries. There was an impressive progression through the Catholic training scheme. Would-be priests at Douai had a regulated day from 5 a.m. to 8.30 p.m. night prayers; they followed a seven-year course, mostly starting at the third or fourth levels, taking logic and four years of theology on top of a basically pre-Reformation-type grammar schooling.

This was more career-orientated than the Anglican cleric's undergraduate studies at Oxford or Cambridge. Some of the Douai students had come from St Omer, where entry at fourteen required Latin proficiency. The focus of academic study was Latin, and Latin composition was trained systematically. St Omer's recruits in turn came from schismatic and clandestine English 'grammar' schools.

To the left of the established church, the Protestant nonconformists gradually diverged from the Church of England, moving more noticeably into theological discord after Archbishop Laud had pushed the state church to the right. While they remained within the state church, Puritans were not banned from grammar schools and universities. Their idea of Christian ministry took hold, furthered by new colleges, for example Emmanuel and Sidney Sussex, founded to educate a preaching ministry, and by Puritan patrons, such as the earl of Huntingdon, who encouraged individual preachers and the prophesyings and exercises for improving clerical learning while President of the Council of the North. The education of Puritan ministers was not structurally different from that of 'ordinary' Anglicans, but their inclinations led them to place more emphasis on sermons in their ministry. Here too there was overlap with teaching, some schoolmasters doubling with ministerial roles, or being appointed lecturers, or giving sermons by invitation, and some deprived ministers succeeded in taking refuge in schoolteaching.

As dissent grew more radical, however, breakaway groups parted company with the orthodox educational institutions. Dissenters were barred from the universities in 1662, and as a result forward-looking dissenting academies were founded to replace both the top level of grammar schooling and the universities for dissenters. These academies originally provided ministry teaching; their more commercial programmes do not concern us here. It is unwise to generalise about dissenting academies. They were established at different dates and by different denominations, but some accepted students of other, so long as Protestant, persuasions; some were in large towns, others in remote places, some had only one tutor, some half a dozen, some lasted only a few years, some outlasted our period, some had intermittent existence, some moved with a leading tutor, some ended with his death. Libraries and apparatus and funding mechanisms could pass from one institution to another. But all this diversity apart, in relation to training a ministry, the academies generally warmed to the opportunity for occupational specialisation. Though inheriting, along with ejected Oxbridge dons, inevitably something of the pre–1662 university syllabus in philosophy, theology and classical languages, the academies applied subjects more purposefully for ministerial training. Latin, Greek and Hebrew were valued for biblical studies, but the academies saw the value in diminishing the use of Latin as the medium of instruction and in applying the students to the study of English oratory, composition and literature as a more helpful preparation for vernacular preaching. They also saw the value of elocution, and some academies habitually sent students on local preaching and pastoral practice during their studies. A broader curriculum embracing history, political theory and practical sciences was justified, partly in the abstract interests of a well-educated, respectably intellectual ministry (less of a desirability in the eyes of certain Baptists and Quakers), and partly in recognition of the practical necessity of training ministers who could also earn a living as schoolmasters, and even as medical practitioners.

It must be acknowledged that the clerical profession, orthodox and unorthodox, embraced a vast range of abilities, intellects and enthusiasms. It included men who owed their appointment to favour rather than to ability, and men who settled down perhaps a little too comfortably into a routine they had themselves rendered undemanding. There were also time-servers, giving rise to the Vicar of Bray song. But for others the education for the calling continued as they exercised it. The clergyman's role is one which is enriched by maturity. Bright young graduates may bring new ideas and enthusiasms to a parish, but a good understanding of relationships with parishioners only comes of getting to know them, and maintaining one's own reputation and their respect. Without organised exercises and refresher courses, there were widely available aids for clerics to improve their sermons, deepen their theology and broaden their scriptural study. Sermon publication in early modern times was prodigious, and theological disputes were also printed in huge quantities. No Church of England clergyman, in a basically all-graduate profession, should have been incapable of continuing his own education, and though some livings were financially ill rewarded, access to books should not have been impossible with mutual support from fellow clergy, and institutional libraries. Nonconformist preachers may have been of more amateur training, but there was movement between the streams as the careers of the Wesley brothers show: their Anglican rector father had been educated at a nonconformist academy and they themselves became known as 'Methodists' in their Oxford days, and saw themselves as evangelical revivalists within the

Church of England, but founded a movement which embraced Anglican clergy and unordained travelling lay preachers.

Law

The Reformation abolished the canon law degrees at the English universities, but did not entirely eradicate some study of canon law, nor terminate the activity of the church courts, which continued to operate a form of Roman civil law, except during the Puritan Revolution. Civil law was a postgraduate study at the universities, but could always be embarked on by undergraduates. They did not save time by this option, since extra years of dialectic and philosophy were prescribed for them, but they may have saved effort, since the regulations were lighter. Employment for civilians lay in the church's courts – from archdeaconry up to provincial level – and also in the courts of Admiralty, and Chivalry, and alongside common law in the courts of Requests and Chancery. The profession of civil law was a sub-profession of the church but became laicised in the sixteenth and seventeenth centuries.[27] Only twenty-seven of the 200 men in Levack's study *The Civil Lawyers in England 1603–41* (1973) took holy orders, with three more taking minor ones. So it is more appropriate to consider civilians generally under the heading of law, though individuals who took holy orders may relevantly be considered as churchmen.

The main law operating in England was the common law, which was studied at the inns of court and chancery in London and practised in the central courts of Common Pleas, King's Bench, and Exchequer, and on the assize circuits and peace commissions throughout the provinces. The common law provided criminal and civil actions, and will concern us first.

The majority of lawyers in England were common lawyers. Both common and civil law had a hierarchy of practitioners, and distinction between the upper and lower branches of the profession developed over this period. Attorneys and solicitors formed the lower branch of the law, which Prest describes as the mechanical level. He recommends viewing the early modern legal profession as 'a fairly solid core of institutionally affiliated lawyers, surrounded by a very broad fringe of more or less marginal practitioners'.[28] The legal profession did not enjoy a monopoly of all legal activity. Yeomen farmers, merchants and tradesmen could all be found acting as attorneys and scriveners in local arrangements, and conveyancing did not need an attorney or solicitor. The Scriveners' Company, founded in 1617, had a monopoly of conveyancing in London until the mid-eighteenth century. Justices of the peace did not have to be legally educated; some were professionals, others had some exposure to legal training, but many were obviously comparatively amateur and eager to pick up the necessary expertise from manuals for justices aimed specifically at gentlemen not conversant with legal study.

Some estimate of the numbers of those professionally employed in law is available. Gregory King's estimate of 10 000 lawyers (not counting barristers) in 1688 is considered too low by Prest. In 1633 an estimated 1725 attorneys were attached to Common Pleas and King's Bench, and between 400 and 450 barristers were practising at Westminster in 1638. Both careers were expanding at the time. Prest estimates a fivefold growth in attorneys between the early sixteenth and early seventeenth centuries, and a threefold growth of barristers between the 1570s and 1630s, in a period when the *per capita* incidence of civil litigation reached an all-time high. Numbers of barristers certainly declined after the Restoration, and there was only limited recovery in the early eighteenth century; Duman estimates a practising bar of at most 300 in 1785.[29]

The education for legal practitioners had, it is generally agreed, originally been based in the law courts themselves, and attending the courts remained a serious commitment for the ambitious student: Prest cites Thomas Wentworth as attending Star Chamber after his continental tour in 1613, and Simonds D'Ewes attended Star Chamber until called to the Bar in 1623, and thereafter attended Common Pleas.[30] The first formal instruction helpful to law students seems to have been provided by the inns of chancery; in the mid-fourteenth century Clement's Inn was providing training in writing documents and handling writs, and law students soon latched on to this. By the early fifteenth century the chancery inns were performing this capacity in a much more organised way, forming preparatory departments for the four inns of court (Gray's Inn, Lincoln's Inn, the Inner and Middle Temple), a role which ceased in the early seventeenth century. By this time, almost half the inns of court entrants were coming on from Oxford or Cambridge, compared with only 13 per cent in 1561. Before the Restoration, when admission to more than one inn became common, men were normally admitted to just one of the inns of court, and were thence members of it for life, though actual residence there could be slight, intermittent or non-existent. By gaining admission, members were not binding

themselves to any strict period of study or a career: neither the entrant
nor those admitting him necessarily expected such a degree of commitment. (Some 6 per cent of admissions were honorific anyway, and some
of these civil lawyers.) Prest calculates that there were 12 163 admissions
to the four inns of court between 1590 and 1639, and that 2138 men
were called to the Bar in the same period, a ratio of 1 to 5.9.[31]

Those who made the grade had been exposed to aurally-based training within their inn, involving three specific elements: (1) the everyday
debate of controversial questions in 'case putting', mounted at the inns
over meals; (2) moots or mock trials requiring justification of interpretation of law, with pleadings in law French; and (3) the following of a
number of 'readings', that is, lecture courses with incorporated case
discussion, held in the two 'learning vacations' per year, over three or
four mornings each week over two to three weeks. Each 'reading' was
dedicated by the elected reader to a chosen statute or part thereof. So
integral to the legal profession were these proceedings (evolved as
teaching methods in the fifteenth century) that the ranks of bencher,
barrister and student took their identification from them. The seniors of
each inn who presided at the moots were the benchers of the inn, who,
in the early sixteenth century, would have already prepared and given
their 'reading'. Serjeants-at-law were originally chosen only from
benchers, and the judges were chosen from the serjeants. Those who
were called to argue and plead before the benchers at the moots were
the barristers, or outer or utter barristers, standing at the Bar as in a
proper court; inner barristers or junior barristers were students, on the
other side of the Bar. The procedure of 'call to the Bar' marked the
transition between ranks. In the early sixteenth century this was still an
internal promotion within one's own inn, but from mid-century it began
to be taken as the qualification to plead in the higher courts of law. In
1598 the judges recommended that a man should have been a member
of his inn at least seven years before being called to the Bar, and eight
years in 1630, but this did not mean seven or eight years of resident
attendance and study. By 1590 all four inns had regulations concerning
requisite minimum attendance at a number of learning vacations (either
four or six, immediately preceding call) and participation in a given
number of moots, before a man could be called. After call, he was
supposed to fulfil certain post-call obligations to attend vacations and
moots, in other words, to contribute to the education of the juniors.
In 1559 no less than ten years of further experience was expected
before the man called to the Bar began actual practice in the courts in

Westminster Hall, but by 1614 only a three-year gap was expected, and by the 1630s barristers were appearing almost immediately after call. Moreover, serjeants-at-law were being promoted directly from outer barristers, whether or not they were benchers. The most demanding contribution to the teaching of the law came if a barrister was elected a reader, when he had to mount a feasible lecture course, to be delivered just once: this had been tied in with promotion to the bench of his inn, but with a limited number of vacations and a great increase in barristers, whether or not one had 'read' had to become less significant. The reader also had the obligation to adjudicate moots and exercises in the six months between his election and the learning vacation assigned to the reading.

Such was the basic manner of the progression in a career in the upper branch of the law in the period between the Reformation and the Civil War, but it has to be recognised that the system was riddled with exemptions, redefinitions of obligations and failures of enforcement, enabling individuals to make more rapid progress than this outline implies. Educationally, the career path involved listening and absorbing, then contributing to the open case-putting, then preparing for moots at various levels, thereby beginning to contribute to the education of those below. Taken seriously, these were challenging exercises. Preparing a reading was a far greater task and even attending it was quite hard-going. In the increasingly unwieldy numbers, readings and exercises declined, and more time was spent in private study, which was becoming easier in terms of available tools, with the growing publication lists of legal texts and treatises and guides to the very methods of learning law. By the eighteenth century, self-education and pupillage was the way to learn the law.

The English common law was not separated into digestible parts such as contract, tort, family law and so on to learn, but was approached as 'a formless, confused jumble of undigested particulars', rendering its study both demanding and tedious. Even men who were going to make good, such as Sir Henry Spelman and Simonds D'Ewes, recorded their early discouragement with a subject they found difficult and unpleasant, in Spelman's words, 'a foreign language, a barbarous dialect, an uncouth method'.[32] Studious law students read cases from the Year Books and Law Reports, and digested them and wrote them in commonplace collections, using printed abridgements and digests and institutional books such as Littleton's *Tenures*, which went through over seventy editions before the Civil War.

In the context of professional development, education at the inns of court has to be viewed in terms of its legal content and its desirably disputatious method. It should not, however, be disregarded that membership of the inns before the Civil War was an educational experience of a broader kind, exposing members to a lively male society including bibliophiles, political activists and theatre-lovers. Under the early Stuarts men from the inns were very active in London's intellectual society. But after the disruption of the Civil War, when no exercises were performed between 1642 and 1647, 'readings' ceased and case-argument exercises ossified. The use of the inns of court as gentry finishing schools fell away, and the inns became professional clubs for practising lawyers, abandoning their educational role. Prest sets the whole history of the inns as educational institutions in context by concluding that the Civil War contributed to the end of the educational boom overall. 'Admissions to the inns dropped steadily towards their mid-Hanoverian low, while the importance and prestige attached to education by the national economic and political elites declined very rapidly.'[33]

The attorneys and solicitors who made up the lower branch of the law were increasingly separated from their superiors in the profession, but before the Civil War the professional demarcation between attorneys and barristers was unclear. From the mid-sixteenth century onwards the benchers of the inns and the judges were issuing orders forbidding the admission of attorneys and solicitors, and in 1617 some sixty barristers and students of Middle Temple complained that the 'glory of this society is faded by the swarms of attorneys which are now admitted'. There was some overlap: thirty-two members of the Middle Temple, including several barristers, were practising as attorneys in 1635. As the two levels of the profession pulled apart, the inns of chancery swung from being preparatory colleges for the inns of court and devoted themselves to the training of the lower branch, and in the provinces attorneys got by with local legal apprenticeship.

Civil lawyers were a much smaller professional group than the common lawyers. Levack's study of those practising in England between 1603 and 1641 who had law doctorates from the universities, identified 200, compared with a contemporary estimate of 2000 common law barristers at the start of the seventeenth century.[34] These were of course the elite civilians, in status somewhere between the ordinary barristers and the serjeants-at-law practising in the Court of Common Pleas: there was of course a wider profession of less qualified officials and lawyers below them. The education of this elite was at the universities, and their nine or ten years of study, it must be said, prepared them inadequately for practical work, being largely theoretical study of traditional sources such as Justinian's *Corpus Iuris Civilis*, and commentaries, little of which was applicable in English ecclesiastical or international maritime law, wherein their main career outlets lay. The university training in civil law included no moots bringing familiarity with court procedures. So, in effect, after gaining technical 'qualification', many of the doctors of law remedied the practical deficiencies of their education by undergoing a virtual training year in London, by joining Doctors' Commons, a college of doctors of law who were practising advocates in the provincial courts of the Archbishop of Canterbury, or the civilian courts of the Admiralty and Chivalry. In origin, in the early sixteenth century, a convenient residential and dining fellowship of professional civil lawyers, Doctors' Commons developed a practical initial training scheme by insisting those who joined it spent a 'silent year' in the Court of Arches learning procedure and pleading. Doctors' Commons was the pathway to prac-tising in the five Canterbury provincial courts (those of Arches, Audi-ence, Prerogative, Peculiars and the Vicar General) and the courts of Admiralty and Chivalry. The society also exerted educational influence by having a library and providing contact between those starting their careers and old hands. To be a judge of one of the Canterbury provin-cial courts, or a regius professor at one of the universities, the legal doctorate was needed, but this educational qualification was not an absolute necessity, even for quite high advancement in the church courts. The 1604 canons insisted that a man could become a chancellor, commissary or official to exercise any ecclesiastical jurisdiction so long as he was at least twenty-six years of age, learned in the civil and ecclesias-tical laws and 'at the least a master of arts or bachelor of law'. At the start of the seventeenth century there were fears for the future of civil law in the curriculum. More civilians were attracted by the 1630s, but the Civil War brought temporary destruction. The Restoration brought back the church courts, but the civilians never again had the honour they had enjoyed in the Middle Ages and late sixteenth century, and the civil law education seems in fact to have been attracting non-professionals. Levack regards the profession as almost moribund by 1750.

Despite the specialisations of legal education, successful students did not necessarily stick to the one career. Among the 200 doctors of civil law studied by Levack can be found men who turned their hand to church ministry (which they could have done without a doctorate or BCL), to practising medicine, and to schoolteaching.

Medicine

Practitioners of medicine in early modern England entered upon the career in a variety of ways. There were two forms of qualifying, and a requirement to be licensed, but non-qualified and unlicensed practitioners patently existed, as is known from their prosecution. The university faculties of medicine produced physicians in small numbers. Apprenticeship within the profession produced barber-surgeons and apothecaries. In London the College of Physicians, founded in 1518, later the Royal College, was a graduate body which licensed medical practitioners to work within seven miles of the capital. There was a struggle between the College and the universities right into the 1720s over the College's restricting influence, and the universities' desire that their graduates should be able to practise without the College's licence. Outside London, the Oxbridge medical degree qualified one to practise, as did an episcopal or archiepiscopal licence, and it has been estimated that those licensed by the church outnumbered university doctors by two to one. The Regius Professor of Physic at Cambridge admitted in 1635 that serving men and apothecaries could be licensed to practise physic 'without giving any public testimony of their learning and skill in the profession'.[35] However, Jean Vanes was favourably impressed by the sixteenth-century standards of the barber-surgeons at Bristol. At the end of the century they had a hall and dissecting rooms, and examinations for apprentices. Their ordinances show professional concern for the patient and the dignity of the calling, and offer free treatment to the poor. Ships' surgeons had to have their sea-chests examined by the Master of the Company and two others to ensure they were adequate for the voyage ahead.[36] The Southampton apprentices' register shows his son John apprenticed to John Stepto, barber-surgeon, for eight years in 1615, and a family of barber-surgeons training in the 1630s and 1640s: Andrew, son of John Peale of Southampton, barber-surgeon, deceased, was apprenticed to his brother Martin, barber-surgeon, for seven years in 1637, Martin's own son Peter was apprenticed to his father, described as 'barber-surgeon licensed in physic' for seven years in 1647, and another apprentice was taken by Martin in 1653, who appears to be a stepson, though the entry is badly summarised.[37]

Women, barred from the universities, had long penetrated this medical field as midwives, for which they needed an episcopal licence to practise, except for a brief period in the Interregnum when they were licensed at Surgeons' Hall in London, after examination by other midwives and surgeons. However, the ecclesiastical supervision was erratic. The episcopal licence in surgery was open to women, and Moscucci cites the case of Mrs Elizabeth Frances, who was licensed in surgery and obstetrics in 1689, with a testimonial from two surgeons, two physicians and a male midwife, asserting that she was 'very well instructed and practised in the art of midwifery and also in the knowledge of medicines which may be of use to women in their several maladies'.[38] How Mrs Frances had been very well instructed is not known. There were books for midwives by midwives, for example, Mrs Jane Sharp's *The Midwives' Book* (1671) and Sarah Stone's *Complete Practice of Midwifery* (1737). The existence of such works suggests some theoretical study by literate learners. But midwives generally received no formal training and learned by their own experience of childbirth and that of their friends and neighbours. By the end of our period male midwives were undermining the public confidence in female ones, and the social status of midwifery underwent precipitous decline.[39] General nursing, which is likely to have been performed by women, had no specific training or control, and was of little better than servant status. Though the situation sounds to the modern mind dangerous, it must be remembered that on the one hand some non-qualified male licentiates and unlicensed male practitioners had had some, if incomplete, university education, and on the other, that the university medical curriculum was in any case of no great practical value. The College of Physicians rejected Richard Reynolds, MD Cambridge 1567, a few years later, as 'very ignorant and unlearned'.[40]

The study of medicine at university level changed noticeably. Only 177 medical degrees were awarded at Oxford in the sixteenth century, but over 950 in the seventeenth, when Cambridge produced even more physicians than Oxford. Both universities declined as medical centres in the eighteenth century, though there was advance in the field in Edinburgh and among dissenters.[41] Throughout our period Oxford and Cambridge had the monopoly in England of producing university medical graduates, but a more advanced medical education could be obtained abroad at Padua or Leiden, and accredited here by incorporation.

During the early modern period the science of medicine progressed from the study of ancient authorities to the experimental observation of physiological phenomena. Knowledge was still transmitted via lectures and disputations, and the ancient authorities were not discarded: in 1636 Laud's statutes still prescribed Hippocrates and Galen at Oxford. However the informal curriculum was broader than the statutory one. Dissections and autopsies were commoner after 1650. At both universities there were close links between chemistry and medicine. Students paid willingly to attend extra-curricular scientific lectures. At Cambridge John Yardley, MB 1704, recorded the syllabus of the Veronese-born chemist John Vigani. At the same period, the physicians were also doing astronomical and biological work. Dr Robert Glynn's lecture course at Cambridge in 1751, the year before his MD, comprised animal oeconomy, operations of medicines, and the history of diseases. In 1752 he was giving medical lectures on the structure and use of the principal organs of the human body.[42]

Without much structured encouragement, intellectually curious individuals developed more scientific, experimental ways of thinking. William Stukeley, who entered Corpus Christi College Cambridge in 1703, and gained his MB degree in 1708, recorded in his diary in 1706: 'at this time my tutor [Fawcett] gave me a room in the college to dissect in, and practise chemical experiments... I often prepared the *pulvis fulminans* and sometimes surprised the whole college with a sudden explosion. I cured a lad once of an ague with it, by fright.' Of an enterprising disposition, Stukeley as a student dissected the family cat.[43] Stukeley became a fellow of the Royal College of Physicians, but eventually gave up medicine and took holy orders.

Stukeley was at Corpus, but Caius, where Isaac Newton was master, had a strong tradition of scientific scholars. Caius was the refoundation of Gonville Hall by Dr John Caius, who had studied at Cambridge and Padua. He published a book on the sweating sickness (1552), which has been described as the first medical monograph in the English language. Dr Caius was a president of the College of Physicians and lectured on anatomy to the barber-surgeons in London. William Harvey, the discoverer of the circulation of the blood, incorporated MD in 1602 at Caius; he held the College of Physicians' Lumleian lectureship founded in 1583 to further physicians' knowledge of anatomy. Another Caius man, Francis Glisson, MD 1634, became Regius Professor of Physic at Cambridge in 1636. He published a Latin treatise on rickets in 1656, and did valuable work on the nervous system and alimentary canal.

Medical and scientific studies were neither easy to pursue, nor reliably encouraged by authorities in this period. Theology had too cramping a hold over intellect for daring experiments to be encouraged. Obtaining human bodies for dissection was difficult and dangerous. In 1724 Parliament rejected an application for corpses of felons in Cambridgeshire and Huntingdonshire to be available for dissection by Cambridge's medical faculty.[44]

In London there was some co-operation, as well as rivalry, between the physicians (the most prestigious practitioners, also allowed to practise surgery) and the barber-surgeons and apothecaries, who were the poorer people's doctors. Caius's career shows the co-operative side. But the physicians were not pleased when Nicholas Culpeper, the apothecary, published an English translation of the physicians' Latin pharmacoepia of 1618, revealing its secrets in the vernacular out of sympathy for the commonalty.

In postscript, it should be said that two very striking, and very different features about university men studying, teaching and furthering science in this period are that their work was not introverted and exclusive, and that their academic careers interknitted with practical employments. Some of the most notable discoveries, and some of the most practical applications, came from men who were not earning a professional livelihood from scientific practice. The outstanding example is Stephen Hales, who was a Cambridge doctor of divinity (Oxford conferred the same degree on him) and perpetual curate of Teddington. He had entered Corpus Christi as a pensioner in 1696, and was elected a fellow in 1703. About this time, according to Stukeley, he was applying himself to chemistry, with Stukeley, and the two were repeating Robert Boyle's experiments and attending Vigani's lectures. In 1705 Hales constructed a planetarium. He was an outstanding enough botanist to be regarded as the 'Father of Plant Physiology', and made remarkable advances in the understanding of kidney stones, blood pressure, shipboard hygiene, and ventilation. The word polymath describes him perfectly, but others too, before the separation of specialisms, crossed many disciplines. The previously mentioned Francis Glisson, scholar of Caius 1617, illustrates the combination of academic and practical strands in a career. He became a fellow in 1624, and Greek lecturer in 1625, but graduated MD in 1634 and became Regius Professor of Physic in 1636. He also practised as a physician in Colchester, and later became Reader in Anatomy at the College of Physicians in London, and became its president in the period 1667–69. Such men illustrate that advances came from men who were not theoreticians in ivory towers, though Swift's scientists in Laputa are obviously a satire on such careerists, but were also alive to the conditions in towns and on ships. As with other professions, there was interactivity: Margaret Pelling argues that many medical practitioners were part-timers, also offering trades and services, from selling ale and food to schoolmastering.[45] John Favour, DCL, practised medicine alongside his ministry in Halifax.

Schoolteachers

Throughout the period schoolteaching was a heterogeneous occupation, with the most prestigious and the least having little in common beyond in some way purposing to teach some skill to the young. The existence of an ill-defined tail to the profession makes an estimate of its size hazardous. Cressy reckons 200–300 grammar schools modelled themselves on several dozen leading schools; these would rarely have a staff exceeding two teachers. Many more elementary and private schools would only have one. Teaching done outside institutions is even harder to estimate. Although schoolmasters are included in Prest's survey of early modern professions, their inclusion is almost constantly treated everywhere by writers in negative terms. Writing of late medieval schoolmasters (between 1307 and 1509), Nicholas Orme concluded that they never managed to develop a national organisation and could not be regarded as a profession. Cressy makes the same points about Elizabethan and Stuart England: that teachers had no professional association, no uniform training, little of the financial reward of lawyers or churchmen, and amid such diversity, no professional solidarity. The [head]masters of the endowed grammar-school foundations had little common cause with the humblest chaplains teaching in chantry schools in the early sixteenth century, nor with the teachers in the elementary schools of the eighteenth, though at least the SPCK recommendations for charity-school teachers showed concern for upholding minimal standards, and considering personal aptitude.

The educational attainments required of schoolteachers were undefined, and any ways of testing them irregular. The absolute minimum required, for any teacher, is to know just enough to remain ahead of the pupils. So the teachers of vernacular reading had only to be able to read in English well enough to pass on the skill. That they included women, for whom no advanced education was institutionally available, indicates the low level of attainment necessary. Very little is known about the teachers of vernacular reading, but Spufford identified a third of the elementary teachers in South Cambridgeshire between 1574 and 1628 as graduates.[46] At the same time, an unflattering picture comes from Francis Clement's *The Petty School* (1587), complaining that children were almost everywhere either taught in private by 'men and women altogether rude and utterly ignorant of the due composing and just spelling of words', or else in common schools most commonly by boys, seldom or never by any of sufficient skill.[47] Teachers of elementary Latin needed only ability to handle basic grammar: anyone teaching Latin throughout a grammar school needed at least to have completed such a course himself, and preferably a university degree which would indicate competence in the language. According to Orme the average English grammar school of the later Middle Ages required its master to have studied the grammar course to at least the level of his highest pupils, and to be of good character, but that it was not absolutely necessary to be celibate cleric or university graduate. Only a handful of schools by 1509 required the masters to be graduates: even among the endowed schools such were a small minority. Although a degree in grammar was obtainable in the fifteenth and early sixteenth centuries, it does not seem to have been this specialist degree which was intended by those school foundations with statutes specifying graduate masters, and most of the identified ones had the standard BA degree, and some the MA. The grammar degree was not awarded after 1548, by which time there had been a vast improvement in the foundation teaching of Latin in schools, achieved by the first generation of humanist Latin teachers, largely themselves of graduate status, following Lily's lead. The growing numbers of grammar-school foundations requiring a graduate master in the sixteenth century were using the university's Arts degree, not a specifically vocational course for teachers, as indication that the appointee would have studied Latin more than adequately for schoolteaching purposes, and also have the basic cultural exposure common to university graduates of the day. This use of the BA and MA degrees as the benchmark of selective status was, as already shown, common to both ministry and teaching, and furthered an overlap and intertwining between those professions, which also pertained beneath the graduates among the nongraduate clergy and teachers.

Late medieval schooling, still coloured by its ecclesiastical roots, had strong clerical associations. Clerical teachers of grammar (including those in minor orders) were sufficiently the norm for it to be necessary to state exceptions when school founders decided either that masters need not be clerics, or indeed should not be. Whereas the graduate embarking on a church career had to advance up holy orders, the graduate following a teaching career did not, and of course, before the Reformation, a big consequential difference was that the schoolmaster was acceptably of lay status and could marry. In these circumstances succumbing to matrimony may have led some graduates to turn from an intended church career into teaching, before the legalisation of clerical marriage in 1547, reiterated in 1559. Subsequently, marrying was no obstacle to continuing in the church, and thereafter the choosing of a teaching career may have been more deliberate, and less an enforced second-best for a man who had taken a wife. However, the professions continued to overlap. One suspects that appointing bodies were playing safe, thinking that if a man satisfied the church's requirements, he must be acceptable for teaching.

The graduate status of clergy and teachers rose together, and in the better grammar schools masters were usually graduates, but a large tail of non-graduates working at humbler levels made the overall graduate percentage (worked out from licensing statistics where elementary teachers were more likely to escape attention and record, thus understating the number of non-graduates in an unknown total teaching workforce) lower than in the church. Of licensed masters in London, 27 per cent were graduate in the 1580s, 59 per cent in the 1630s, the percentage thereafter declining sharply.[48] Others had acquaintance with university but had not completed a degree. It is clear that religious conformity and sobriety of character were valued above actual academic competence, and religious conformity became a tightening straitjacket with requirements to subscribe to the Oaths of Supremacy, Articles of Religion and the Act of Uniformity.

The ideal qualifications of schoolmasters may be deduced from school statutes phrased to prevent unsuitable appointments. Cressy cites Sir John Deane's Free Grammar School at Witton, founded in 1558, which required a 'learned, sober discreet and unmarried' master, over the age of thirty, undefamed, with a degree or degrees from Oxford or Cambridge. This paragon could be removed if he later declined from these admirable qualities and proved dissolute, inclined to drinking, whoring, dicing or gaming, or entangled with unsuitable occupations.[49] The statutes for Sandwich School in 1580, seeking Lincoln College's assistance in making the appointment, required an MA if possible, approved by the ordinary, and examined for learning, discretion of teaching, honest conversation, and religion. Archbishop Harriet's school at Chigwell in 1629 required the Latin master to be a graduate, at least

twenty-seven, skilled in Greek and Latin, a good poet (!), sound in
religion (neither papist nor puritan), of grave behaviour, of a sober
and honest conversation, no tippler or haunter of alehouses nor puffer
of tobacco, apt to teach and 'severe in his government'.[50]

Thus far it emerges that the training of schoolmasters was unspecialised – basic literacy itself, grammar-school or university Latin, for high-
fliers a degree, in all cases embedded in orthodoxy and sobriety. The
earliest attention to pedagogical methods and techniques was not drawn
by training institutions (none existed), but by the writings of individual
practising teachers, for example Ascham's *The Scholemaster* (1570), more
suited to private tutoring, Coote's *English Schoolmaster* (1596) for both
professional and amateur teachers, and Brinsley's *Ludus Literarius or the
Grammar School* (1612). The earliest advocate of vocational teacher training was Richard Mulcaster, headmaster of Merchant Taylors' 1561–86
and High Master of St Paul's 1596–1608. Samuel Hartlib envisaged a
special type of school for 'scholars' who were to teach others humane
arts and sciences. But no such specialising institution, or even course,
was devised. By the first decade of the eighteenth century the SPCK's
recommendation for its charity schoolmasters sets out a useful specifica-
tion, though it does not indicate how the individual was to train. The
charity schools wanted a master who was a member of the Church of
England, of sober life and conversation and at least twenty-five years
old. He had to frequent Holy Communion, be of meek temper and
humble behaviour, and be 'one of a good genius for teaching'. Reiter-
ating the point about religious orthodoxy, he had to be able to give a
good account to the parish minister, and indeed had to be approved by
the minister before being presented to be licensed. He had to keep
order in his family, and write a good hand, and understand the grounds
of arithmetic: all this for £30 per year, and a house. (For charity school
women teachers see below.) The SPCK abandoned any idea of running
a training college, but it did act as an employment agency of sorts, and
got a pupil–teacher recruiting system going.[51]

It had long been the case that senior pupils in grammar schools had
been used in an assisting capacity, not just in the embryonic role of
prefects, but in a pedagogic capacity, for example at Manchester Grammar School, where entrants to the school who could not read already
were to be coached by a senior pupil, and this was a not uncommon
provision in school statutes. Some of this virtual apprenticeship gave the
pupils involved an inkling of the master's job. At schools with more than
one master, the second (and more rarely any third or fourth) was

normally very much junior in status and pay, often called the usher; he was generally assigned the less palatable hours (starting earlier, and having shorter breaks) and the junior forms, and less demanding subjects. At Chigwell the second master needed all the qualifications of the Latin master but had also to write fair secretary and Roman hands and be skilful in ciphering and casting of accounts, to teach his scholars. The ushership was a form of paid in-service training, and many careers rose from such a start. Indeed, it was the intention in the grammar schools founded by Archbishop Holgate at York, Hemsworth and Old Malton in 1547–48, that the usher, if qualified, was to succeed the master, in any vacancy, with the ushers of the other two schools next considered. In this way teachers learned as they went along. But the trouble for the whole 'profession' was that many did not go along, gaining experience, but fell in and out of the career intermittently, and worked in schools themselves of only temporary duration. All these factors combined to keep schoolteachers, taken as an unwieldy whole, inferior to the ministers of religion, and comparatively amateur, with the gap between their attainments really too wide to support any generalisation about their education. However, one kind of evidence suggests quite respectful contemporary opinion of schoolteachers, and this is the not uncommon title-page identification of schoolmaster authors with their schools and profession, indicating that this enhanced rather than diminished their credibility as experts with the book-buying public. Writers whose title pages proclaim their schoolmastering include John White, William Walker, Charles Hoole and John Clarke. Schoolmastering was not something to conceal, and for a writer putting forward educational theories, or publishing well-tried pedagogic practices, his long experience of teaching was a good selling-point.

So far here the teaching profession has been handled as though it were exclusively male. This was never the case; even in the Middle Ages the occasional schoolmistress is recorded, and women filling the role of governess worked in aristocratic households. In our period women are found teaching at two levels: the vast majority of them in elementary education, where the term 'dame school' covers a nursery schooling of very varied quality, and a few in fashionable girls' schools or young ladies' academies. The poorest dame schools were uneducative child-minding facilities: Eachard in 1698 described the sending of children at two and three years of age to a schooldame to keep them out of harm's way rather than to learn a letter. But not a few of the children destined for grammar schools and literary fame began their education in a dame school, including Dr Johnson. The charity schools provided a frame-work for women teaching; their salaries were £ 24 per annum where the men's were £ 30, and their work was more structured than that of the schooldames. The private girls' schools evidently paid more attention to accomplishments, but Mrs Makin's ambitions for her establishment at Tottenham were higher, as shown above.

Education for Other Careers

Commerce, Trade and Administration

Compared with the medieval scene, the sixteenth century was commercially far more active and advanced, and the seventeenth positively modern. Some guilds had been requiring literacy from apprentices from the fifteenth century to cope with small trade 'paperwork', but the need for skills in literacy and numeracy to operate any enterprise from a provincial bookshop to a global trading joint-stock company expanded enormously in the early modern period. The bureaucracy of business generated accounts, invoices, stock inventories, receipts, shares and other sophistications such as bills of exchange, all requiring handling with understanding.

There was of course a wide range of participants from big financiers, none more impressive than Sir Thomas Gresham, down to small traders keeping their own books. Some of the grammar-school foundations offered writing and accounting from the fifteenth century, for example Rotherham. The ordinances of many traditional grammar schools show, however, that writing was not part of the curriculum and was taught by a different teacher, often a local scrivener, as an extra, for which boys were released, for example on Thursday and Saturday afternoons at Bristol. Some grammar schools came to develop practical classes in arithmetic, especially in the eighteenth century. Throughout the dissenting academies' history individual institutions offered a secular, or 'commercial' option alongside the ministerial training, often a three-year course where the ministerial one was five. The students on these courses generally had specifically vocational subjects. Students at Sheriffhales (1663–97) engaged in practical exercises such as surveying land, composing almanacs, making sundials and dissecting animals.[52] By the 1770s at Warrington the commercial stream took in the first year elementary mathematics (arithmetic, algebra and geometry), French, and universal grammar and rhetoric. In the second they took mathematics, including trigonometry and optional navigation, natural philosophy and astronomy and French, and in the third further philosophy, chemistry and morality. Essays, translations and specimen letters were done as exercises. Writing, drawing, bookkeeping and shorthand were available if desired. What was unusual about Warrington was the 'pick and mix' availability of the syllabus, where course fees were separately charged, allowing the student to take what he chose.[53]

Such commercial courses were a new development, but on a more individual scale and by more informal and piecemeal facilities the need for this kind of education had been recognised and met far earlier in the period. Particularly for merchants trading overseas, grocers and mercers, apprenticeship contracts might even specify foreign experience as part of the training. The examples which follow are taken from the edited Southampton general apprenticeship registers.

In 1610 a master contracted to keep his apprentice, indentured for seven years, in Spain for two years 'to learne the langued'. In 1629 another was to be instructed as a merchant and 'in the French tongue', though it is not said where. In 1633 an apprentice was to be instructed in the trade of grocer 'and other merchannts affaires' and to be sent by his master 'one yeare of the terme into France'.[54] Some of the contracts illuminate precisely the kind of sheltered practice the apprentice might enjoy in the later years of his term. David Jenvy, bound to William Smith, mercer, for seven years in January 1649, to be instructed in the trade of mercer and 'the art of merchandizinge beyond the seas', was to be allowed to 'trade and trafficque for himselfe', with a stock of £50, when he went to sea, which was to be in the last two years. In 1651 a gentleman's son, Thomas Nicholls, was apprenticed to William Smyth, mercer, for seven years, to be employed in the last two in France or any other foreign parts by consent of his father. For those two years the apprentice was 'to have the benefitt of the master commissions after such rate as other marchants then doe allow, and if they amount not to £20 per annum the master is to make it up soe much'.[55] With such an apprenticeship behind him the trainee merchant could enter confidently into action on a larger scale. In order to cope one needed the full training of the merchant's counting-house, and at sea and in foreign parts. Small wonder formal education at Eton seemed useless: concerning young Robert Ellison, then sixteen and at Eton, John Baker, a director of the Royal Exchange Assurance Company, wrote: 'I find Mr Ellison's son is now at Eton. He cannot come from thence into a merchants' [*sic*] compting house without being some months at school in London to learn to write and also accounts.'[56] Much was learned from practice, but there were already textbooks in appropriate subjects such as John Herford's *An Introduction for to lerne to recken with the penne or counters* (1537), Robert Recorde's *Ground of artes* (1543), Humphrey Baker's *Wellspring of Sciences* (1546) and Thomas Masterson's *Second Book of Arithmetic* (1592). James Peele's books on accountancy stress what would still be good practice: legibility, accuracy, sorting and archiving bills and correspondence both incoming and outgoing, and double-entry bookkeeping.

In private administration, for example as estate stewards, and in public, for example as civil servants, there were many individuals who bestrode classification, being perhaps small landowners on their own account, and purchasers of office for whom it was an investment rather than a career. The high-fliers had been educated at grammar schools and university: Samuel Pepys, at the Navy Board, was a Magdalene man. Grammar-school boys who did not aspire to university must have been reasonable recruits to clerkship, and more elementary scholars who could read and write and cast accounts had the makings to fill the lower local jobs. D. R. Hainsworth, writing of estates stewards in Prest's *The Professions in Early Modern England*, comments that they could all read and write and keep accounts but had not passed straight from education into a single line of employment – they normally matured by experience in more than one sphere. There was practically no institutional provision for educating intending entrants into these careers. They had to find an appropriate private school, or negotiate with teachers of particular commercial subjects, or pick it all up as they advanced in employment, and from a whole range of instructive textbooks. What can be said about the aims of this kind of education is that they were specific, limited and usually short-term: that is, the student entered upon the learning for a particular purpose and then went off to practise the skill. Students of these subjects were not learning for life before choosing a career.

Technology and Craft

Technological and craft skills were most commonly learned through apprenticeship, which was rarely for less than seven years. The 1563 statute of artificers forbade anyone to exercise any art, mystery or craft unless apprenticed for at least seven years. It reinforced a wedge between skilled crafts, requiring various levels of property ownership in the apprentices' fathers, and less skilled crafts where anyone could be apprenticed anywhere. Already the Tudor Poor Laws of 1536 and 1547 had lighted upon apprenticing vagrant children as a solution to social problems, and legislation of 1563, 1597 and 1601 refined the practice. The separate registers kept at Southampton for registering general apprenticeships and for poor children bound as apprentices may be used to illustrate the differentials. Of 650 entries in the general register, 261 (40 per cent) related to the better-quality mercantile crafts including grocers, merchants or merchant adventurers, mercers and drapers; fifty-six (8.6 per cent) to victualling trades – brewers, butchers, bakers, chandlers, vintners, innholders and fishmongers; ninety-seven (15 per cent) to clothmaking occupations; 140 (21.5 per cent) to handicrafts producing mainly clothes and shoes; nineteen (3 per cent) to metalworking (the largest number being seven goldsmiths); seventeen (2.6 per cent) to building crafts; eight (1.2 per cent) to shipbuilding; thirty-six (5.5 per cent) to other crafts, dominated in numbers by twenty-nine coopers; with six sailors/mariners and a fisherman (together forming one per cent) and six barber-surgeons, one barber and one notary (together 1.2 per cent). One case is not identified. The poor child register, analysing the first and last hundred identifiable trades (from 1609–45 and 1669–1708) produces the following breakdown: in the two respective batches of a hundred (figures for the second batch being given in brackets), no apprentice (one) entered mercantile trades; nine (six) entered victualling, nine (eighteen) building, thirty-six (thirteen) clothmaking, thirty-three (fifty-seven) entered an assortment of handicrafts including blacksmithery, cobbling, shoemaking and tailoring, one (none) entered labouring, two (none) husbandry, seven (four) fishing and sailing; none (one) gardening and three (none) were musicians.[57]

The benefits of apprenticeship can be seen to have exceeded the transmission of skills in those agreements where, at the end of the term, the apprentice was to be given tools of the trade. Thomas Cossen, apprenticed to a tailor in 1619, was to have a pressing iron, a pair of shears and 10s at the end, as well as the almost standard provision of double apparel. William Wilde, indentured to a shipwright in Blackwall, Stepney, in 1627 was to have at the end axe, adze, auger, malle (maul), claw hammer, handsaw, chisel, caulking iron and mallet, a handsome and helpful endowment. John West, apprenticed to Richard Barnard, cordwainer, in 1659 was to have at the end 'working geere of all sorts belonging to ye trade', and Thomas Ratcliffe, apprenticed to a plumber that year, to be instructed in the trade of plumber and hellier (roofer) was to have 'working tooles of all sorts for a hellier'.[58] These agreements underline the single vocational aim of the apprenticeship, the preparing of a youth to earn his living in the practice of a qualified skill. Literacy and numeracy might be understood to be part of this preparation, either obtained before indenture, or as an agreed part of the contract. Giles New, apprenticed for nine years to Andrew Emerye, clothier, in 1631 was to be instructed in the trade of clothier and to write and cipher. Thomas Neale, apprenticed to a blacksmith for thirteen years in 1633, was to be kept at the writing school during the first three years to learn to read and write.[59] The latter case, though in the general register, is in the formulae of the poor child register and indeed describes the child, son of a yeoman late of Southampton, as a poor child aged about ten, bound by the churchwardens and overseers of All Saints with the consent of the mayor and justices. The earlier instance was a less impoverished case, since the master was expressly rewarded with the interest on £50 of the apprentice's money for the first eight years, but the longer term, and the fact that the apprentice's father was dead, suggests we may be handling here a younger apprentice still in need of formal education.

In the poor child register, apprenticeship of many of the boys may be treated here as craft training. It appears to have been for longer, commonly nine, ten, twelve and even sixteen years, up to the early 1630s, then declining to around eight and a half years. Children of both sexes were handed over at any age from three to eighteen in ninety-five analysed cases between 1609 and 1680, and finished serving at any age from fifteen to twenty-five, most commonly at nineteen to twenty-four. Some poor children learned a specified craft, for example feltmaking, fulling, fishing, weaving and kembing (wool-combing). As with the general apprentices, sometimes the master was bound to help the qualified apprentice set up. James Blumpey, apprenticed to Hugh Tanner of Durley, cooper, for eight years in 1645 was to have 'all manner of tooles fitting for his trade of everie sort', and Thomas Osman, son of Jane, born at 'The George' in the parish of All Saints, was put at three and a half years to Richard Morris of Eling, cooper, for twenty and a half years, to have at the end a 'sett of tools fitt to bee used in the trade of a cooper'. William Neale, apprenticed to a tobacco-pipe maker, was to have at the end of nine years 'one mould of tinn to make pipes with' and 10s. Nicholas Post, apprenticed to Hugh Rogers of the Minories London, weaver, for eight years to be instructed in the art and trade of silk weaver was luckier, being promised 'a loome with ye appurtenances fitting to sett himself on worke'.[60] The whole aim of craft apprenticeship can hardly be better summed up.

Education to Improve the Poor

Poor-law apprenticeship, whereby the churchwardens and overseers of the poor, with the assent of a couple of justices of the peace or involvement of the mayor, bound children, could lead to craft training, though often in the less elite crafts, as deliberately educational and vocational as the craft training of better-born apprentices. However, this was not always the case. The law was administered to reduce the parish's liabilities for unsupported children, to find them in modern parlance foster-parents who could expect recompense either by means of the child's labour, or especially where it was very young and unproductive, by money from the authorities and/or charitable trusts, either supplied with the child, or in instalments. One is less confident of the educational value of this experience, especially it must be said, for girls.

It tends to be assumed that boys apprenticed in this way learned the skill of their master, but sometimes the details provided make the instance less, not more, clear, though the purpose of learning some living remains the same. Thomas Gill, put out to Peter Gage of Wimborne Minster, clothworker, for fourteen years in 1656 was to be instructed in 'a lawful vocation for to gett his living'. A girl who appears to be his sister Ann was put to a husbandman at Wimborne for fourteen years 'to be taught and enstructed in som lawfull employment': there is a marginal note 'Ann Gill aged the daye abovesaid 3 yeres'.[61]

There was not, of course, the range of crafts open to girls, so it is small wonder that for many the parish apprenticeship was domestic service. About the clearest statement in the Southampton Register of a poor girl being taught a distinct skill is the case of Hannah Shackle, bound to Lydia Austen, widow, for seven years to learn the art trade or mystery of sempstress in 1669. Dorothy Cawte, aged about fifteen, was placed with Robert Houchins sergeweaver and Joane his wife for seven years in 1631 to be taught 'the use of her needle', while Joane Farre in 1631 went to Thomas Austen shoemaker and his wife Suzan for twelve years 'to be instructed in the making of cutt work'. A girl who appears to be her sister Elizabeth went to a tailor and his wife for eight years 'to be instructed in sowing and spynning and the like'. Mary Jenkins went to Elizabeth Woodland for eight years in 1633 'to learne to knitt etc.' Hanna Cawle, aged about ten, went to a sailor and his wife for ten years 'to learne to spinne and to knitte'. Joane Nash went to Thomas Johnson barber and his wife for seven years to be instructed in needle-work and housewifery in 1639. Even girls were to be taught to read in some cases, in one of which both master (Gideon Renough) and appren-tice (Sara Tollervey), being unable to sign, put their marks. No specific skill was promised to Ann Stevens, bound in March 1658 for five years to a couple 'to be taught and employed in such household employments as they shall employ her about'. The case of Ann Shud in July 1663 is interesting, not because she went to a couple for ten years 'to teach her in som good employment to get her living', but because the entry records that £3 from Nathaniel Mills's charity was given to the master, 'which the said donor gave to place a boy but in regard a boy cannot conveniently be found to be placed according to the said testator's will, therefore the mayor and alderman have placed the said child'.[62]

Parish apprenticeship, from the end of the sixteenth century, was dedicated to enabling the poor to be self-supporting in their working lives, and to getting them off the community's back as cheaply and quickly as possible. The records leave us able to see the humbler crafts thought suited to the poor's situation, with here and there mention being made of reading ability. But how the parish apprentice was to come by this facility is often left unsaid: it is not very likely to have been in the household of a master who had to register his own participation in the contract with a mark. It is unlikely that a girl of fifteen would need seven years to learn to use a needle, and there was a limit to the amount of housewifery which could be learned, however long one spent in the household of an ordinary barber, sergeweaver or labourer. Much of the girls' time must have been plain drudgery, and the apprenticeship of boys to unspecified husbandry is likely to have been a similar servitude. Obviously in real crafts children's first efforts would be clumsy and in effect a waste of materials, so with child apprentices the masters had to be recompensed for the years before the child became an asset econom-ically. Setting aside twentieth-century qualms about the individual assignment of an individual child to relatively unsupervised masters/

mistresses, it is clear enough that the educational element in parish apprenticeship was rudimentary and strictly utilitarian.

Both these qualities were carried forward into the institutionalised framework of the eighteenth century's provision for the education of the poor. The beneficiaries of the charity schools and Sunday schools were living at home, except for those who qualified for institutional care, generally orphans or workhouse children. So they did not need the foster-parenting of the parish apprentices. Nor did they need the craft apprenticeship to be provided by the schools: that could follow for those lucky enough to get into it. Out of some 20 000 children passing through English charity schools by 1733, over 15 000 had been placed in what was meant to be decent employment by school administrators. Some 7000 boys and nearly 1400 girls had been apprenticed, and 3000–4000 of each sex put into service. The schools themselves provided the training in reading and ciphering mentioned occasionally in indentures, allowing the boys writing and arithmetic, but largely confining the girls to the same skills as the parish girls: reading perhaps, but not often writing, and knitting, spinning and sewing. The only major change from the parish apprenticeship (which continued into the nineteenth century) to the charity schooling was the institutionalisation of the religious instruction, hammered home remorselessly at every opportunity, along with the underlying lessons in obedience and submission. Throughout the period the aims of education for the poor remained the same: to teach them industrious habits, make them self-supporting, and to preach at them their station in life and their obligations to their 'betters'. It was not an unrealistic upbringing for their situation at that time.

4

EDUCATIONAL FACILITIES

The layout of this chapter is designed to handle the facilities for learning, taking the opportunities as an age cohort would progress through them; however it is much easier to distinguish elementary, secondary, further and higher education today than it was to separate their equivalents in early modern times, so the subdivisions have a touch of anachronism about them. There was no overarching system decreeing the age at which to proceed from one level to another, and there was overlap.

Some form of elementary schooling was utilised by all who learned to read, but in some cases the provision was made institutionally and in others through private tuition. Social class influenced both access to and the duration of education. Basic literacy, reading of the mother tongue, with or without writing, was as far as some children got on the academic ladder, on which others never even started. With or without basic literacy, unskilled labour was the lot of many. Needy families had their children working for money as early as seven years of age, and agricultural proficiency was generally attained by the mid-teens.

For the most part, in the sixteenth and seventeenth centuries, only the children of yeomanry and above could enjoy the luxury of school attendance beyond the age of employability. It is generally agreed that children began school around six to eight years of age, but some started younger, others older. Spufford argues that children beneath the yeomanry might have been at school long enough to learn to read, but by the age they should have progressed to writing they had been put to work. On this argument, reading ability would have been very much more widespread than writing ability. After two or three years of full-time education a child would have outgrown elementary schooling, but some attenders were erratic or little more than part-timers. Paradoxically, some children's poverty pulled them into charitable education, at establishments like Christ's Hospital, at the later charity schools, and in workhouses. Workhouse conditions varied greatly: at Stroud two hours a day was recommended for each child to spend learning to read, in 1722; at St Giles in London (*c*.1726) children between the ages of five and nine had two half-hour periods a day to be taught reading, and the older ones the same time for writing and accounting.

Those who went on to grammar school seem to have done so between eight and eleven, and stayed there up to six or seven years. However, there are incompatibilities here too, for we hear of younger individuals at grammar school. Josiah Langdale had been at grammar school before he was eight; his education came to an abrupt end on the death of his father. James Fretwell remembered being removed from the hornbook class at Kirk Sandall Grammar School at the tender age of four years and seven months, when his reading proved better than expected. These individual cases may be reconciled with the general rule by regarding these young pupils as attending virtually preparatory departments of the grammar schools concerned. The grammar schools clearly expected their intake to be able to read already, that is, to be past the elementary requirements. St Paul's and Merchant Taylors' required entrants to be able to read and write and know the Catechism, and St Albans and Shrewsbury required them to have started Latin accidence. The big difference between elementary and grammar schooling was the learning of Latin.

Any distinction between grammar schools and boarding schools, for boys, was blurred because boys who lived too far from any school to travel daily might stay with a local householder in the vicinity of a school, without that school itself offering or supervising boarding facilities. Furthermore, schools which had a full boarding facility also had day pupils. Boarding schools for girls are a different species; since girls were nowhere institutionally offered the full rigour of the Latin curriculum there could be no overlap of their boarding schools with grammar schooling.

The grammar schools took children younger than the age for entering apprenticeship, which was generally between the ages of thirteen and eighteen. Apprentices were generally expected to have had some basic education; even in the fifteenth century guild regulations were requiring apprentices to be literate. Some apprenticeship contracts specified that the apprentice was to be released for formal schooling for a period at the start of his time. It does not seem likely that most apprentices would be recruited from boys who had had a few years of grammar schooling, so one must consider whether the apprentices came straight on from rather late elementary education, or whether their early elementary schooling, if any, had been followed by work experience. Both patterns can be seen: the elementary school founded at Marlow (1624) was for children entering between ten and fourteen, and had provision for apprenticing the boys, while Edward Barlow was apprenticed in textiles at Manchester at about thirteen, having had a variety of local jobs over the previous year or two, following rudimentary schooling between the ages of seven and nine.

Grammar and boarding schools and private tuition all passed boys on to the universities at ages around sixteen to eighteen, where they would stay four years to gain BA and seven to reach MA, if they completed the courses. Completing the degree or not, some went on to the inns of court, joining other students there who had not necessarily been at university first. For the 'milords' whose education culminated in the Grand Tour this was undertaken in their late teens or early twenties.

Elementary Schooling

Internal organisation was not a strong characteristic of schools in the late Middle Ages and is scarcely touched upon in contemporary documentation, which implies it was of small import. At the elementary level of ABC, song, reading or petty schools there must have been many educational enterprises (one hesitates to call them institutions) involving only one, not necessarily full-time, teacher and perhaps only half a dozen pupils, operating in a room in a house or church. Chaplains of medieval chantry foundations taught spelling and reading in addition to their religious duties, for example at Aldwinkle from 1489, where this teaching was to six poor boys of the parish.[1] The previously cited 1530 Canterbury convocation order to rectors, vicars and chantry priests to instruct boys in the alphabet, reading, song or grammar, provided schooling without setting up dedicated schools or masters. Chantry certification refers to ABC, reading and song teaching at schools which were not generally continued. The children at chantry schools seem to have been aged anything from four to ten, and in theory some could have been girls, though song schools were designed to train choirboys in particular. Seven or eight was the common starting age for elementary education when Brinsley wrote his *Ludus Literarius* (1612).

After the dissolution of the chantries it was not until the seventeenth century that the charitable endowment of elementary schools began to any great extent, though a sterling example was created in London with Christ's Hospital, founded in 1552 for 'fatherless children and other poor men's children' of both sexes, who were lodged, fed, clothed and taught in the old Greyfriars building. Sir William Borlase's school at Marlow, founded in 1624, was specifically to teach twenty-four poor children to write, read and cast accounts. They were to study for two years and there were provisions for binding the boys to apprenticeships, making this a well-integrated school of practical use. The Red Maids' School at Bristol, founded in 1634 under the will of alderman John Whitson, began as a charitable institution for forty girls, daughters of freemen of Bristol, apprenticed to their schoolmistress for seven years, learning reading and plain needlework. In the later seventeenth century the charitable provision of education for the poor continued. Jones, in *The Charity School Movement* (1938), estimates some 460 endowed elementary or English schools existed by the end of the century. Some elementary education was available in institutions which were not primarily schools. The Clerkenwell College of Infants set up in 1685 taught reading, writing and trades, and an early inspection disclosed its children 'well lodged and well clothed, kept neat and clean, taught to read and write and well instructed in the religion of the Church of England', and the Bishopsgate workhouse scheme, launched in 1699, taught reading, writing and arithmetic to children over seven, who were well fed and clothed and part self-funded by their spinning, knitting of stockings, and making of their own clothes and shoes. The Female Orphan Asylum opened at Lambeth in 1758 took girls between nine and twelve and apprenticed them to the matron for seven years. During this time they learned to cut out and make their own linen, understand plain cookery, and clean kitchen and other household furniture. They were also to be able to read a chapter of the Bible, write legibly and cast up a sum. Only then were they placed in domestic service or trade.[2] Most elementary schooling, however, lacked the security of endowment, and all of it lacked any review of academic quality.

For its clientele of young children, its availability was crucial. Adam Martindale had to go two miles to school in St Helens in 1630, and remembered this as 'a great way for a little fat short legged lad (as I was) to travel twice a day' at seven years old. Across the Pennines young James Fretwell had to be placed with a widow as he could not keep up with the older local boys walking to school.[3] To be effectively available, elementary schooling had to be very localised. Charles Hoole was pointing to this when he wrote in 1660 of children starting school at the age of four or five in towns, but at six or seven in rural areas, because of distance.

Elementary education until the end of the seventeenth century had evolved for utilitarian ends, and was largely located according to local demand and support. With the exception of a few institutions like Christ's Hospital and the Red Maids' School elementary schools were impermanent enterprises. Some were started and run by persons who hoped to make a living, or supplement one, by teaching locally; others were set up in response to local demand by a few parents or benefactors, in which case the chances of permanence were higher, especially if there was any endowment. What is generally called 'the Charity School movement', promoted by the London-based SPCK, was on a different scale. This was joint-stock financed promotion of education for the lower classes with a religious and social agenda. Aiming to take the children of the labouring poor off the streets and indoctrinate them with a Christian and useful education, at the subscription of the better-off, the movement set up schools for thousands of children of both sexes, between the ages of seven and twelve to fourteen. Jones considered the charity school as part of the eighteenth-century 'age of benevolence', and stressed the thousands of schools and pupils involved, many of whom were subsequently placed in apprenticeship or service. Thirty years on, in the Leicestershire context (an area claimed as a major success for the movement), Joan Simon questioned whether there was a charity school 'movement' at all.[4] Clearly the SPCK reports claimed credit for many schools which in fact already existed, and historians' enthusiasm has led to too many schools being swept into the category. Schools set up to 'rescue' unemployed youth from idleness and irreligion were what was new, and distinct, and not every school where 'poor children' (by an assortment of definitions) could benefit from charitable subvention of their education and maintenance should be included. The greatest impact of the charity schools was in London and Westminster, where it is claimed fifty-four schools were teaching 2000 pupils by 1704,

132 teaching 5225 by 1729, and 179 teaching 7108 by 1799. Bristol and Newcastle were also active.

Modern scholarship is also suspicious of accepting 'eighteenth-century benevolence' too credulously. In the charity schools proper religious instruction was foremost. Previous schooling had had pious intentions involving the sharing of religious principles understood and approved by both parents and teachers, but the charity-school proselytising was more of a war by the teachers and their employers on the vices prevalent in the pupils' background. Only secondarily to hammering out the evil came the teaching of reading (of religious material) and writing, to boys, with some going on to arithmetic. The girls were seldom taught writing and even less often arithmetic. Knitting, spinning and housewifery were their practical specialities. Modern liberalism finds the religious indoctrination of the Charity School movement unpalatable, and its aim to produce a tractable workforce abhorrent. But to be realistic, it did result in thousands of children learning to read. Some of these would be able to build on this skill, which would not otherwise have come their way. The Charity School movement did not set out to promote upward mobility socially, but this was really the first attempt at mass education, and suiting the next generation to the sort of life it was likely to lead had a certain practicality.

The lowly level of the elementary school is underlined by the obscurity of its workforce. Most of the identifiable schoolteachers were employed in grammar teaching, and the cream of them were university graduates. Elementary or petty teachers were supposed to be licensed, but rather less concern was shown to keep record of their subscriptions. The licensing system was regarded as only necessary for grammar schoolteachers by the early eighteenth century. Many of the male elementary teachers combined the job with others of no great status, baking, shoemaking or parish clerking. (This may not actually have detracted from their patient direction of struggling pupils, for the most highly educated do not always communicate well with those who have difficulties in learning.) The women teachers could not normally have had much education themselves, obviously, and are generally dismissed as contemptible, but again, may have been in individual cases kindly and patient communicators, provided too much was not asked of them. However there were extraordinary exceptions. Elizabeth Elstob, the highly respected Anglo-Saxon scholar, impoverished after her brother's death, was discovered elementary teaching under an assumed name in the Evesham area by George Ballard, the sympathetic researcher into learned women. She died in post as nursery governess to the Duke of Portland's children. Schoolteaching was not professionally trained at any level, and some of the worst examples must be expected to have been among the elementary teachers. Mulcaster (*The First Part of the Elementarie*, 1582) declared good scholars would not abase themselves to elementary teaching; Richard Hodges (*The English Primrose*, 1644) confirmed teaching reading of English was so tedious and grievous that it would not please scholars. Nevertheless, the elementary teachers were deemed a professional market. John Hart's *An Orthography* (1569) was a manual on teaching reading, followed the next year by his *A Method of Comfortable Beginning for all Unlearned*, which used pictures and phonics to teach. Francis Clement's *The Petty School with an English Orthography* (1576), which claimed to teach a child to read in one month, and dealt with writing as a subsequent skill in the 1587 edition, was followed by *Bullokar's Book at Large* (1580) and Mulcaster's *Positions wherein those Primitive Circumstances be examined which are Necessary for the Training of Children* (1581) and his earlier cited *First Part of the Elementarie*, William Kempe's *Education of Children in Learning* (1588) and Edmund Coote's *The English Schoolmaster* (1596), which claimed to get its readers up to grammar-school or apprentice literacy. Coote himself was a master in the Free School of Bury St Edmunds, but was willing to disclose the secrets of the profession to amateurs. The book went through twenty-six editions by 1656, and the last edition emerged in 1704. From these works it can be seen that children learnt pronunciation as well as visual letter recognition.

Locke recommended that children should learn the alphabet by playing with dice and playthings with letters on them, and so 'cozen'd into a knowledge of letters, to be taught to read, without perceiving it to be anything but a sport'.[5] The first basic equipment of elementary teaching was the criss-cross row arrangement of the alphabet on parchment or paper, or the hornbook, a tablet of wood with the alphabet incised on it or written on parchment or paper fastened to it, with a thin horn covering for protection. Commonly it had the Lord's Prayer set out on it, the Creed, and sometimes the Ten Commandments. The hornbook dates from the early fifteenth century, and remained in use into the nineteenth.

After learning letters, the child was given religious material to practise on, namely the primer, psalter and catechism. Primers, which were books of devotion, were sometimes published with ABCs as prefaces, which indicates their educational as well as religious use. These were the basic elementary (but originally Latin) readers, read before grammar studies began. Their availability was massively increased by printing. By the 1520s the London bookseller John Dorne had primers costing from 3*d* to 6*d*. The first approved primer wholly in English was *A Primer in English* (1534). A standard primer was authorised in 1545, in English and Latin versions. Catechisms of Christian principles poured forth in the religious changes of the sixteenth century, and were used in schools, in English for the elementary pupils. Locke, however, thought the learning by heart of the Lord's Prayer, Creed and Ten Commandments should be kept separate from learning to read, and that when the child could read, 'some easy pleasant Book suited to his Capacity' should be given to him. He recommended Aesop's *Fables*. Addressing himself to gentlemen's sons, he thought it 'seasonable' to begin writing as soon as the child could read English well. He paid attention to the correct holding of the pen and the position of the paper, arm and body, as well as the forming of letters with the aid of copy-sheets.[6]

Grammar Schooling

Grammar schools were attached to cathedrals in the Middle Ages, and formed part of prominent collegiate establishments. They were in some cases part of a tiered educational structure, such as Eton, tied to King's College Cambridge, and some university colleges had their own grammar schools, such as Magdalen. There were also town grammar schools, which often overlapped with some form of ecclesiastical endowment, and some chantry foundations provided grammar schooling (which survived the Dissolution better than the chantries' elementary teaching provision).

In the medieval grammar schools one master, or a headmaster with an usher or assistant, was the common complement of staff, so patently there could not have been a separation into several classes taught in separate rooms by individual teachers at this date. (On the other hand, even before the end of the medieval period there were specialist teachers for specified subjects. Thus Archbishop Rotherham's College had teachers of song, grammar and accounting, and Bishop Stillington's foundation at Acaster Selby masters of song, grammar and scrivener craft.) Eton, Winchester and Westminster, schools closely connected to the university colleges, were England's most prestigious early modern schools, with St Paul's, Merchant Taylors' London, Bury St Edmunds and St Bees singled out by David Cressy as 'stars of second magnitude', a ranking embracing several dozen schools. Over the country, a further 200–300 grammar schools were modelled on them.[7]

The teaching of the whole school together, not in separate classrooms, is reflected architecturally. The commonest feature of the purpose-built school was a large room or hall for teaching. Malcolm Seaborne, in *The English School: its Architecture and Organization 1370–1870* (1971), tabled four large early grammar schools which provided between thirteen and twenty square feet per pupil. In chronological order these were Winchester (1382), 45' × 29' for seventy scholars and ten commoners; Eton (1440), 76' × 24', for seventy scholars and twenty commoners; Berkhamsted (mid-sixteenth century), 70' × 27' for a maximum of 144 pupils and Guildford (1557), 65' × 21', for 100. Thame, built in the later sixteenth century, had a schoolroom 50' × 20', Enfield, of similar date, one 52' × 22', and Ashbourne, built at the very end of the century, one 46' × 22'. The early seventeenth-century school at Burnsall in Wharfedale was 43' × 20', and Blundell's school at Tiverton was 100' × 24', for 150 boys. Schoolhouses in the fifteenth and sixteenth centuries were unlikely to cost much over £100. This was the cost at Birstall in 1556, Pontefract in 1583 and Thornton in 1599. After the Restoration the schools remained similar in size: Witney had a central schoolroom 50' × 22', and Guilsborough one 54' × 20'. Appleby Magna, built in 1693–97, cost £2800.[8]

In early modern England grammar schools for 100–150 boys remained common, but a few grew noticeably larger, by pulling in boys to board in the town or providing accommodation for them (see the next section). Shrewsbury School had 266 pupils by 1562, and 360 by 1581; significantly, in 1586 Camden called it the largest school in England. Schools' growth promoted their subdivision into forms (not yet requiring separate classrooms). St Paul's, refounded in 1509, had sixteen boys and a head boy in each form, and nine forms. The 1574 statutes of the Free Grammar School at Leicester provided for seven forms, the top three being under the main schoolmaster, the next three under the head usher and the lowest under the under-usher. A breakdown of forms from Wolverhampton Grammar School in 1609 shows there were eleven boys in the junior or accidence form, averaging 8.8 years of age, fifteen in the second form, averaging 9.7 years, and fifteen in the form described as 'under the usher', averaging 10.6. The next form, called the latter or lower part of the third form, had eight boys averaging twelve years, the next, the former or upper part of the third form, eleven, averaging 13.5. There was then a second form of seven boys averaging 15.5 years, and a head form of two boys, one aged seventeen and one eighteen. All sixty-nine boys were taught in the same room by the two masters. They were grouped by difficulty of work rather than strict age. A similar age-span emerges from William Kempe's writings (1588); his first form teaches the boy the beginnings of Latin and moves him at eight to the second form and practice of Latin; he finishes at fifteen after Latin, Greek, logic, rhetoric, arithmetic and geometry. By 1775 the breakdown at Eton consisted of a lower school comprising first, second and third forms, and an upper school comprising fourth, remove, fifth and sixth forms.[9] The curriculum at Leicester described in Chapter 2 may be cited to indicate the progressive work undertaken in forms.

There is not much information about the furnishing of grammar schools. Hull corporation refurnished the school there in 1452 and the works included providing a canopied pew and desk for the master, and a form for the boys. Libraries, or at least a few books for the boys, emerge quite early. John Elwyn of Hedon left all his grammar books to St Augustine's chapel at Hedon in 1465 for the benefit of the boys learning grammar at school there. Actual housing for the books is mentioned by the end of the sixteenth century. Seaborne cites the history of Guildford in this context. In 1586 the gallery which linked the usher's and master's houses on the first floor was adapted to house books bequeathed by the Bishop of Norwich, and this is one of the earliest references to a school library, and an example of a chained library belonging to a school. The books bequeathed were largely Lutheran and Calvinist commentaries on the Bible. By 1648 new bookshelves were provided. By contrast most grammar schools of the time had only a few dictionaries. The few books were chained at Boston in 1578 and at Cheltenham in 1586. Leeds Grammar School got a separate library building in 1692, and in 1707 Sedbergh's library had sixty-two books.[10]

The textbooks for the grammar schools in the Middle Ages had been the grammar of Aelius Donatus, Priscian's *Institutes of Grammatical Art* and the *Doctrinale* of Alexander of Villa Dei. The first published grammar book in England was John Holt's *Lac Puerorum* of 1497, and John Stanbridge was another pioneer. William Lily's grammar book of 1513 became popular and was the base of the authorised textbook which dictated grammar learning for two centuries from 1540. Lily's grammar, really a composite work involving Lily, Colet and Erasmus, went through over 300 editions, and had huge print runs, making privileged profits for its monopolist printers. It was printed as a small book (5.5 in. × 3.5 in.) of some 200 pages. Books called *Vulgaria* were devised to help grammar students master vocabulary and rules, and these invited the translation of homely sentences which throw light on commonplace activities of Tudor school life. From composition (making Latins) the boys went on to imitate classical stylists, such as Cicero, and to write themes, or formal argumentative essays, and verses in Latin. (Locke thought Latin should be taught informally, like English, by conversation rather than rules. He believed composing themes and verses in Latin was a waste of time.[11]) Latin was taught as a spoken language via colloquies, orations and disputations, though the spoken element declined.

Pupils were expected to provide their own pens, paper and even candles. Some schools, including Merchant Taylors' and Manchester, positively forbade children bringing food and drink into school. The children worked from 6 or 7 a.m. until 9, with about a quarter of an hour's break then; they resumed after this until 11 a.m., when they had a couple of hours out for dinner. From 1 p.m. until 3 they worked again, and after further short break, until 5 or 6 p.m. Later starts and earlier finishes were allowed in the winter months. Part of Monday was normally spent examining Sunday's sermon, and Friday was largely revision. If there was a half-day holiday this was usually Thursday afternoon and termed a 'remedy'. Much teaching remained oral and aural, though Merchant Taylors' had written examinations three times a year. The first visitation of the school in 1562 found the ushers, 'being northern men born', had not taught the children to speak distinctly or pronounce their words as well as they ought.[12] (The headmaster, Mulcaster, was from Cumberland.)

For grammar masters the predominant salary rate at the start of the sixteenth century was £10 per annum. The 1547 injunctions to cathedrals lacking a free grammar school ordered them to pay their master £13 6s 8d, along with providing a rent-free house, and the usher had half this sum, plus a chamber. By Elizabeth's reign many grammar masters had £20–£25 per annum. The master of Norwich Grammar School had £20 from 1562 to 1602, then £26 13s 4d until 1610, £40 until 1636 and then £50; Birmingham paid £50 in 1655 and £88 15s in 1702; Kirkleatham, built in 1709, paid £100 per annum.[13]

Boarding Schools and Private Tutors

Boarding schools and private tutors existed throughout the period, and were also a facility for some girls. Two distinctive schools had late medieval foundations: Winchester, founded by Bishop Wykeham in 1382 and Eton, founded by Henry VI in 1440. These were both church colleges, and the scholars on the foundation were only part of the collegiate community. Wykeham stipulated that seventy scholars were to be admitted, between the ages of eight and twelve, already competent in reading, song and elementary Latin grammar. They could not stay on beyond eighteen, and New College at Oxford was their intended next move. The scholarships were to be given at first preference to kin of the founder, next to inhabitants of manors belonging to the two colleges at Winchester and Oxford, then to inhabitants from ten counties which contained college lands, and only if any places were still left to anyone from the rest of England. In addition a small number of commoners were admitted, that is, pupils paying fees. Eton was established on similar lines. The wide-ranging geographical recruitment was only compatible with boarding provision, and as the schools were collegiate institutions this could be expected to be within the college. The scholars slept eleven or twelve to a room in a block of chambers, with fellows, master and usher sharing chambers on the floor above them. They dined in hall with the warden and fellows, and attended services in the college chapel. Winchester was teaching 120 boys in 1679 and reached 186 in 1778, Eton – which reached over 200 by 1678 and soared to 522 in 1765 – had particular cachet, attracting boys from all over the country.

Other schools with more local recruitment had cause to offer boarding facilities, for example, cathedral schools, where the boys formed the nucleus of the choir, lived close to the cathedral and had to be seen to be a properly behaved adjunct of the church, not just boys coming together for lessons. The choristers' house at Lincoln dates from 1616. Secular schools in remote and sparsely populated areas took day boys and boarders. At Shrewsbury in the Elizabethan period the boarding was entirely outside the school, with local householders, not part of the school organisation. At Leicester during the headship of Gerrard Andrewes (to 1762) boarders at the Grammar School reached about thirty in number. By the seventeenth and eighteenth centuries there were many boarding schools for boys, of varied quality. There was a pull to the South-East from the provinces, and as provincial families rose in social ambition and wealth they set their educational sights higher. The curriculum of the good boarding school was no different from its day equivalent, so movement between the two was not difficult, and indeed schools could be both day and boarding.

By the eighteenth century, boarding at 'preparatory' level was also well established. Mary Woodforde's diary records her four-year-old son leaving home in 1687 'to board at Mr Wallace's, to go to school'.[14] In 1746 Edward Gibbon was sent, at eight, from his home in Putney to board at a preparatory school in Kingston-upon-Thames, kept by the Rev. Dr Richard Wooddeson. His comments are telling:

> there is not, in the course of life, a more remarkable change than the removal of a child from the luxury and freedom of a wealthy house, to the frugal diet and strict subordination of a school; from the tenderness of parents, and the obsequiousness of servants, to the rude familiarity of his equals, the insolent tyranny of his seniors, and the rod, perhaps, of a cruel and capricious pedagogue. Such hardships may steel the mind and body against the injuries of fortune; but my timid reserve was astonished by the crowd and tumult of the school.

His own personal agony was increased, he saw, because he was not good at sports, and was reviled for his ancestors' Tory politics.[15]

Private home tuition was still an approved practice at the end of the seventeenth century; Locke patently preferred it. Weighing up the balance of keeping a son at home or sending him away ('both sides have their Inconveniences'), he concluded the faults of private education infinitely preferable to the so-called improvements learnt among schoolboys. Locke thought the son under a tutor at home would do much better than the one 'put into a mixed herd of unruly boys'. Himself the product of Westminster School and Christ Church, Oxford, a tutor there, a private tutor to Lord Shaftesbury's heir, and Grand Tour governor of Caleb Banks, Locke was not unsympathetic to institutional schoolmasters, appreciating that the task of teaching two or three boys in a house was very different from facing three or four score in a school. With the luxury of a private tutor, the child could learn at his own pace, free of an enforced curriculum. Locke prescribed arithmetic, geography, chronology, history and geometry, learned through Greek and Latin as the child's language and capacity grew.

He did not, however, recommend Greek for gentlemen: Greek was for scholars.[16]

Families of social ambition sent daughters away to school, but girls' boarding establishments placed less emphasis on academic subjects and more on accomplishments. Upper-class girls at the start of the period enjoyed access to private tutors, and later to specifically girls' boarding schools. They did not enjoy access to grammar schools from any level of society. Antonia Fraser makes the point that upper-class girls were fortunate if they had several well-spaced brothers, and so could take advantage of lessons with them: examples are the Russell daughters, cited above. Earlier, Thomas More generously provided his daughters with the same quality of education as his son. Private tutors produced the mid-Tudor female prodigies, and many of the less startling successes of the seventeenth century. These private tutors were often not careerist teachers (as Ascham undoubtedly was), but young men, divines or poets, on their way to a church or literary career, as was the case with the poet Andrew Marvell, briefly tutor to Lord Fairfax's daughter from 1650, then to Oliver Cromwell's ward, William Dutton, and in 1657 John Milton's assistant as Latin secretary to the Commonwealth. Rather than one tutor, some girls had a string of visiting masters – at Fyfield Rectory Mrs Walker employed dancing, writing and singing masters. The private school proprietresses were often governors and managers, employing specialist male teachers, not themselves instructing. Private fee-paying schools for girls seem to have been a creation of the early seventeenth century. The first known one is the Ladies' Hall at Deptford mentioned in 1617. Individual schools are instanced in Stepney in 1628, and soon in Enfield and Waltham, and especially Hackney. Mrs Perwich's school there, existing in 1643, exceeded 100 pupils, from all over England, girls of a class which brought their maids with them. Ralph Josselin's wife took daughters to school at Chelsea in 1682. The London schools had a certain social pull, but the provinces were reasonably provided. A Mrs Amye ran a school in Manchester for at least thirty-five years from 1638 to 1673, and Ralph Thoresby took his sister to Madam Falkland's school there in 1684. In 1697 Celia Fiennes commented on 'a gentlewomen's school as good as any in London' at Salford. 'As good as any in London', however, may not have amounted to very much. There was no inspection of any schools, and no obligation to maintain minimum standards, and girls' boarding schools probably varied in quality far more than boys' boarding grammar schools.

Even the veneer of culture aspired to by the paying parents may
have been thin. Bathsua Makin's advertisement for her school in 1673
embodied the nearest creation to a girls' grammar school, requiring
the intake, at eight or nine years of age, to be able to read already, as the
grammar schools required of their boys. Mrs Makin's criticism of the
'frisk and dance' curriculum of others is telling.[17] Bad private schools
for girls were lampooned by Swift and Steele, and precocity and shal-
lowness in English gentlewomen cannot be denied. On the other hand,
learned women were scoffed at throughout the period. The overall
impression is that the girls' private boarding schools took girls off
their parents' hands during adolescence and taught them at best com-
mand of English and French, and decoratively a good deal of dancing,
singing, instrumental music, drawing, painting and ornamental craft-
work (not the plain sewing of the charity school drudges).

Not all girls' boarding establishments were the resort of well-founded
fee-payers. The charitable boarding element descended to some
fairly appalling levels. Individual charitable foundations like Christ's
Hospital at London (originally co-educational) selected deserving poor
children and clothed, fed and housed them as well as teaching them
reasonably useful skills. The poor children on some foundations were
the genteel poor: the Godolphin School at Salisbury was opened in
1784 (founded 1707) for eight orphan gentlewomen and a mistress;
later this school was redefined to benefit specifically clergy daughters.
But the boarding 'hospitals' of the Charity School movement were less
satisfactory.

It is a fact that some of the most notable women scholars of the period
had received no regular education either in school or by sustained
formal private tuition, but had learned from male relatives who, extra-
ordinarily, encouraged them to learn regardless of their sex. Mary Astell
(b. 1666) daughter of a Newcastle Hostman classed as a gentleman, is
believed to have been the protégé of her bachelor uncle Ralph, a Cambridge MA, curate of St Nicholas Church, Newcastle, but this is not
proven and he died when she was thirteen. No other part of her educational experience can be even this hazardously accounted for. It does
appear that she only learned French in adult life, confessing herself in
correspondence dated to 1693–94 as unable to read Malebranche in the
original, yet she assumed in the *Serious Proposal* that most ladies understood French, and recommended they read Descartes and Malebranche
in it, rather than novels. Lacking the classical linguistic education, she
achieved a fine argumentative logic and crisp style in English.

Apprenticeship

Apprenticeship in early modern England embraced a wide spectrum of society and range of skills and crafts. Already a traditional form of training in the Middle Ages, it was organised everywhere on similar lines. The apprentice was bound to his master to learn his craft, meanwhile living in his master's house and working in his shop, picking up the skills of the trade over a traditionally seven-year period, at the end of which the apprentice achieved mastery of the craft. There were a few opportunities for the apprenticeship of girls, for example in silk processing. A boy might be apprenticed to the widow of a craftsman, and certainly might finish his apprenticeship so bound after the death of his master mid-term. More curiously, there are known examples of boys apprenticed to married women to learn their craft while their husbands were still alive and pursuing a different trade. Most of the problems of apprenticeship had been experienced and provided for before the start of our period. In corporate towns apprenticeship was regulated by the guilds and the municipal authorities. Both had an interest in ensuring that too many entrants did not flood into a craft, upsetting the balance between the supply of and demand for labour, and both wanted standards of quality maintained for the good repute of the town's trade. In towns guilds controlled the number of apprentices a master could take. The joiners and carpenters at Worcester in 1692 were concerned about 'who may keep two apprentices at same time, who may only keep one, within what time before the expiration of such apprenticeship the master or mistress may take another apprentice'.[18] The freedom of the guild and town was only given after due testimony to competence and good behaviour. In the countryside crafts relating to agriculture and building could take apprentices with less regulation.

There was a proper enforceable contract, creating basic obligations for both parties. The apprentice was bound to take reasonable care of his master's property and reputation, the master to teach the apprentice properly, house, feed and clothe him suitably, and, if so bound, release him for a certain amount of schooling. In 1567 Simon Forman, at Salisbury, was to be allowed to go to grammar school for three years.[19] Many agreements incorporated a premium paid by the apprentice or his father or guarantors, and bonds for surety. Ways of discharge had been worked out, where the agreement broke down.

A new facet was added to apprenticeship by the Elizabethan and subsequent Poor Laws, which charged authorities with overseeing the apprenticeship of pauper children. This type of apprenticeship was differently motivated. Instead of a voluntarily entered agreement between a master and an apprentice, guaranteed by the youth's parent or some other relative or friend, this was a compulsory outplacing of a child who was a liability to poor relief by the parish poor officials, the churchwardens and overseers. It could take place in a corporate town and end with the apprentice having a craft like any other apprentice, but it also operated in the countryside where children were mainly apprenticed to husbandry or housewifery, and much of the time used as cheap labour. It was a charitable deed to set up, or contribute to, existing trust funds to pay premiums of parish apprentices, but it is interesting to see, as is clear from the Southampton poor child register, that some of these funds were given to a master to take his own child as apprentice, thus subsidising the child to stay at home. In these cases the child was likely to be rather less destitute than the children the original donors had intended to help.

The 1563 Statute of Artificers specified a seven-year duration for apprenticeship, but this was not always upheld. Boys embarked on the training usually in their teens. Edward Barlow entered a textile apprenticeship in Manchester at thirteen; Thomas Holcroft, a shoemaker's son, was apprenticed in shoemaking at sixteen; Bristol soapboilers commonly apprenticed their sons to others of the trade at sixteen or seventeen. The evidence from the seventeenth-century autobiographies produces a mean age of 14.7 for entering apprenticeship, lower than the mean of sixteen for going to university, and higher than the normally thirteen-year-old entry into agriculture. London apprentices tended to be older: seventeen to nineteen. Ben-Amos believes that about 1400 youths a year entered apprenticeships in mid-sixteenth-century London, doubling by the early seventeenth century, and that about 10 per cent of the population was apprenticed in London, Bristol, York and Norwich, with 5 per cent or so apprenticed in smaller towns. Rural apprenticeship was possible but many would-be apprentices left the countryside for the towns. In London and Bristol in the mid-sixteenth century, respectively 90 and 80 per cent of the apprentice population was immigrant, falling to 85 and 75 per cent in the early seventeenth century, and to about 50 per cent later in the century. Mercantile and distributive trades, such as drapery, grocery, mercery and merchant tailoring, attracted gentle and yeoman younger sons, but most urban apprentices were sons of husbandmen, craftsmen and labourers entering smaller crafts, along with the pauper apprentices. In forty-four Bristol apprenticeship agreements recording premiums, the highest sum was £ 70 paid to a mercer in the 1650s, the lowest £1–£4 paid to a shoemaker, buttonmaker, tiler, ropemaker and mariner between 1615 and 1630.[20]

Some apprentices, parish and other, were bound to family or friends, but most were not, and started their training performing menial tasks in the master's house. Judging by the Southampton evidence, many apprentices were their master's sole apprentice, but some masters had simultaneously more than one in training. Peter Legay, merchant, took his son as an apprentice in 1643 for seven years; in 1646 he took James Fauntleroy for seven years, at the end of the year he added Francis Sampson and James Oviatt for seven years, and in 1650 John Browne.[21] The apprentice's earliest unskilled labours were offset by his later cheap labour performed for his master when near to qualification. Sixty per cent of London apprentices never completed training in the sixteenth century, and still 50 per cent in the late seventeenth century. In Bristol in the mid-sixteenth century about 3 per cent of the apprentices were female, as were 2.2 per cent in a sample from 1600–45. Ten per cent were female in Southampton, and it is thought more might be found in smaller towns and villages. The trades included cordwaining and turning as well as more obviously female crafts such as sewing and lacemaking. The Bristol evidence suggests women's apprenticeship was declining in prestige, and becoming more associated with parish relief.

Apprenticeship was certainly an educative experience, both generally and technically. It took the apprentice sometimes many miles – the average distance travelled to London in the early sixteenth century was 115 miles, and 60 miles in the 1710s. It sometimes brought the apprentice into urban life for the first time, and often into the company of strangers, requiring rapid adaptability and responsibility. It taught specific skills, and set quality. If all went well, the apprentice emerged between twenty-three and twenty-six with a trade for life. Some places even had loan stocks to help the newly-fledged craftsman set himself up in trade, and sometimes the master was pledged to set him up with appropriate tools.

Universities and Dissenting Academies

Oxford and Cambridge emerged from the Middle Ages as universities of the masters' type where the teachers dominated. Colleges had been founded since the thirteenth century, and were originally essentially religious foundations benefiting graduate fellows mostly studying theology or civil or canon law. Medieval undergraduates had lived in lodgings or latterly, as the university tightened discipline in the fifteenth century, in halls (at Oxford) or hostels (at Cambridge). All this changed dramatically in the late fifteenth and early sixteenth centuries, as the colleges began admitting large numbers of undergraduates, and accepting responsibility for their actual tuition and progress.

At the start of the period an undergraduate entered the Arts faculty in his mid- to late teens, and spent, if he persisted, four years studying a course dominated by logic and philosophy. The methods of instruction were the lecture and the disputation. After four years, a student who had mastered the texts and fulfilled the necessary exercises for the BA degree would be admitted to the degree and required to 'determine', that is, be tested in public disputation. After three more years of study, concentrating on philosophy, natural, moral and metaphysical, he could 'incept' and become a Master of Arts. At this stage he originally owed it to the university to perform one or two years of teaching, as a regent master. This 'necessary regency', until it broke down at the end of the Middle Ages, provided the university with a constant supply of cheap, youthful teachers, who gave the standard ordinary lectures on the set texts, making no financial demand on the university. After this the undeterred student could go on to the so-called higher faculties of theology (later divinity), law (civil and canon, until the abolition of the study of canon law at both universities in 1535) or medicine. Although the Arts faculty generally provided foundation courses for study before entry to the higher faculties, there were exemptions. The friars had struggled against the university authorities to enjoy the right to proceed straight into theology with only an Arts foundation which they had gained within their own orders, but friars disappeared from the universities at the Reformation. The law faculties permitted direct entry, but lengthened the courses by two years for such entrants. Both universities offered degrees in music by the end of the fifteenth century. At both universities, it should be stressed, individuals could gain exemption from statutory requirements, by means of graces or dispensations granted for a fee for a wide range of reasons, and amounting to tailoring of the conditions to suit them.

Given this basic structure, the Faculty of Arts, as the supplier of the broad foundation course, could be expected to be the largest faculty, and with the removal at the Reformation of the monks and friars who had swelled the theology faculty, and the canonists from the lawyers, this dominance became even clearer. During the fifteenth century the Arts curriculum shifted towards modernity at both universities, but more markedly at Cambridge, where in 1488 the first two years of the degree, formerly spent on Aristotle's Organon and medieval terminist logic, gave way to two years' study of humane letters, diminishing the weighting of logic and natural philosophy in the prescribed studies. Just as striking as the syllabus reform, and perhaps of rather greater consequence, was the change in teaching provision, where the blanket obligations of necessary regency gave way to salaried lecturers, a process begun at Cambridge in 1488, and modified at Oxford over the sixteenth century. At both universities, from the later fifteenth century, the colleges themselves had begun to supplement the university's provided teaching with closed or open lectures, and specific tutorial provision for the undergraduates. Movements in these directions began in the late fifteenth century, but became a characteristic feature of the first half of the sixteenth.

Sixteen colleges were founded between 1500 and 1750, at Cambridge Christ's (1505–06) absorbing Godshouse, St John's (1511), Magdalene (1542), Trinity College (1546) absorbing the King's Hall and Michaelhouse, Emmanuel (1584) and Sidney Sussex (1596), and at Oxford Brasenose (1509), Corpus Christi (1517), Christ Church (1546), Trinity (1554–55), St John's (1555), Jesus (1571), Wadham (1612), Pembroke (1624), Worcester (1714) and Hertford (1740). The dating of the foundations testifies to the vigour, and later decline, of the universities, and the expansion was even greater than is implied by the number of new foundations because existing colleges built new blocks and opened up cocklofts to increase accommodation. Characteristically, the pre-Reformation foundations were dedicated to improving the quality of the late Catholic clergy; the mid-sixteenth-century ones reinforced the appropriate changing orthodoxy, and Emmanuel and Sidney Sussex promoted the Puritan ministry. Throughout our period colleges retained regional linkages established and reinforced by founders and benefactors. Thus Exeter College gave preference to the South-West, Christ's and St John's at Cambridge and Queen's at Oxford to the North, and Jesus College Oxford to Wales. In general terms Cambridge recruited from the North and East, and Oxford from the West, including Wales. Both universities drew students from the South, but not as heavily as might have been expected, given the regional variations in the population and economy of England.

The medieval colleges had been essentially clerical seminaries, and training clergy remained the principal object of university education, but the numbers of well-born students heading for careers in law and politics increased. Between 1575 and 1639 50 per cent of Oxford's entry came from sons of the gentry, and it seems that some of these were gaining scholarships to the disadvantage of poorer students. Harrison, in his *Description of England* (1587), commented on founders' intentions to benefit poor men's sons being overturned: 'now they have the least benefit of them, by reason the rich do so encroach upon them. And so far has this inconvenience spread itself that it is in my time a hard matter for a poor man's child to come by a fellowship (though he be never so good a scholar and worthy of that room).'[22] Poor students were admitted, and managed to make ends meet by taking on work as bible clerks, or as sizars, servitors and batellers, doing menial work such as waiting at table. Fee-paying commoners became the largest group in the undergraduate population. At the other extreme were the gentleman or fellow commoners, who paid higher fees to share the fellows' better-quality food, and had other privileges, including fancier gowns. Entry for sons of the influential had been provided for by college founders from the late fifteenth century, but the class seems particularly notice-able in the eighteenth-century shrunken universities, ostentatiously throwing money around and being disruptive.

College founding dropped off after 1624 and university entry peaked around 1640 before the disruption and ejections of the Civil War. After the Restoration and further ejections the universities were in some decline for the rest of our period: they were constrained by religious requirements, which barred them to Catholics and Protestant noncon-formists, and a more utilitarian view of education made them less popular. Mordechai Feingold shows at length, however, that they were not as fossilised by the continuation of ancient pedagogic methods such as disputations, nor as conservative in matters of syllabus, as used to be thought. The statutory requirements were not incompatible with inno-vation.[23] Regarded largely as clerical training institutions, however, they had little attraction for otherwise-minded careerists. At Oxford the intake of 460 in the 1660s was down to 310 by the 1690s and under 200 mid-century, with the noble and gentry recruits diminishing mark-edly.[24]

Educationally the colleges offered their junior members a protected environment to study, with tutorial supervision, admittedly of varied quality, within the college, and access to facilities offered by the university itself, though the universities were becoming little more than regulatory and examining bodies. Chambers in a college were commonly shared, and the traditional space-deployment (private carrels for study, communal area for sleep) was being reversed. The colleges had their own libraries, chapels, and great halls where communal meals were taken. The standard of accommodation and food was more luxurious than in the Middle Ages, because the gentry-born clientele expected it, but students were responsible for providing much of their own comfort, and sold off their furnishings to their successors. Conscientious tutors supervised their pupils' finances as well as their studies, and excessively holy ones nagged at them to mend their ways: John Wesley was not above suspicion of indoctrinating his pupils, while others hardly bestirred themselves. Qualifying exercises and examinations being laxly administered, students, especially gentleman commoners, could please themselves whether they studied or idled. V. H. Green cites the case of Arthur Annesley, a gentleman commoner admitted to Lincoln College in 1750, who spent £176 5s in a year. For comparison, a Lincoln College resident fellow received a stipend of a little under £100, and a non-resident one £60 18s 2d in 1765.[25]

Senior members of colleges were not all occupied in educational purposes: that is, they were neither studying for further degrees themselves, nor actively involved in teaching students. Many, quite obviously, were filling in time until they obtained church preferment, were non-resident, and were waiting, impatiently if they wished to marry, for their college to provide them with this from the advowsons it held. The recruitment of teaching dons seems to have been a somewhat chancy affair. It was not generally a profession for a lifetime, and though the teaching by fellows would be more continuous than the medieval system of necessary regency with its very rapid turnover, it was generally undertaken on the way to a vicarage, rectory or even the episcopal bench. Fellowships were not unattractive propositions, and the remuneration of fellows compares favourably with grammar-school masters. Green estimates that the average stipend of a fellow at Lincoln College in 1607 would have been £14 16s $2\frac{1}{2}d$, however, this was exclusive of free rooms and services and a few minor allowances and fees from tutorial pupils. By c.1750 a resident fellow at Lincoln was getting between £50 and £70 in addition to fees, and fellows' income was improving steadily through the eighteenth century.[26] The initial stipend of regius professors in 1540 was £40 per annum, which was obviously then very attractive. The creation of regius and other endowed professorships and lectureships meant that there were holders of these specialist lecturing positions, but their expertise and dedication to the subject varied immensely. Edward Waring, who became sixth Lucasian Professor of Mathematics at Cambridge at the age of twenty-five in 1760, did not lecture because his 'profound researches...were not adapted to any form of communication by lectures'. Richard Watson, later bishop of Llandaff, appointed to the professorship of chemistry at Cambridge in 1764, placed on record that 'he knew nothing at all of chemistry, had never read a syllable on the subject, nor seen a single experiment in it', though apparently he put together a course of lectures within fifteen months.[27] What is surprising, today, is the frequency with which professors and other lecturers changed subject, as though outstanding in many diverse areas. Francis Glisson, lecturer in Greek at Cambridge in 1625, became Regius Professor of Anatomy in 1636. Watson himself moved from chemistry to divinity. Scholarship does not seem to have had much chance of tipping the balance in financially desirable appointments. There were many college fellowships tied regionally, affecting the election of new holders, and there were many patrons pushing clients into elective appointments by jobbery, certainly in the eighteenth century. Newly-founded professorships, for example in anatomy, astronomy, geometry and ancient history, encouraged new areas of learning and research, but if the syllabus did not change it was difficult to build these into study programmes. Fortunately many students were enterprising and attended lectures beyond their immediate requirements, paying extra fees to do so. It was very much a situation where the universities and colleges offered students opportunities but left them to decide whether or not they took advantage or simply enjoyed the life. However, compared with the inns of court, the universities' tutorial supervision is much praised.

The universities had their own libraries, built up from their abysmal state after the destructiveness of the Reformation. By 1600 Cambridge University Library had about 950 books, by 1602 the Bodleian 2500, and 16 000 books and manuscripts by 1620. Sir Thomas Bodley was the great benefactor to, and campaigner for, Oxford's library, and one of his most valuable gifts was persuading the Stationers' Company in 1610 to give the library a copy of every registered work printed in England; even after the 1709 Copyright Act, however, only about 10 per cent of English publications were registered and deposited c.1710–26.[28] The Radcliffe Camera was opened as a library in 1749, named after the benefactor John Radcliffe, the physician. Gradually the appreciation that education needed more equipment than books and the spoken word became productive, and Oxford acquired its botanical garden (1621) and chemical laboratory (1683), part of the Ashmolean, which also had a library. College libraries also existed, but in all, undergraduates had restricted access.

The dissenting academies came into being after 1662 for the education of nonconformists driven out of the universities. Taking their institutional identification from Calvin's Geneva Academy, they varied immensely in size, longevity, efficiency, organisation and method. The one-tutor academy was not unusual and entrants overall are only estimated at about fifty a year in the 1660s and 150 a year in the 1690s. Numbers increased, but also fluctuated, in the eighteenth century. Northampton Academy had forty students in 1730, sixty-three in 1743 and twenty-nine in 1747. At Homerton Academy, founded in 1730, the usual complement of tutors was three; Warrington Academy had six.[29] Compared with the universities, the academies were small and unstable institutions, in some cases so dependent on one tutor that they would move with him, or close at his death. Richard Frankland's academy founded at Rathmell in 1670 moved seven times before its closure in 1698 at his death. From the 1660s until the end of our period and beyond, academies were being founded and refounded, some only lasting a few years. The early ones, not unexpectedly, showed the influence of the old university curricula and were staffed by Oxbridge graduates and in some cases fellows – Francis Tallents at Shrewsbury had been vice-president of Magdalene – but they started life without the resources of institutional libraries, buildings and endowments. Libraries were appreciated accumulations and in some cases outlasted the institutions. Taunton Academy's valuable collection was removed on its dissolution in 1759 to the library of the second Exeter Academy, and after the suspension of this institution was loaned to Hackney College 1786–96, then returning to Exeter, and later still passing to Manchester College, then at York.

From the start some academies were purely ministerial training establishments, while others also took students intending to enter 'civil stations' and commerce. The emphasis in the ministerial courses tended to be on Latin, Greek and Hebrew for scriptural study, on English language and literature as aids to preaching, on a core of divinity/theology, and on a wider range of subjects studied to enhance ministerial intellect and interpreted to this end, that is, teleologically. The students entered generally at fifteen or more, though at Warrington the minimum age was only thirteen. The full ministerial training course was commonly of four or five years' duration, the commercial course of three, some parts being common to both. After the Toleration Act (1689) the academies' activities could be more open and funding bodies were set up, such as the Presbyterian Fund (1689), Congregational Fund Board (1695) and Coward Trust (1738), which supported ministerial training by giving financial assistance to both academies themselves and to selected students attending them.

Early students lived with the tutor. At Sheriffhales (1663–97) this was in a spacious mansion he already had. Later students were mostly non-resident. Collegiate-type accommodation was not particularly characteristic of academies. Warrington's move into rather appropriate-sounding accommodation in the town in 1762 left it with debts which contributed to its dissolution, and did not lead to the students living as a disciplined community – indeed, their rowdiness led to the institution's downfall. For the students costs were lower than at university, which led to some Anglican students attending. At residential Northampton in 1729–51 students paid £4 per annum for tuition and £16 for board, and a guinea for their room. This is considered above-average pricing for academies. Kendal at about the same date charged eight guineas for board and lodging and four guineas for tuition. Warrington in the 1770s was unusual for pricing courses separately and allowing students to select and pay only for what they took.

For the most part academies had to take over and adapt existing buildings and build up their libraries and apparatus. Hoxton Academy, founded in 1701, was given a grant not exceeding £50 by the Coward Trustees in 1741 to buy books. Homerton Academy was left a collection of books by the Rev. Richard Rawlins, minister of Fetter Lane, London, who died in 1757. It was estimated to have 5000–6000 books by 1793. Warrington was given, by his son, Dr Benjamin Grosvenor's books after his death in 1758, and was loaned, by his brother, the books of the Rev. Samuel Stubbs who died in 1753. Philip Doddridge, the tutor at Northampton throughout its life, used the ploy of asking students entering the second year to pay a guinea for the library, if they intended to stay the full course, otherwise half a guinea, and another guinea for scientific apparatus, which he also acquired by gift from friends. The Coward Trustees voted five guineas for improving electrical apparatus at Daventry in 1707, and £15 for an observatory in 1771. The impression given is of careful, thrifty husbanding of resources.

The standards of education varied enormously. Individual academies began with differently emphasised intentions and developed different focuses and strengths. Individual tutors and educational fashions made particular marks. The early Baptists distrusted university education, and some of them still feared it as inculcating pride as late as the 1750s. Bristol was the most notable Baptist Academy, its reputation established during the thirty-eight years Bernard Foskett was tutor there. Richard Frankland's students were of such good repute, despite the Rathmell Academy's peripatetic history, that some were accepted straight into the final year of the MA course at Edinburgh University. Northampton flourished from 1729 under Doddridge, famous for his broad comparative teaching methods and use of English as the medium of instruction. Doddridge kept abreast of scientific advance and was a friend of Isaac Watts. The pair of them influenced the overall outlook of academy education, Doddridge's own lectures being handed on to many other institutions. Doddridge himself, in 1728, describing his own education at Kibworth Academy under John Jennings, indicated that passages from *The Spectator* and *The Tatler*, both serious and humorous, were assigned to the students for translation from English into Latin, which should have brought a breath of fresh air. In 1733 Doddridge was cited to appear in consistory court over 'teaching and instructing youth in the liberal arts and sciences being not licensed thereto by the ordinary of the diocese', but George II intervened to stop the case in 1734. Warrington failed after perhaps being too ambitious on too wide a front, but its tutor Joseph Priestley's legacy to education was considerable, in placing history and politics in the curriculum, as well as pursuing the chemistry he advanced. Priestley observed the gap between education for the counting-house, as he put it, consisting of writing, arithmetic and accounting, and instruction in abstract science, leaving unprovided the gentleman destined for active life, but not one of the learned professions.[30] When Methodists were driven from Oxford in 1768, John Wesley, who had corresponded with Doddridge, was ambitious in his plans for developing higher education at Kingswood, commenting: 'if those who have a tolerable capacity... do not advance more here in three years than the generality of students at Oxford and Cambridge do in seven I will bear the blame for ever'.[31] There was a huge range of quality within academies at large. Some could envisage rivalling and improving on university education; some were barely adequate ministerial training colleges.

There was never an iron curtain between dissenting academies and the two English universities: seven of Frankland's pupils went on to study Arts at Cambridge, and Joseph Butler went from Samuel Jones's tuition at Tewkesbury to Oriel College, becoming eventually bishop of Durham. Another of Jones's pupils was Thomas Secker, later Archbishop of Canterbury. Less surprisingly, there were links between academies and Scottish and continental universities, particularly Dutch ones. It is clear that whatever the denominational persuasions and personal changes of loyalty in individual men's lives, a good nonconformist education could hold its own in comparison with a good orthodox one.

Recent work has tended to play down the direct influences of Scotland and Holland on the academies and has diminished the claims of innovatory methods made by earlier historians for particular tutors, for example Doddridge. The effect is not to disparage the merits of these features, but rather to place them among tendencies of the time, set in motion in small ways by less noticed experimenters and then pushed into prominence by one man or academy. Simultaneously the contrasting reputation of the universities as sluggish and in decline has been challenged, making the educational gap between the universities and academies less striking. The role of the dissenting academies should not be pushed to the back of our minds for these reasons. Much of their work and achievement remains impressive. Their students tackled old traditional subjects like the ancient languages with no fall in standard, and applied them usefully in occupationally orientated ways. Tutors opened up biblical study and theology in some cases with a fearlessness of controversy and comparison which contrasted with the universities' more hide-bound conformity. The academies were aware of the latest ethical/moral science thinking. In natural sciences they were from the start experimentally minded and their mathematical syllabuses are generally regarded as broader than Oxford's. In more radical treatment of curricula they advanced both English language and literature, and modern history and political/constitutional studies. Some academies offered modern languages, and Warrington employed a native French speaker as tutor. Music had little appearance at the academies, but shorthand was frequently taught.

Teaching methods were less traditional than at the universities. It must be remembered that many academies had only one, two or three members of staff teaching a small number of students over many courses. The university-style lecture on a standard text was not normal academy practice. Reading a variety of texts and free discussion of opinions was more common in the academies and better educationally. Teaching by the medium of English was more effective. In these educational advances (as we would view them) the academies were helped, compared to the universities, by their somewhat self-selecting intake of serious students. Though ill discipline at Warrington was a cause of the collapse of the second academy there, students of many academies emerge as seriously-intentioned young men eager to read and discuss. There was not the automatic, thereby potentially mindless, progression into dissenting higher education which was a feature of closed scholarships from feeder schools to Oxbridge. Students were not attracted to the academies for their social prestige, nor for the social life, which compared ill with the universities and inns of court. The 'smart' element must have been markedly less in the academies. It is easy to idle in a luxurious setting, and the atmosphere in the small town or rurally-sited academies, with tutors and students forced to do their best with limited resources, must have been light years different from what Gibbon called 'the port and prejudice' of Oxbridge colleges in the eighteenth century. Northampton's rules, for example, clamped down on the comparatively innocuous luxury of cheese on toast: 'as making toasts and butter and toasting cheese has been found to be more expensive than can conveniently be afforded on the usual terms here, that custom is to be disused except by the parlour boarders'.[32] There was much serious application in the academies, and John Wesley knew what he was competing with when he laid the ambitions for Kingswood.

Inns of Court and Chancery

In his *Survey of London*, following the section 'Of schools and other houses of learning', John Stow wrote 'besides all this there is in and about this city a whole university, as it were, of students, practisers or pleaders and judges of the laws of this realm', listing the Serjeants' Inns, the four inns of court, or greater inns, Gray's Inn, Lincoln's Inn and the Inner and Middle Temple, and eight inns of chancery, or lesser inns, then existing: Clifford's, Thravies', Furnival's, Barnard's, Staple, Clement's, New Inn and Lion's Inn. A ninth, Chester's or Strand Inn, had been demolished in Edward VI's reign in the building of the Duke of Somerset's house, and a tenth, as indicated in Fortescue's *De Laudibus*

Legum Anglia (1468) had disappeared – 'where it stood, or when it was abandoned I cannot find'.[33] Admissions to the four inns of court increased from about forty a year in the early sixteenth century to a high point of 300 in the early years of James I.[34]

Fortescue's description, the earliest literary account of the inns, made plain the costly exclusiveness of the company:

> no student could be maintained on less than £13 6s 8d a year, and if he has servants to himself alone, as the majority have, then he will by so much more bear expenses. Because of this costliness there are not many who learn the laws except the sons of nobles. For poor and common people cannot bear so much cost for the maintenance of their sons.[35]

Stow repeated the point – 'the younger sort are either gentlemen or the sons of gentlemen, or of other most wealthy persons', maintained privately. Prest asserts that the cost of keeping a student at the inns of court in the period between 1590 and 1640 was £40 per year, and that those admitted, as far as can be ascertained, were in origin 48 per cent gentry, 40 per cent peerage and squirearchy, and 8 per cent bourgeois/ professionals. By 1700–09, when admissions were averaging 120 a year, 45 per cent came from the peerage and squirearchy, 32 per cent from the gentry and 22 per cent from the bourgeois/professionals. As the inns lacked the universities' sponsored scholarships and sizarships (though there were some discretionary dispensations and reductions of fees for sons of benchers and senior barristers and suchlike), the recruitment remained upper-class. Social expenditure was demanding: servants, dinners, drink, clothes and fees for dancing or fencing lessons and music tuition made for sizeable bills. Simonds D'Ewes received £10 quarterly while a student at the Middle Temple in the early 1620s, and later reflected that he had groaned under 'continual want or short stipend'.[36]

Institutionally the inns were voluntary unincorporated societies of fourteenth-century origin. Legal inns existed in London by the 1320s, the period when laymen ousted clerics on the judicial benches of the common law. They offered residential facilities during law terms. The provision of specialist accommodation was the origin also of the inns of chancery, which met the needs of the clerks of the chancery when the chancellor's household dispersed into hostel accommodation run by senior clerks. By the mid-fourteenth century Clement's Inn was offering a diplomatic training for chancery clerks, which common law students latched on to and began to turn to themselves. During the early fifteenth century the chancery inns became providers of preparatory training for lawyers, and the inns of court recruited from them. Before the start of our period some of those admitted to the inns of court had already spent a year or more at one of the universities, and this educational pattern became more common. Whereas 13 per cent of the entrants came on from Oxford or Cambridge in 1561, almost half did by 1601. The connection between the inns of court and chancery weakened as the latter became in the seventeenth century the focus for the lower legal branch of attorneys and solicitors.

The inns of court, the more important of the inns, thus developed as educational institutions from professional clubs, and for about a century, from the 1540s to the 1640s, flourished as both legal training centres and high social class finishing schools (a trait already showing in Fortescue's day); after the Restoration their popularity as purveyors of general education to the gentry and above declined, and they reverted to professional associations with their educational aspect less marked. It had always been a development rather than a design, and consequently the establishment was pedagogically speaking rather informal in its structure and methods. The training of the lawyers has been described in discussing educational aims in Chapter 3. It embraced discussing cases informally, participating in moots and attending readings by senior barristers. Serious students also betook themselves to observe the actual courts at work, and read on their own legal records and commentaries in full or digest form. The inns were building up libraries in this period, and some students themselves purchased books for private use. Some quite outstanding private libraries were collected by lawyers in this period – Robert Ashley left the Middle Temple 5000 works in 1641. At Lincoln's Inn, in 1609, there was instituted a levy on members at their call to the Bar to be spent on library purchases, and a common library was opened in 1631. It had only 224 books in 1646, and ninety-five of these were works of divinity.[37]

There was apparently no testing of aptitude before admission to the inns, little supervision of students when they had been admitted, and the regulations were concerned with minimum attendance and participation, not with eliciting if any intellectual profit had been gained therefrom. However, it has been relevantly suggested that the inns' lack of supervision was less serious once many of the ambitious students were embarking on study there after benefiting from the experience of being more straitly 'tutored' at university, where college tuition had become widespread by 1575. There was no specific provision academically for those who, increasingly in the sixteenth and early seventeenth centuries, attended the inns merely as finishing schools, who often stayed only about two years. It may be, as Prest suggests, that these amateur dilettantes did not particularly impede the progress of the career lawyers and students, but one wonders how many students occupied a hazy middle ground, with spells of reasonable application and fits of disinclination before, eventually, opting to go one way or the other. Such a group could not have been helpful to their more purposeful fellows, though those who did not complete the law course should not all be assumed to have entirely idled away the opportunity.

In terms of the facilities the inns of court offered their members, we have to consider four centrally located residential institutions in the capital which, over the period, underwent a good deal of expansion followed by some decline in numbers. On the borders of London and Westminster, the inns were at the hub of the legal world, by design, and close to the excitements of the City and Court, which was an added attraction to the student body, and certainly offered more distractions than Oxford or Cambridge. The Temple area retains something of an ancient university atmosphere, and not surprisingly, since the inns were a kind of college and their architecture reflected it. Thus they had halls (the Middle Temple's hall of 1562 apparently served as model for the new hall at Trinity College, Cambridge), gatehouses (that of Lincoln's Inn dates from c.1520), gardens (Francis Bacon laid out the gardens of Gray's Inn) and residential accommodation, which was pushed up to five or six storeys in expansionist times. Members of the Long Parliament heard several sermons in Lincoln's Inn chapel. Like the university colleges, the inns had certain regional leanings: Gray's recruited from the North, East Anglia and Kent; Lincoln's from East Anglia, the South-West, and Wales and the Marches, the Inner Temple from Devon, the Midlands, Wales, Yorkshire and the East, and Middle Temple from the South and South-West. Like colleges, too, they had disciplinary problems, exacerbated by their situation at the heart of London/Westminster. The younger members (entrants to the inns of court were commonly in the 16–20 age group) were notorious for disorder and violence, which was reined in by stricter regulation over weaponry. There was no real supervision, and much temptation from the nearby theatres and brothels. Revels were held within the inns on Saturdays from All Saints to Candlemas, and masques and plays were performed. Targeted by

Catholics in Elizabeth's reign, the inns became religiously of interest to the government, and had much autonomy as peculiars. By the late sixteenth century all four inns supported a permanent preacher, and by the run-up to the Civil War were seen as conservatively Puritan, in contrast to the universities, which Laud had hectored into Arminianism. Technically they were orthodox institutions, with utter barristers and benchers required to take the Oath of Supremacy and all members required to attend chapel or church.

The inns had effectively the complete monopoly of common law professional qualification. Their trainees, recruited from the upper classes socially, had lived communally, in the capital, close to the central courts of the justice system they studied. Whereas university graduates had emerged from two universities, and within them, from some quite broadly recruiting colleges, the common lawyers had all been funnelled through the four inns of court. With a more specific vocational orientation than the universities, too, the inns might be expected to promote an 'Old Boy' monopoly of a very exclusive kind. Paradoxically, they were more important in the educational spectrum than they would have been as narrow training schools just because of their generally cultured influence on that majority of their students who did not proceed to the Bar. In Prest's striking phrase, 'what caused the inns to fail as law schools boosted their success as liberal academies', and this was their permissive discipline and lack of supervision, which was wholly in line with the most liberal interpretation of education. By the eighteenth century, the inns provided no formal legal education, though a man had to be enrolled for seven years and eat dinners in the hall of his inn for twelve terms before being called to the Bar. Among those so called, Duman asserts: 'many must have left the inns as ignorant of the law as when they entered'.[38]

The Grand Tour

Young men from the highest social classes rounded off their education with a leisurely Grand Tour on the Continent. The Grand Tour was not simply the practice of being sent abroad for formal education, at a school, academy or university: that went on, both before and after the particular Grand Tour's heyday, which was the seventeenth and eighteenth centuries. The Grand Tour was a far less structured experience, though there was some attempt to formalise the learning aspect when a tutor or governor (sometimes termed 'bearward') was dispatched with the young man. The Grand Tour was a legacy of the discovery of Italy consequent upon the Renaissance. France and Italy were on the regular itinerary, though some travellers penetrated the Iberian peninsula and others went further east into the German empire and Switzerland, and even Greece. The tour could be tailored to individual tastes, for example, viewing fortifications and military reviews for young men from military families. The men who embarked on the Grand Tour, however, were rarely anticipating having to earn a living in the future: they came of the landed classes and expected to inherit comfortable independence. The Grand Tour filled a gap between school and/or university or inn and inheritance. It was undertaken by youths who had been through the classical education and could be expected to be interested in Roman monuments, sites of classical battles, and homes of Latin poets. It was invariably spoken of as an educational experience, but there may have been an element of status symbol about it, and some reduction of family tension while a young upstart was abroad to sow wild oats. Young men went at different ages, under varying degrees of supervision, for divergent lengths of time. If they went rather young, the most they could be expected to absorb was some foreign language facility: some contemporaries thought young minds needed to be twenty-five or so to make valid mature comparisons between countries and benefit much from the experience, but most were back home by then, and married, and fathers themselves: as Locke put it: 'he must be back again by one and twenty, to marry and to propagate'.[39] Indeed it was not unknown for the travellers to be already married when they set out, even though it seems odd to us to think of young men leaving wives in England to undertake an educational tour with a tutor.

The classic Grand Tour embraced Paris and Rome, and Venice, Florence and Naples. Parents who were nervous of metropolitan sophistication sent sons to French provincial cities to polish up the language, for example Orléans, Angers, Tours and Besançon. Dutiful sons sent home serious prose letters about what they were seeing and learning. Those caught up in sex, gambling and drinking tended to be less communicative: eventually their trails of debt began to become apparent.

The Grand Tour was for the monied. J. B. Black in *The British and the Grand Tour* (1985) cites Ashe Windham as having £600 per annum in the 1690s, and Viscount Boston spending £566 during twelve months in

1715–16, while Robert Carteret roused parental criticism for spending over £1850 in 1740–41.[40] From this expensive experience men came back, Black considers, 'better-informed xenophobes'. There is no way of arriving at a balance-sheet to reflect the benefits imbibed or the value for money achieved from this experience. Too often the Grand Tour is taken at its own estimate of being a mind-broadening educative experience without it being asked how. Is it so self-evident? Hooray Henry characters could spend months on the Continent without becoming any wiser, and probably only doing damage to the reputation abroad of English gentlemen.

However, it is in educational terms that the Grand Tour should be considered here, and when so treated it slides into place very well. First, it was undertaken by young men who had the standard classical upbringing. They had a grasp of Latin, and Virgil tripped lightly off their lips. They were in this respect going on a 'follow-up' illustrative tour: having long studied humane literature, they could now admire the settings. So the tour was bound to the earlier educational experience of those who undertook it.

Second, a good many travellers did successfully improve their linguistic skills abroad, not just by going there, but by deliberate study. Thomas Wentworth spent six months improving his French at Orléans in 1612, and became fluent in French and had some Italian and Spanish.[41] In this way, students supplemented their English education.

Third, those individuals capable of more artistic cultural development flourished on a diet of Italian art, opera, and architecture, especially of Palladio. Here the Grand Tour bound their limited earlier education to their future tastes and collecting habits. Black was favourably impressed by the eighteenth-century tourists' diary criticisms of Italian music, based on a high level of musical culture in London, and reinforcing this on their return. Similarly, many were discerning critics of art, and in the eighteenth century the English elite was expected to dabble in architecture, and their commissioning power, if they baulked at designing for themselves, was exerted in the light of their experience. Paintings, drawings and statuary were brought back from the Continent (including some fakes). The outcome was an impressive stately-home civilisation. Thus the Grand Tour was all of a piece with high-class education and culture. Frederick Calvert, the sixth Lord Baltimore, having gone further east than many into Greece, Constantinople and the Balkans, in 1763–64 wrote reflectively: 'what I saw in my travels recalled strongly to my remembrance the classical education I was so happy as to receive at Eton college'.[42] Such was the felicitous fulfilment of the educational aim. This was not achieved by those who ruined their health whoring and drinking, ruined their finances gambling, and scuttled about the Continent evading tailors' bills.

Informal Opportunities: Adult Education

Where a society's provision of childhood and adolescent education is in any ways deficient, there is more call for adult education for those who seek to remedy their own weaknesses. Education being in this period neither compulsory nor universally accessible even for those who desired it, many reached adulthood with unsatisfied educational needs. Adult education is one of the most heartwarming facets of education, for it is one of the clearest illustrations of applied human aspiration.

Thomas Kelly, in his history of adult education, reckoned it as old as the Christian church here, and part of applied religion. After the Reformation, stress on individual reading of the vernacular Bible inspired some adults from social classes which had not generally aspired to such literacy before, to take reading lessons. Writing of the late sixteenth century, Kelly commented on the 'development of that movement towards a working-class culture based on the bible'[43] which had its origin in Lollard bible-reading in the fifteenth century and lasted until the nineteenth century, a culture which essentially brought literacy to the fore. The SPCK enthused over teaching servants to read at night, and John Wesley also encouraged adult education among his followers. The aims of this kind of teaching were religious and social, to enlarge the circle of those who could read their bibles and benefit privately thereby, and by directing their thoughts and lifestyles to better things, to turn poor working folk from idleness and drunkenness to holiness and sobriety.

The facilities in our period were patchy, depending on individual enthusiasts for both establishment and maintenance. In the sixteenth century in England some Puritan ministers undertook the instruction of adults in their spare time, and attracted pupils; some groups of self-improvers got together to pursue a godly end by what we might term group-therapy techniques, the ablest helping the rest. Only at the very end of the eighteenth century was to come the Sunday school movement and such experiments as the More sisters' evening readings, from which adults could benefit.

A second area of adult education was more directly vocational. Here, too, the second half of the sixteenth century saw significant developments, particularly in London. Public lectures on mathematics were given in London in 1588, under City patronage, and continued for at least four years. Though the lecturer was a Cambridge graduate, the purpose was practical rather than academic, and the impulse came from the Spanish Armada scare, when a new premium was attracted to such skills as navigation and gunnery. In 1582 the Lumleian lectures in surgery were established at the College of Physicians, beginning in 1584, for 'learned or unlearned'. Lumley's lecturer spoke for three-quarters of an hour in Latin, and only in the final quarter in English, which must have been restricting to his audience. The Gresham College plan, mentioned earlier, for lectures in Latin in the mornings repeated in English in the afternoons, indicates similarly a breaking-away of instruction from the ancient medium to one more commonly understood. By the end of the seventeenth century public lectures on sciences were widespread in London and in the later eighteenth century spreading in the provinces, and attended, incidentally, by middle-class women. In the same period evening classes for seamen and mechanics appeared in Newcastle from the 1750s, Salford from 1772, and Leicester from 1788. Kelly sees the former as the origin of university extension teaching, and the latter of mechanics' institutes and technical colleges. The Spitalfields Mathematical Society (1717) was largely an association of weavers, working out mathematical exercises and experiments with scientific instruments.

The third area of adult education continued the mind-broadening leisured education of the socially better-placed, who had a better educational grounding to start with. This took the form mainly of gentlemanly societies or clubs, combining social conviviality and artistic or scientific research or experiment. The Society of Antiquaries in London researched mainly history and genealogy; the Royal Society was characterised as a gentleman's club for the discussion of scientific matters. Literary and antiquarian societies throve in the provinces in the eighteenth century, and debating societies flourished in the later half of the century in London and leading provincial towns. Birmingham's Lunar Society originated between 1768 and 1775, bringing Boulton, Watt, Darwin, Wedgwood and Priestley together in a marriage of manufacturing and experiment. Of varied standing and longevity, these voluntary associations were primarily of reasonably well-educated men of poly-math interests.

A new feature of the late seventeenth century, London coffee houses (numbering over 2000 by the end of the century) were remarkable for their educational leavening and social breadth. John Houghton, a con-temporary, commented that they made 'all sorts of people sociable, the rich and the poor meet together, as also do the learned and unlearned',[44] but it would be the leisured or lightly employed who had the time to linger to discuss intellectual topics. Some of the coffee houses were the bases of specific debating societies: James Harrington's Rota Club met at Miles's Coffee House in New Palace Yard; James Salter's coffee house, in Cheyne Walk, opened in 1695 and offered a public museum. Coffee houses spread to the provinces, but by 1800 coffee-house culture had gone down-market to working people, partly attracted by the availabil-ity of newspapers there when the taxes on such papers made them expensive.

Emerging musical societies, lending libraries and museums all increased facilities for getting hold of information, but largely benefited those who already had an above-average cultural grasp. Humphrey Chetham left his library to trustees in 1653 'for the use of scholars and others well affected'.[45] A century later the first gentlemen's subscription library in England was founded in Liverpool in 1758 with a guinea entrance fee and a yearly subscription of 5s. Select though some of these societies clearly were, their members' participation in times not particularly conducive to their enterprise is impressive. The seven-teenth- and eighteenth-century voluntary associations of gentlemen and upper middle-class people sowed the seeds of extension to work-ing-class clienteles in the nineteenth.

Societies where learned papers were read, experiments conducted, or issues debated, involved meetings and the rubbing-off of minds against one another, and were largely confined to men. But anyone literate could read in privacy. Printing totally transformed the availability of books, which burgeoned in our period, with educational consequences. As early as Elizabeth's reign a wide range of educational works was being printed in English, many for working-class readers. Pious bene-factors distributed bibles and other religious works. While books were becoming cheap enough for wider private ownership, they were still dear enough to deter purchase. In 1697 Dr Thomas Bray raised a plan for establishing a lending library in every deanery in England because he thought a third of the clergy too poor to buy necessary books, and they were more comfortably off than many. In the eighteenth century two kinds of subscription library emerged, private ones set up by societies for members, specialising in polite literature of an improving and informative kind, and commercial ones run by booksellers and specialising in fiction. These are all testimony to more reading by more people, as is the growth of newspapers in numbers, circulation and influence, both in London and the provinces.

5

EDUCATIONAL ACHIEVEMENTS

Stone argued that most societies are judged by the achievements of their cultural elites, but that what made seventeenth-century England remarkable was the appreciation and practice of cultural activity by 'the whole of the rural and urban propertied classes'.[1] Clearly it is one-sided to judge the achievements of education by the creativity of a tiny cultural elite, but if the focus is widened to take in all the people appreciative of intellectual culture it may embrace a larger body than is normally considered the 'propertied classes', an elitist term in itself. In this chapter it is proposed to take four focal points, the clearly cultural elite comprising writers of literature, philosophy and history on the one hand, and their scientific equivalents in mathematics, natural sciences and architecture on the other, then the literate elite of the magistrates and governing classes, then the receptive audience of the written word stretching into lower social ranks, and finally the ebb and flow of basic literacy.

The Cultured Elite

Certainly rated on the achievements of its cultural elite, early modern England scores highly. In the arts and humanities it produced Thomas More, William Shakespeare, John Milton, John Dryden, Daniel Defoe, Alexander Pope and Henry Fielding to offer a selection of leading writers of plays, poetry, satire and novels. Among philosophers and thinkers it produced Francis Bacon, Thomas Hobbes and John Locke. In mathematics and sciences, including medicine, it produced William Harvey, Robert Boyle, Edmund Halley and Isaac Newton, and in architecture Christopher Wren. It is disappointing, but perhaps significant of the value contemporaries placed on education, that comparatively little is known about the educational experiences of these intellectual giants. There are no records from the appropriate date for Stratford-upon-Avon Grammar School, where it is assumed Shakespeare received the only formal education he had. More is believed to have attended St Anthony's School in London and Canterbury College Oxford, and was admitted to Lincoln's Inn in 1496; he spent about two years in the household of Archbishop Morton, c.1490–91. Pope, whose father was Catholic, was a sickly child and is considered largely self-educated. Milton attended St Paul's school and Christ's College Cambridge: St Paul's also produced Halley, who went on to Queen's College Oxford. Dryden attended Westminster School, and Trinity College Cambridge. Based on this particular selection of cultural giants Westminster and Trinity shine out, as Westminster also produced Locke and Wren, the former proceeding to Christ Church, the latter to Wadham College. Trinity produced Bacon, who went on to Gray's Inn, and Isaac Newton. Boyle and Fielding both went to Eton, the latter studying for about eighteen months at Leiden. Harvey was educated at the King's School Canterbury, Caius College and Padua. Defoe attended the dissenting academy at Newington Green. Hobbes was educated at Magdalen College, but is a better educational illustration in his activities as a tutor than as a pupil and student. He was a tutor in the Cavendish family, escorted pupils abroad, and became tutor to Charles Prince of Wales in 1647.

It is not difficult to reconstruct the general intellectual development of the literary and philosophical giants from the classic grammar-school education (whether they had received it from public school, lesser provincial grammar school or family tutor) supplemented by arts courses at the universities and more rarely by studies at a legal inn. It is more difficult to capture the development of the mathematicians and scientists. Newton apparently had no mathematical training at all before going up to Trinity from Grantham Grammar School in 1661. He began to crack gravity while at home in Woolsthorpe during the 1666 plague, but left it aside until urged to publish by Halley. Newton made the first reflecting telescope known in 1668. Wren's training in geometry and arithmetic may have come from his brother-in-law William Holder, rector of Bletchington.[2] For the scientists in particular extra-curricular experiment and observation was the way to make progress, and to a considerable extent the high-fliers in these fields were self-educated, and mutually supported by groups of those like-minded.

Indeed, in all intellectual spheres it is very clear that much progress was made not only by gifted and studious individuals working away on their own, but by associations of minds sympathetic to furthering cultural or scientific interest, and these associations included the pioneers and embraced many less brilliant enthusiasts. Wren was one of the founder members of the Royal Society, where anatomy, mathematics and astronomy were furthered. In 1663, sixty-five of the known earliest 115 members of the Society were definitely university men, and only sixteen definitely not academic. But many of the seventeenth-century members are classed as 'merely dilettantes seeking amusement'.[3] Other associations furthering scholarship were founded throughout the early modern period. The College of Arms, founded by Richard III, formed in the late sixteenth century a pushful centre of heraldic, genealogical and historical research. William Camden, author of *Britannia* (1586), was Clarenceux King of Arms from 1597. Sir William Dugdale, the famous antiquary of Warwickshire and monastic historian, was Garter King of Arms in 1677, and Elias Ashmole wrote a history of the Order of the Garter in 1672. Ashmole was a member of the Royal Society, and presented his collection of curiosities, left to him by John Tradescant, to Oxford University in 1677, forming the start of the Ashmolean Museum. The Society of Antiquaries included such scholars as Camden, Sir Robert Cotton, founder of the Cotton Library, and John Stow, a merchant tailor turned historical researcher; it seemed politically dangerous enough to incite James I's suspicions and suppression, and was refounded a century later.

It is clear that the giants of the intellectual elite formed only the peak of an educated group shading imperceptibly into less prominent levels, and one significant quality in the stars of the next magnitude is their polymath adequacy. Thus Camden, cited above as an antiquarian and herald, educated at Christ's Hospital, St Paul's School, Magdalen, Broadgates Hall and Christ Church, was headmaster of Westminster School and taught Ben Jonson, playwright, poet, and lecturer in rhetoric at Gresham College. Sir John Vanbrugh, whose education seems particularly obscure, was not only a playwright and architect but also Clarenceux King of Arms. Many professional clergy exercised specific other talents one might not expect. Cuthbert Tunstall, who became bishop of Durham and was politically useful as president of the Council of the North, published in Latin the first book on arithmetic printed in England, *De Arte Supputandi* (1522). William Stukeley practised medicine before becoming a parson, but is also famous as an early archaeologist and fossil man. Gilbert White, curate of Selborne, his birthplace, and fellow of Oriel, was a naturalist and author of the *Natural History and Antiquities of Selborne* (1789). Lawrence Sterne, educated at Jesus College Cambridge, held ecclesiastical livings in Yorkshire but is better known for *Tristram Shandy* (1759–67) and *A Sentimental Journey through France and Italy* (1768).

A remarkable number of women writers emerge in this level, particularly after the Restoration. Janet Todd claims women writers constituted 'a substantial minority' of authors in the eighteenth century, and cites Samuel Johnson's 1753 reference to 'a generation of Amazons of the pen'.[4] The women were not the equals of the male literary giants, but their success in publishing in such numbers, given their inferior educational opportunities and prejudices against them, is remarkable. Aphra Behn was the most outstanding, probably the first Englishwoman to earn her living by writing, a playwright of witty, bawdy Restoration drama, author of a number of novels, and a poet. So exceptional is Behn's literary career that it is scarcely more remarkable that she was apparently also a spy in Charles II's intelligence service, based in Antwerp for nine months in 1666. Nothing is known of any formal education she may have received, but it is believed that she went with her family to Surinam in her early twenties, which provided material for her novel *Oroonoko* (1688). Behn was able to translate from French. Another capable linguist was Katherine Philips, 'the matchless Orinda', whose translation of Corneille's *La Mort de Pompee* played in Dublin and London; she was translating Corneille's *Horace* when she died of smallpox. The daughter of a London merchant, she was educated at Miss Salmon's school at Hackney, and married at sixteen; her output was far less than Behn's, but more virtuous, and she was much admired by later women writers and indeed by contemporaries such as Dryden. Mary Astell was 'perhaps the first respectable woman prose writer in England', now highly valued as the first widely read feminist. Astell did not only concern herself with women, however, being alert to current religious and political controversies. Conservatively Anglican in religion, and Tory in politics, she argued fearlessly with male opponents when necessary, and won much respect, though not all could take her criticism. Bishop Atterbury, given a sheet of remarks on his sermon against

Benjamin Hoadley, spluttered about their 'extraordinary Nature, considering that they came from the Pen of a woman. Indeed one would not imagine that a woman had written 'em. There is not an expression that carries the least Air of her Sex from the beginning to the End of it.'[5] Astell's education is believed to have been private, with her curate uncle, and many women writers were daughters, wives, sisters of or otherwise related to clergymen. Their range of writing, and networks of contacts and patrons, are fascinating subjects, but only the educational aspects are relevant here. Elizabeth Carter, poet, essayist, translator and letter writer, was educated by her clergyman father alongside her brothers; Sarah Fielding, novelist sister of Henry, had been at boarding school in Salisbury, but it was only later that she learned Greek and Latin and studied English literature privately. Many women writers lamented their lack of Latin, though Mary Hervey was praised by Lord Chesterfield for wisely concealing her perfect understanding of Latin in 1750. An impressive number of women writers had sufficient French, Italian and German to publish translations; some had Latin, Greek and Hebrew, even Spanish, Portuguese and Arabic. Elizabeth Carter had all these, and published in 1739 translations of Algarotti's *Newtonismo per le dame* (*Sir Isaac Newton's Philosophy Explained, for the use of Ladies*) and Crousaz's *Examen de L'essay de M. Pope sur l'homme* (*An Examination of Mr Pope's Essay on Man*), and the long standard English translation of the Stoic Epictetus, published by subscription in 1758. That there were subscribers for the latter and readers for the former, tells us something about their education as well as hers. Some of the women writers were involved in education, for example Bathsua Makin and the enterprising Hannah Woolley, who boldly chided parents for 'letting the fertile Ground of their Daughters lie fallow, yet send[ing] the barren Noddles of their sons to the University'.[6]

Almost 500 writers feature in Todd's *A Dictionary of British and American Women Writers 1660–1800* (1987), many of the Americans born in England. Their creativity extended to novels and plays, poetry, essays and polemics, letters, journals, travel diaries, spiritual autobiographies, biographies of their husbands, translations and straightforward instruction manuals, from Woolley's *The Cook's Guide* (1661) to Jane Sharp's *The Midwives Book or the whole Art of Midwifery discovered* (1671). A few entered the comparatively new field of journalism; Delarivière Manley succeeded Swift as editor of *The Examiner* 1711, and Eliza Haywood published *The Female Spectator* from 1744 to 1746. The professional female writer remained a rarity, and most women writers wrote only a few works of varying merit; still, their achievement deserves attention. Many published only incidentally in a life of landed sufficiency; so more of them will be met in the next section, testifying to the literacy of the governing class.

The Literate Elite: Magistrates and Governors

The renaissance programme for educating governors achieved rapid general acceptance among the governing classes and formed the pattern of elite education throughout the period. The basic building-block in this educative process was grammar schooling, which, alone, proved sufficient to enable many men to go far. In *Mount Tabor* (1639) Richard Willis wrote of his own education and career: 'It was not my happiness to be bred up at the university, but all the learning I had was in the free grammar school called Christ's school in the city of Gloucester.' There he was given 'extraordinary help by the new schoolmaster brought thither, one master Gregory Downhale of Pembroke Hall in Cambridge'. Willis's account of this master's career is worth citing as it contains several not uncommon features, most importantly perhaps the transitoriness of schoolmastering as a mere phase in a man's overall career. The teacher arrived at the school 'but a bachelor of arts', a good scholar, who wrote both the secretary and Italian hands exquisitely well, evidently worth noting; he then proceeded to the master of arts degree, and abandoned schoolteaching to become a nobleman's secretary, rising to be secretary to Lord Chancellor Ellesmere. Willis, 'though furnished with no more learning than he taught me in that grammar school', took the same line, becoming in turn secretary to Sir Fulke Greville, Lord Brooke, chancellor of the exchequer, Lionel Cranfield, Earl of Middlesex, treasurer, and Sir Thomas, later Lord, Coventry, keeper of the great seal. 'Though I were no graduate of the university, yet (by God's blessing) I had so much learning as fitted me for the places whereunto the lord advanced me.'[7] In the recurring stress on Willis's lack of university education, and reliance solely on grammar schooling, there may be detected perhaps the writer's consciousness that his education might be deemed deficient, although his success proves its adequacy.

Willis patently recognised that his attendance at the Gloucester free grammar school had been his making; Dover Wilson cited the extract because Willis was an exact contemporary of Shakespeare, whose own formal education is believed to have been entirely provided at the grammar school of Stratford-upon-Avon. Shakespeare, however, son of an alderman who apparently could not sign his name, does not appear to have been mindful of a debt of gratitude. He encapsulates the schoolboy's perspective in the famous passage in *As You Like It*, II. vii, shows a dry pedant playing with Latin words and figures in the schoolmaster Holofernes in *Love's Labour's Lost*, IV. iii, and echoes the distrust of education by the unlettered when his Cade accuses Lord Say: 'Thou hast most traitorously corrupted the youth of this realm in erecting a grammar school' in *2 Henry VI*, IV. vii. The *Taming of the Shrew* and *Love's Labour's Lost* feature educational progress as a theme, however.

At its most select level, the grammar-school education was provided by the public boarding school. Edward Gibbon, the historian, who had been briefly, and due to illness intermittently, at Westminster School, in the rather unusual circumstances of having an aunt keep a boarding house there, enthused support for

> the common opinion that our public schools, which have produced so many eminent characters, are the best adapted to the genius and constitution of the English people. A boy of spirit may acquire a previous and practical experience of the world; and his playfellows may be the future friends of his heart or his interest. In a free intercourse with his equals, the habits of truth, fortitude and prudence will insensibly be matured.

However these schools did not teach 'relevant' subjects, for one might emerge from Westminster or Eton

> in total ignorance of the business and conversation of English gentlemen in the latter end of the eighteenth century. But these schools may assume the merit of teaching all that they pretend to teach, the Latin and Greek languages: they deposit in the hands of the disciple the keys of two valuable chests; nor can he complain if they are afterwards lost or neglected by his own fault.[8]

This shows clearly enough the continued dominance of the Latin and Greek education even though it was not 'relevant' to eighteenth-century business or gentlemanly conversation. Indeed, this irrelevance may have been perceived as the very liberality of the arts. However, Locke had launched a more utilitarian view at the end of the seventeenth century, considering time spent writing Latin themes, declamations and especially verse wasteful.[9]

Many did have what Willis termed the 'happiness to be bred up at University', taking this advantage (assuming it so to be) with them on to the local bench or into Parliament, as shown in Chapter 3. The governing classes gained their position more by birthright than by education, but a particular educational pattern was beginning to follow from birth into a certain social class. J. H. Gleason's study of justices of the peace in Norfolk, Northamptonshire, Somerset, Worcestershire, Kent and Yorkshire's North Riding between 1558 and 1640 shows a clear advance in educational experience in the magistracy over the period. Patently the educational pattern was spreading into even outlying provinces. However, attendance at university or legal inn is not proof of educational profit therefrom, nor did the gentry influx last. John Earle, in *Microcosmographie* (1628), began a definition 'a young man of the university is one that comes there to wear a gown, and to say hereafter he has been at the University'.[10] Gibbon himself enthused over his velvet cap and silk gown, which distinguished a gentleman commoner from a plebeian student. He had been at Magdalen College for a period spanning fourteen months in 1752–53. Gibbon regarded his time at Oxford as the most idle and unprofitable period of his life, but it did not have to be so for a man. He admitted he could not share the filial piety to the university expressed by Robert Lowth, professor of poetry 1741–51, bishop of Oxford 1766 and London 1777, but quoted him:

I was educated in the University of Oxford. I enjoyed all the advantages, both public and private, which that famous seat of learning so largely affords. I spent many years in that illustrious society, in a well regulated course of useful discipline and studies, and in the agreeable and improving commerce of gentleman and of scholars, in a society where emulation without envy, ambition without jealousy, contention without animosity, incited industry and awakened genius.[11]

Thus Lowth could find well-regulated study where Gibbon found idleness and stagnation, a generation (at most) apart. Gibbon was not ineducable, as his development at Lausanne showed, but he was not responsive to Magdalen's regimen at the age of fifteen to sixteen.

Gibbon praised the eighteenth-century public schools, although they did not teach the gentleman studies relevant to business or conversation. 'The calling of a Gentleman', Locke had written, 'is to have the

Knowledge of a Man of Business, a Carriage suitable to his Rank, and to be Eminent and useful in his Country according to his Station.'[12] The usefulness of the governors' education must have varied considerably and should not be exaggerated. Quarter Sessions records show us the local squirearchy administering the law, according to the rules, though with some discretion, but there were no opportunities for doing the job better for knowing Virgil or Aristotle, or for being interested in political theory. Even Locke regarded Latin as 'absolutely necessary for a gentleman' (but not for trade). He also thought 'it would be strange to suppose an English gentleman should be ignorant of the Law of his Country', at least from the perspective of the English constitution and government.[13] Yet the use of the legally expert clerk of the peace as the legal adviser to the magistrates underlines the fact that they were expected to be amateur executives in terms of legal knowledge, even if some had been at the inns of court for a time. The English preference for the amateur over the professional, elevating as it does motive (public service) over achievement (bureaucratic efficiency), was fully established in these years, and Gibbon's comment testifies to the survival of high repute for an irrelevant education in some quarters.

If not needed to shine on the bench, a 'good' education might have been expected to show in the cut and thrust of parliamentary debate, but again this proves not necessarily so. Gibbon, elected to two rotten boroughs in his career, admitted to remaining silent: 'after a fleeting illusive hope, prudence condemned me to acquiesce in the humble station of a mute', and he booked the experience complacently as beneficial to himself: 'the eight sessions that I sat in parliament were a school of civil prudence, the first and most essential virtue of an historian'. When appointed a Lord Commissioner of Trade and Plantations in 1779 he enjoyed the emoluments, commenting 'our duty was not intolerably severe, and . . . I enjoyed many days and weeks of repose, without being called from my library to the office'. This seems richly hypocritical considering Gibbon's own criticism of his second Oxford tutor: 'Dr [Winchester] well remembered that he had a salary to receive, and only forgot that he had a duty to perform.'[14]

The Reformation had brought a great change to society because it reduced the dominance of churchmen in the state. Education as the gateway to entry into ecclesiastical professions gave way to education with more open, lay opportunities. So complete was this process eventually that it is often forgotten today that a clerk was originally a cleric, and the idea of an unprofessional person as a 'mere layman' contrasted him expressly with a professional ecclesiastic. The changes built up slowly, with impetus and reaction interplaying in the mid-sixteenth century. There was formal bookish education for laymen before the Reformation, but there was very much more of it afterwards. Late Tudor schoolboys were learning without commitment to any single career. Different atmospheres prevail in institutions which are essentially training students for particular purposes and institutions which are essentially educating students to achieve their intellectual potential for application as they choose. This was the strength of seventeenth-century Oxford (with which Cambridge was in close harmony), offering 'a panorama of knowledge . . . a solid foundation upon which the student could proceed to build, independently, for years to come'.[15] Turning out parsons and schoolmasters remained the universities' most obvious functions, but the leavening of this with polishing up the cultural attainments of men of independent means, provided this sector did not swamp the institution with 'smarts', benefited all parts of the social mix. Bishop Lowth had valued exposure to 'gentlemen and scholars'.

It would be anachronistic to imply that the universities were widely open to talent in our period, or that their intake was a broad social mix. The matriculation registers from the universities, along with some college lists, enable classifications to be drawn, but these are not as clear as they might seem. Entrants of lower social status paid lower fees, so some may have exaggerated downwards. However, eldest sons of esquires and above could take the BA degree in three years instead of four, offering a different kind of saving, so some may have exaggerated upwards. Students not bothering to matriculate at all, or evading it for religious purposes, skew the analysis of social participation in higher education further. For the period 1575–1639 Stone reckoned, allowing for misrepresentation and omissions, that 50 per cent of the Oxford entry comprised sons of gentlemen and above, 41 per cent were sons of plebeians, and 9 per cent sons of clergy.[16] The plebeian class, though obviously socially inferior to the gentlemen and above, and separable from the clergy, is however too imprecise to be helpful. It included the sons of merchants, yeomen, non-clerical professionals, artisans, husbandmen and labourers. Examination of the entrants at Gonville-Caius and St John's Cambridge between 1558 and 1700 shows 'pitifully small numbers' of entrants of rural parentage from south Cambridgeshire and Ely not claiming to be of gentle or clerical background. The imprecision of the evidence permits democratically minded enthusiasm over 'poor boys' being given opportunities to achieve great things, and examples can be cited. John Richardson of Linton is cited by Spufford as one of the rare careerists of peasant stock: he became Regius Professor of Divinity at Cambridge in 1616 and was one of the translators of the Authorised Version of the Bible.[17] But the general evidence supports those who believe university education remained elitist, for a largely privileged intake. Most of the students began comfortably up the social ladder, and it was the better-born even of these who enjoyed also the inns of court and the Grand Tour. The legal inns' intake was more socially restricted than the universities' because of the costs, regulations, and the comparable lack of sponsorship. The universities and the inns of court were not fostering social engineering in the early modern period, but it suited them to show pride in the few exceptions to the norm they could glow in having made great.

In this governing class, the educational achievements of the women remained firmly sublimated to their menfolk. Margaret Roper (née More), Lady Jane Grey, Mary Sidney Countess of Pembroke and Lady Brilliana Harley are examples of women from the first half of the period who showed outstanding intellectual capacity, not only similar to their brothers' and husbands', but applied to the same sort of classical and literary interests. But this was rare. Other aristocratic and gentry wives of the period were capable managers and shrewd individuals, as some show in diaries, two of the earliest female diarists being Lady Margaret Hoby and Lady Anne Clifford. The Puritan Hoby seems to have been initially motivated by religion to begin an almost 'confessional' diary. Lady Anne, who had had Samuel Daniel as her tutor from the age of nine to twelve, was motivated by a fierce dynastic sense and proprietorial determination, practically expressed in the archival Great Diary as well as her personal journal. But later women diarists had more participation in the action to record. Mary Cowper, née Clavering, was lady of the bedchamber to Caroline, wife of George I, and began her diary in 1714 as a record of court life to refute 'the perpetual Lies that One hears'. Elizabeth Percy, Duchess of Northumberland, was another lady of the bedchamber who kept a diary, written between 1752 and 1776. Her grandfather, the Duke of Somerset, who died in 1748, criticised her as a prig and a bluestocking, which typifies the widely disapproving attitude to women's learning which post-Restoration generations held. (The term bluestocking derives from the salon circle of Elizabeth Montagu.) Some women diarists reveal awareness of their sex's educational disadvantage: Caroline Girle (later Powys), who began keeping a travel journal in 1756 at her father's desire, complained in 1760 that she was unable to describe a fort she had seen for ignorance of the technical language required: 'the terms of fortification are quite out of female knowledge'. She thought 'women might be made acquainted with various subjects they are now ignorant of, more for want of instruction than capacity'.[18]

Margaret Cavendish, née Lucas, Duchess of Newcastle, was the first Englishwoman to publish extensively. Privately tutored as a girl, she grew up with an undisciplined mind, lacking even elementary principles of grammar. Heedless of being thought eccentric, she published poems, philosophical speculations, essays, plays and letters. Among this variegated output is the first biography of a husband to be published by an Englishwoman (1667) and the first autobiographical work so published (1656). She used her status to gain an invitation to visit the Royal Society in 1667. Her piece of writing most pertinent to the present study is her letter dedicating her *Philosophical and Physical Opinions* to the two English universities in 1655, seeking a better deal for women,

> kept like birds in cages to hop up and down in our houses, not suffered to fly abroad to see the several changes of fortune and the various humours ordained and created by nature, and wanting the experience of nature, we must needs want the understanding and knowledge, and so consequently prudence and invention of men.[19]

Margaret Cavendish wrote, as she openly declared, out of restless ambition for fame, but many well educated women of the gentry class wrote works which were only published after their deaths. Anne Finch, later Viscountess Conway, daughter of the Commons speaker Sir Henry Finch, wrote a philosophical notebook which was translated into Latin and published on the Continent in 1690, and retranslated for publication in English in 1692. Anne Fanshawe's *Memoirs*, written for her son in 1676, were first printed only in 1829. Celia Fiennes wrote travel accounts of journeys within England between 1685 and 1703 which were only published in 1888. They are artless as literary works, but observant and entertaining and now useful to social historians for many details such as comparative prices. Anne Halkett, wife of Sir James, daughter of Thomas Murray, provost of Eton (and tutor to Charles I) and his wife Jane, née Drummond (herself once governess to Princess Elizabeth) was educated by tutors under her mother's supervision. In widowhood she tutored children of the Scottish aristocracy. Selections from her religious writings were published soon after her death in 1701, but her autobiography was only published in 1875. Lady Mary Wortley Montagu, née Pierrepont, reared by a governess and self-taught in Latin, was famous for her wit but wrote her works 'only for myself '; the *Embassy Letters* from the time of her husband's ambassadorship in Turkey were published the year after her death. Lady Mary railed against what she called the unjust custom of barring her sex from the advantages of learning.

The early modern market for sermons and theological tracts took off with printing and grew prodigiously, with arguments protracted in print through counterblasts and vindications. Over one thousand and probably over two thousand sermons were printed in Elizabeth's reign and perhaps another two thousand and more by 1640.[20] Who bought these publications? Who watched Shakespeare's plays? Surely these questions show the inadequacy of judging a society by its elite, unless the term is widened to an almost meaningless degree. To read Bacon or Milton, to persist with arid theological arguments, to follow Hobbes, one needs no small intellectual education, though obviously less than to produce them. To follow a Shakespearean play's performance would be easier for the contemporary audience than for one today, from a linguistic point of view, but we should avoid being patronising of the audiences' receptiveness in an age when reading a Shakespeare play is thought a hard option in a secondary education English literature syllabus.

Compared with ploughmen and labourers, the purchasers of *Eirenarcha*, *Britannia*, or *Arcadia* were the cultural elite, but where is their lower line drawn? What about the readers of the chronicles of Hall and Hollinshed, of Berners' translation of Froissart, of Lambarde's *A Perambulation of Kent* (1576), of Hakluyt's *Voyages*? Lambarde's *Kent*, of which 600 copies were printed in 1576, was the first of the genre of published county histories, which developed in the next century, appealing directly to the local gentry, who were often subscribers. What sort of libraries did these gentry have? Sir William More of Loseley House had 140 books and manuscripts in 1556, in English, French and Italian and a few in Latin. These included a variety of English chronicles and classical translations, the Bible, scientific works, works of Chaucer, Gower and Lydgate, ballads and songs.[21] Edward Gibbon's library at Lausanne, on his own estimate, contained 6000–7000 volumes, but Gibbon had had more books than this as other volumes were left with Lord Sheffield. This was an exceptional collection, but Gibbon's comment about his father's books is worth noting.

My father's study at Buriton was stuffed with much trash of the last age, with much high church divinity and politics, which have long since gone to their proper place; yet it contained some valuable editions of the classics and the fathers, the choice, as it should seem, of Mr Law [d. 1761, a notable spiritual writer and his father's old tutor]; and many English publications of the times had been occasionally added.

From this slender beginning Gibbon congratulated himself on forming a numerous and select library, the foundation of his works and the great comfort of his life, in England and abroad.[22] His father, born in 1707, had been given the 'benefits of a liberal education as a scholar and a gentleman', at Westminster School and Emmanuel College, benefiting from his own father's fortune, made in commerce. Gibbon distinguished between his paternal grandfather's education in the world and his father's in institutions approved by polite society. His criticism of his father's library (to which he resorted happily enough on visits home) is surely rather informative. That dismissed as 'trash' was 'of the last age', in other words ephemeral stuff, but this was no doubt reflective of an up-to-date purchasing policy when acquired. Alongside it were 'some valuable editions of the classics and the fathers', the purchase of which Gibbon junior attributed to Mr Law's influence. However the works came to be chosen, they did reach the library, and if other country gentlemen's libraries were expanded over these years with the advice of old tutors and spiritual counsellors we may think better, not worse, of them. John Locke's treatise 'Some thoughts concerning reading and study for a gentleman' was compiled for the thirty-six-year-old Roger Clavel of Steeple in Dorset in 1703. Arguing that reading was for the improvement of understanding, to increase knowledge and better communicate it, the tract recommends, in this order of priority, works to improve the communication skills of writing and speaking, regarding both style and reasoning, and then works of morality, politics (the origin of societies and power and the actual art of government), history (and law), chronology, geography (with books of travel), classical works touching the understanding of human nature, and finally, for diversion, *Don Quixote*. The list ends with a selection of dictionaries of all kinds, several Latin, several specialist, geographical and historical. Many individual titles and authors are recommended, ending with Gerard Jan Vossius, whose works 'lately printed in Holland in six tomes' are described as 'very fit books for a gentleman's library, as containing very learned discourses concerning all the sciences'.[23] This is a demanding reading programme, to which the recipient's initial response was reported as favourable.

Buyers of books do not necessarily profit from them, but unless books were on a large scale only bought as status symbols, shelved for show and never read nor lent, private assembling of considerable book collections in country houses must both reflect and support the educational attainments of subsequent generations. Gibbon's maternal grandfather's library is also worth noticing. James Porten was a businessman, until he failed and absconded; he must have had a reasonable book collection at his house in Putney by 1748, as his grandson recollected: 'my grandfather's flight unlocked the door of a tolerable library, and I turned over many pages of poetry and romance, of history and travels'.[24] Unusual evidence of a woman's library comes from several catalogues and lists, dated expressly to 1702 and 1704, of the books belonging to Lady Anne Coventry. The books, which are listed by abbreviated or descriptive titles, include bibles, prayer books and other religious works including sermons, Miege's *French Dictionary*, Ovid's *Metamorphosis*, Harvey's *Physician*, a French Aesop, Clarendon's *History* in six volumes, many plays, specified as comedies, tragedies and tragic comedies, a complete herbal, Culpeper's *London Dispensatory*, a large book of maps, a paper book of gardening, the whole body of cookery, and the cure of diseases in infants.[25]

The Receptive Audience

There was clearly a tolerably educated iceberg beneath the peaks of the cultured, governing elite. While Gibbon enjoyed his huge private library, the poet Mary Leapor (1722–46), a gardener's daughter, had only a few books: her entry in Todd's *Dictionary* states 'her library at her death consisted of only sixteen or seventeen volumes, including part of Pope's works, Dryden's Fables and some volumes of plays'. When does a shelf of books qualify to be classed as a library? With this meagre collection Leapor, who died of measles at twenty-four, produced verse of her own, began to get recognition in her lifetime and was well known after death as an untutored poet. If we were to take every family possessed of any printed work as part of an audience literate enough to be receptive of written communication and in its small way as a patron of the printing trade, we should have to extend the assessment of the achievement of education radically.

At the lower levels of literacy, people bought books for three reasons: for religious purposes, for instruction, and for entertainment. Religion was a major motivator, inspiring both the learning and the teaching of vernacular reading for those not aspiring to Latin. Religious books formed from the first the largest class of printed books, embracing sermons, bibles and commentaries, prayer books, meditations, books of saints and martyrs, priests' manuals, and from the mid-sixteenth century, polemical tracts. Religion accounted for 40–45 per cent of the output of early printers: Caxton, de Worde and Pynson. Thousands of sermons were printed in Elizabethan and early Stuart England, and thousands of catechisms were printed and circulated widely. Print runs for religious works were large, New Testaments running to 2000–3000. Those who invested in the printed word for religious edification were presumably better than halting readers, and if the reading was a struggle at first they would benefit from it if they persevered. It has to be remembered that in the seventeenth century reading was seen by many as the key to absorbing uplifting material, not as a social skill to advance one's worldly career.

The early part of the period is the great age of biblical translation, beginning with William Tyndale's *New Testament*, of which printing began in Cologne in 1525 and ended at Worms in 1526. By 1557 there had been thirty editions of the Bible and fifty of the New Testament in English, and in 1543 it had seemed necessary to the government to forbid English bible reading to women, artificers, apprentices, journeymen and yeomen and lesser ranks, husbandmen and labourers, indicating the need to deprive these people of access to the English text by legislation since, presumably, they could no longer be assumed to be safely kept from it by illiteracy. A further hundred editions of the Bible followed in Elizabeth's reign, and over 150 between 1603 and 1640. Biblical translation reached its apogee in the 1611 Authorised Version (King James Bible), created by several committees of some fifty scholars, but taking much from Tyndale. The quality of Tyndale's and the Authorised Version is undeniably high – bearing testimony to excellent standards of Hebrew scholarship and English literary style in the translators – and it exposed its readers and hearers to fine quality prose thereafter, which must have had some positive effect on their own appreciation of language.

Religion aside, the obvious saleability of informative secular books testifies to another aspect of the reading public, namely the existence of men and women willing to learn through the written word. At the most erudite level there were published legal and medical textbooks for experts – editions of statutes, year books, treatises on and for justices of the peace, textbooks on surgery and on anatomy: John Banister's *Historie of Man* (1578) had a long life as a textbook of surgery. What is more surprising is the publication of medical manuals for the non-expert, for the 'poorer sort' unable to afford a physician, yet clearly capable of learning from a book. Practical works for specific employments included Fitzherbert's works on husbandry and surveying (both published in 1523), works for seamen and explorers, and the first shorthand manual in English (1588). (Shorthand was much used for taking down sermons.) There were books for hobbies and interests such as gardening, and a growing array of foreign language grammars and dictionaries, even polyglot ones. Travel and history books probably appealed to a comparatively educated readership seeking further edification. Almanacs and plays costing a few pence and halfpenny broadsheet ballads had a large circulation among people who would not buy expensive books. These were bought for entertainment, and pedlars hawked them round the countryside far from the booksellers' shops round St Paul's. By the early seventeenth century there was an increase of literacy in the middle and lower classes and publication for the 'ordinary reader' was reaching down further, supplying material for a market which was opening up among those who were only haltingly literate.

Basic Literacy

There is a fundamental change in societies when the balance swings from vernacular literacy being a minority skill to being the majority's culture. This change was in process in early modern England, but it was uneven. Male literacy was commoner than female, and urban populations more literate than rural. Class made a further difference, with gentry and professionals being most literate, well ahead of yeomen and craftsmen and tradespeople, themselves ahead of husbandmen, with servants and labourers least literate. There were also regional differences, with London most advanced, then the South and Midlands, with the North and far South-West (where the Cornish language was in westward retreat) least advanced in the 1640s; however R. A. Houston's work using northern assize circuit depositions shows a remarkable catching-up by the North over the next century, leaving the North-East one of the most literate areas by the late eighteenth century.

David Cressy's book *Literacy and the Social Order: Reading and Writing in Tudor and Stuart England* (1980) offers a clear discussion of the evidence, the contemporary value placed on literacy, and modern attempts to measure past literacy. It profiles the class distribution of literacy, and studies the overall chronology, suggesting a quickening of literacy around the Henrician Reformation, another energetic advance *c.*1558–80, then stagnation until around 1610, when a revival of progress began which was ended by the Civil War, and resumed from 1660 to 1680 when it faltered again. Cressy estimates that 90 per cent of men and 99 per cent of women were illiterate in Henry VII's reign, and over 66 per cent of men and 90 per cent of women unable to sign their names in the 1640s, but by the end of our period evidence from the archival consequences of Hardwicke's Marriage Act (1754), requiring the signatures (or marks) of parties and witnesses on bound standard forms, suggests illiteracy rates of 40 per cent for men and just over 60 per cent for women.[26]

There are two obvious conclusions: that the overall literacy rate was rising, and that beneath the elites, popular literacy was fairly strictly utilitarian. This is shown by breaking down further urban literacy and trade and craft literacy. The mercantile elites – such as mercers, vintners, drapers, haberdashers and grocers – were approaching the literacy level of the gentry with only 10 per cent illiterate. Skilled craftsmen such as goldsmiths and clothiers were in the next band, with 14–33 per cent illiteracy. The 'industrious sort' such as weavers, fullers and tailors reached down from 37 to 52 per cent illiteracy and blacksmiths, carpenters, millers and butchers were 56–86 per cent illiterate.[27] At the bottom came bricklayers, thatchers and, in the country, shepherds, approaching near total illiteracy. Literacy is found where it was needed, and it may be assumed it was more sought where its acquisition was seen as advantageous to a career, however much stress contemporaries might make on its prime importance for religion. This uneven chipping-away at illiteracy is in fact a major educational achievement, but it has to be viewed in its historical context, not as an abstract and certainly not as a steady progression.

Stone thought the eighteenth century shifted most of the lower middle classes from semi-literate to literate, but these terms are really very imprecise. It is hard enough to define literacy, let alone semi-literacy, and the difficulties historians have are clear from the attempts they make to tighten the meaning with qualifying adjectives. *Literatus* at one time meant literate in Latin, so to indicate a different standard it has been necessary to specify a vernacular literacy, or the person 'literate in English'. However, even vernacular literacy can be subdivided between full literacy, the ability to absorb or express any written communication, and pragmatic literacy, by which is meant practical, get-by literacy sufficient for day-to-day basic written communication, but with no spare capacity as a vehicle for cultural activity. Halting literacy comes at the lower end of this spectrum, where people might sign laboriously, but pen little else, and might painfully struggle word by word through a simple, short, written text.

Whereas today the skills of reading and writing are pretty evenly distributed, in the early modern period this was probably not so. Because reading was taught before writing, and there was no compulsory schooling of children to an age when they would have been exposed to both levels of instruction, reading ability was more widespread than writing ability, which was commonly taught after the age at which poor children might be put to paid labour. There was more to this than the pedagogic timetable, however. While religion remained a major factor in educational purpose, reading was far more essential than writing. Reading opened up the Bible, the prayer book and the catechism for private study, reinforcing the normal aural exposure under ministerial supervision, but there was no need for the religious amateur to write. Quite the contrary: orthodox authorities could fear that indiscriminate teaching of writing could encourage the pouring forth of unlearned, irresponsible and pernicious religious ideas. Thus reading was a vehicle of salvation while writing was not. Responsible authorities could therefore support the teaching of reading (though not always without political qualms) while having graver doubts about the wisdom of teaching writing. From the recipients' point of view, there must have been a similar inclination, for a different reason. Many individuals could find a use for reading – notices, even political lampoons, were posted up from the late Middle Ages; the Ten Commandments and Tables of Affinity were displayed in churches; printing brought much more communication by the written word, and eventually journals and newspapers of even daily frequency within the period. (The bookseller George Thomason collected nearly 15 000 pamphlets and 7000 newspapers published between 1640 and 1663.[28]) So families could see advantage in having a child taught to read. But from the sixteenth to the eight-eenth centuries there were far fewer occasions for ordinary people to write. Private letter writing, diary keeping and recipe copying were not the practices of ordinary folk. Writing skill would not be frequently called upon in normal life, even when one had it, unless one had become recognised as one of the village elders who could be called upon to pen a will or some other important document. So writing ability was probably less widely taught than reading, and writing ability prob-ably more often rusted for lack of practice.

All this suggests the literacy estimates now commonly based on sig-natures to oaths, depositions, wills and marriage registration may err on the low side. The indirect evidence – contemporary comments and assumptions, the scale of printing and nature of the output, and the spread of book ownership – suggest a more literate culture prevalent than the proportion of estimated literates in the population supports. This may be partly because history is a study dominated by written sources, and writers reflect literate values. The evidence for illiteracy is largely the absence of evidence for literacy. There is no certainty about it. The person who leaves behind evidence of personal literacy is unde-niably literate, but a person who has not left such evidence is not necessarily illiterate. About very many individuals there is simply noth-ing known. Even where people appear to register their illiteracy by making a mark instead of a signature it does not mean they were never able to write, particularly if there is only one occasion when there is such evidence about them. Elderly and enfeebled people mak-ing a last will might demonstrate a very weak hand or only manage a mark when they might have made a better fist at it with full vigour and eyesight when younger. Young brides might think it politic not to reveal superior literacy to their husbands. We cannot be sure about the spread of literacy or its depth in those who had perhaps little grasp of it. What we have to ask, to avoid an optimistic overassessment or a pessimistic underrating, is why people should have wanted to be literate and to spread literacy, and how much we can see they were and did.

Literacy was seen as desirable for pious purposes; this was said openly, for example by Comenius. It can be seen being put to this use by the silent purchasers of the huge quantities of bibles and religious works, and by the vociferous entrants into oral and written disputation. Puritan conferences at Wisbech in the 1580s and 1590s were attended by laity carrying bibles who looked up and argued over cited texts.[29] Men and women attracted into the new religious sects of the seventeenth century

were able to aspire to ministry without the formal educational requirements of the orthodox church. John Bunyan came of modest origins, his
father being variously described as a brazier, a tinker, and a nine-acre
declining yeoman tinkering to make ends meet. Bunyan became a
nonconformist preacher and spent about a dozen years in Bedford
gaol, where he wrote books including *Grace Abounding to the Chief of
Sinners* (1666) and worked on what became *The Pilgrim's Progress* (1678/
84). In *Grace Abounding* he tells us it was reading two works owned by his
first wife, Arthur Dent's *Plain Man's Pathway to Heaven* and Lewis Bayly's
Practice of Piety, that first turned him to religion: a resounding illustration of what could come of learning to read and write at a village school
and marrying a wife possessing a couple of serious religious books! The
Quakers allowed women's ministry: Rachel Wilson (1720–75), daughter
of a Kendal tanner, and wife of a shearman dyer, was acknowledged as a
Quaker minister at eighteen, and travelled widely, preaching in Britain
and America.

Literacy also offered advantages to traders and craftsmen and had
been demanded in apprentices in some crafts since the fifteenth century,
while instruction in writing and accounting for worldly business was
already provided in the 'commercial stream' of Rotherham's college.
While some Southampton apprentices were sent abroad to master a
foreign language, other people taught themselves with the aid of
books on French, Italian and Spanish grammar, available from the
sixteenth century. From the same period there were practical books
on arithmetic, surveying and husbandry. *The Merchant's Avizo*, registered
in 1589, got off to editions in 1591, 1607, 1616 and 1640, and is
described as the first handbook for young merchants on managing
commercial correspondence. It was not only literate legal professionals
and amateur justices of the peace, for whom books of statutes and
guides to court administration were available, who turned to the printed
word for instruction. For the higher social classes there were books
catering for hobbies such as gardening, horse management and chess,
and for ladies recipe books and books of the household companion
type. Hannah Woolley published several, including *The Cook's Guide*
(1661), *The Ladies' Directory* (1662), *The Queen-like Closet* (1671) and *The
Gentlewomen's Companion* (1675). The really literate could build up
libraries of more literary works, as Sir William More had done by
1556, and as Roger Clavel was being urged to do in 1703. Ballads and
songs could be a more plebeian taste. Margaret Spufford's *Small Books
and Pleasant Histories* brings out the ubiquity of the printed word. The

stock of one of the specialist publishers of chapbooks, Charles Tias (d. 1664) at his death is worth noting: in house and warehouse there were 10 000 books ready to go out, and 80 000 printed and ready to make up. Only 642 of the books ready for sale were priced in excess of 6*d* (including bibles at 10*s* and 4*s*); many were less than 4*d*. Chapbooks were aimed at rural and urban readers, and were distributed up country by chapmen along with lace, cloth and knives. The range included small godly books, romances, jest books and novels. Samuel Pepys made a collection of a good cross-section published between 1661 and 1668, which Spufford examines. Small wonder Spufford thinks historians of literacy may be too conservative in evaluating the spread of reading ability. Tellingly, she argues that by 1700 printed ballads, chapbooks and plays had already made an indelible mark on oral tradition in England. The volume of surviving evidence of the transmission of information by the written word suggests that seventeenth-century English society demonstrated a literate mentality, before it can be confidently asserted that the majority of its population could read and or write. Between 1500 and 1700, Spufford argues, provincial England was being transformed from a late medieval peasant society, aware of the value of written records, but where reading and writing were experts' skills, to one in which writing and especially reading were used over much wider areas of human activity, including entertainment and self-education, and by more people, including some of the labouring poor.[30] More of the labouring poor gained reading skills in the next few years thanks to the charity schools. Thus eighteenth-century England showed many characteristics of a literate society, that is, one relying on widespread circulation of information and ideas through writing. It was, of course, run by literates for literates, but at the same time it was admitting more newcomers to the literates (for example the charity school pupils) than it was admitting to the establishment, thus giving more people the benefit of literacy in their communities, families, employment and faith, without thereby giving them entitlement to political power. Traditionalists were apprehensive that power was what the educated lower orders would resent being deprived of and come to demand. In the end the chronology was actually narrowly reversed, the 1870 Education Act being a rapidly necessary consequence of the extension of political enfranchisement in the 1867 Reform Act.

    The estimates of literacy based on signatures may be cautiously low, and it may be significant that when scholars concentrate on specific areas, or consider previously unused types of evidence, they seem to discover better than average situations, compared with the generally established picture. Three examples are Spufford's work on Cambridgeshire, Joan Simon's on Leicestershire, and R. A. Houston's on the North of England. The indirect evidence does suggest an impressive amount of literacy about, but one has to remember that for a large number of people, labouring in the countryside and low skilled workers in the towns, reading and writing were 'purely academic', above their heads and concerns. Studying Cambridgeshire villages, Margaret Spufford realised children below yeomen class could hardly be spared for the inessential fripperies of education, and that any focus on peasants' sons penetrating higher education was less important than the question of the extent of basic literacy among the mass of the villagers. Considering the evidence for village schoolmasters, however, she concludes the Cambridge peasantry should have had ample, if erratic, educational opportunities, and the literacy rates should have been fairly high if they were well enough off to take up the opportunity. There is a huge problem of terminology here, which has to be discussed since its emotiveness colours historians' interpretations. How are rural inhabitants appropriately classified in early modern England? Who were peasants? Who were yeomen? Sir William Petty's estimate of the distribution of social classes in England in 1696 ignored these terms, preferring freeholders of the better sort (an estimated 40 000 families with £84 yearly income), freeholders of the lesser sort (140 000 families, with £50 income), farmers (150 000 families with £40), labouring people and outservants (364 000 families with £15 income) and cottagers and paupers (400 000 with £6 10s income).[31] The analysts of literacy by social class are agreed that yeomanry fit below the gentry and generally well clear of the husbandmen, though less distinctly, apparently, in the far north. Spufford is firmly of the opinion that it was the yeomanry and above who could generally spare their children for any education, and that reading remained only of marginal importance below the yeomanry. So it is fairly important to know who these yeomen were, and where they stood. Spufford regards them as peasants, as is clear from her comment: 'amongst the peasantry, only sons of yeomen had much chance of appearing in grammar school or college registers'.[32] She writes of leaseholding yeomen, and classes Bunyan's father as a declining yeoman. The 1543 ban on bible reading supports this case, by including yeomen with artificers, journeymen, husbandmen and labourers, and women. By contrast, Houston, commenting on the rather more generously comprehensive understanding of the term 'yeoman' in the North, points to the legal definition of the term as 'a forty shilling freeholder', and refers to 'a notion of prosperous farmers which is usually implied by the term'. This is in agreement with Cressy's placing of yeomen as landed freeholders with a parliamentary vote, a socially superior class.[33] There is even more room for confusion when the terminology is a translation: *ingenuus* has been translated both as 'gentleman' and 'yeoman'. The problem with the yeomanry is that it was a class in transition, in the fifteenth century a term for gentlemen serving in a royal or noble household, later a small farmer, commonly a freeholder, immediately below a gentleman, later still any small farmer or countryman above a labourer. In Sir Thomas Wilson's *The State of England* (1600) he claimed to know many yeomen in different areas able to spend £300–£500 a year, and some two and three times this much. Their sons, significantly, tripped off to the inns of court and chancery, scorning to be called other than gentlemen. [34] (Even Spufford cites the case of yeoman Nicholas Butler's son Thomas (d. 1622) who styled himself 'gentleman' and had been at Gray's Inn.) Wilson estimated that there were 10 000 yeomen of the richest sort in 1600 and 80 000 yeomen of meaner ability called freeholders in England and Wales. The term yeoman is either so changeable, or so elastic, as to be of no abiding value. Nor do the other terms from which it distinguishes itself help much in trying to draw the social class boundaries. The husbandman is clearly a lower level of working farmer than the yeoman, arguably from the existence of the 'husbandland' of two oxgangs (about twenty-six acres), the descendant of the medieval manorial virgator (with about thirty acres). On this definition of the husbandman, the consideration of Bunyan's father, credited with nine acres, as a yeoman at all, even if one in decline, shows clearly how some members of the yeoman class had sunk well down the level once technically beneath them. The trouble with the term peasantry, overarching these definitions, is that it is looking at people from a different perspective. The word derives originally from locale. The peasant is a countryman or rustic; the term itself pays no attention to the legal and thence social distinction between freehold and villein (later copyhold, later still leasehold) tenure. Yeomen and husbandmen seem to have emerged in the Middle Ages one each side of the freehold/non-freehold line, with all its social nuances. But the line became blurred: tenurial conditions changed and wage labour began replacing labour services and, by our period, the term defies definition. No definition is right or wrong, but the interpreter's inclination colours the emergent picture, and is critical in educational history, for if we count yeomen as peasants we get more apparently upwardly mobile literates from that class than if we do not.

Definitions set aside, Spufford's Cambridgeshire study provides some concrete examples of educational progress in the countryside. Willingham's inhabitants endowed a school by public subscription in 1593, even cottagers giving odd shillings. As probably three-quarters of the subscribers could not sign themselves, this was generous and optimistic investment to give others better chances, and the school went on to produce 'a large number of fully literate villagers'. Fifteen per cent of Willingham wills were signed between 1600 and 1690, though hardly any had been before. Seventy-four per cent of the commoners signed an agreement in 1677–78, those who could not sign being either women or the least well-off men. Although thatchers are classed among the least literate, a thatcher John Tylbrooke of Snailwell left his son an English bible in 1620, and a Willingham chandler John Carter left a son and daughter bibles in 1648. A Trumpington yeoman had ten books in his 'study' in 1669.[35] So a close study of Cambridgeshire produces evidence conducive to a more optimistic estimate of rural literacy than the general assumptions.

Similarly, Joan Simon's study of conditions in Leicestershire showed a more vigorous continuation of educational activity in a time of supposed national stagnation after the Restoration, and devalued the specifically charity-school activity there by showing how many of its claimed achievements were already in train. Houston looking at the North, and particularly the North-East, of England after the Reformation saw clear improvements there in the late seventeenth and early eighteenth centuries, and raises the point that the changing illiteracy profile derived from assize court evidence might prove to have characterised other areas too if similar material is reviewed there. However, might one influence on far northern English education have been an example across the Border?

6

THE BROADER PERSPECTIVE: THE BRITISH ISLES, WESTERN EUROPE AND NORTH AMERICA

The educational patterns in early modern England have now been investigated in some depth, and to place them in perspective it is desirable to consider the situation in the rest of the British Isles, in countries of western Europe, and finally briefly in North America, where European educational traditions were taken by settlers in the seventeenth century.

The most important factor here is the shared educational history of medieval Europe. Viewed from a different perspective, the racially distinctive peoples of western Europe were the common worshippers of western, or Latin, Christendom. Their religion, before the Reformation, gave them a common culture, and membership of an international organisation which expected to be represented in individual countries by agents who could communicate in the church's language of Latin. Consequently each country needed to train cosmopolitan Latinists for high church office; these could correspond with Rome and their peers elsewhere, and travel on church, and indeed state, business using the same tongue for international diplomacy. The English educational system in place at the start of the early modern period was simply the form of western Christian church education which had developed here. Much the same basic situation existed in other countries of western Europe and in the rest of the British Isles, where it had come from western Christianity rather than through particularly English pressure or example.

Scotland

Education in Scotland has long enjoyed a good reputation. The Scots have been seen as a people who particularly value education and its availability for all students capable of advancing through it, regardless of their class of birth, or certainly more regardless of this factor than has been the case in England. Recent critical investigation of the subject has, however, diminished the glory of Scotland's somewhat legendary educational system. There is nevertheless still plenty of achievement to record, and it is very largely the achievement of this particular early modern period.

Lowland Scotland had been part of the Roman Empire but it was Latin Christianity, not imperial rule, which had the lasting effect on Scottish education. Scotland, like England, underwent pagan Viking attack, and lowland Scotland was occupied by Normans after their conquest of England, so the influences on Scottish education were fundamentally the same as those in England. However, the Scottish terrain made for greater communication difficulties, and divided the country into highland and lowland zones characterised by different economies and social arrangements. (This makes generalisations about Scotland even less valid than generalisations about England.) One of the big differences was the existence of two languages, lowland Scots, similar to English, and Gaelic. At the end of the Middle Ages, Scotland, a self-governing kingdom, did not have a particularly strong educational system. It did have three universities, at St Andrews (1410), Glasgow (1451) and Aberdeen King's College (1496). It had grammar and song schools in the main burghs and some smaller towns such as Musselburgh and Brechin, all south and east of the highland zone, and also in insular Kirkwall. There was also a tradition of private tuition among the aristocracy, and internal teaching within the religious orders. The Scottish church as part of western Christendom used Latin, so the educational structure evolved as in England, focused on the teaching and learning of Latin grammar, and at university on the theology and philosophy common to the West. Lowland Scotland reflected the imprint of Anglo-Norman influences, including the importation of some features of English common law, but compared with other western European countries there was a striking lack of professional legal education outside church circles, tied up with the absence of a centralised judicial system until the Court of Session emerged in the late fifteenth and early sixteenth centuries.

Neither the church nor royal government had much penetrated the Highlands, and Scotland emerged from the Middle Ages as two nations, Lowlands and Highlands. This posed particular problems for educationists in our period. Before 1750 few highlanders had more than a smattering of English, except for the clan chiefs and their relations; churches in the Highlands were few and parishes immensely unwieldy. Set against these problems what could be done was limited, and what was achieved was immense.

The Scottish Reformation from the 1560s took an ambitious stance on education. The reformers, led by John Knox, wanted a school in every parish and Latin grammar schools in every burgh, with colleges teaching logic, rhetoric and languages in every notable town. However, there seems to have been little advance before 1600. The distribution of schools in the countryside was patchy, often depending on the minister himself teaching. Old schools were maintained in the burghs and some new ones established. The Universities of St Andrews and Glasgow were reformed in the 1570s, Edinburgh University chartered in 1582, and Marischal College founded in Aberdeen in 1593. In the seventeenth century, after the Union of Crowns (1603) but before the Union of Parliaments (1707), the Scottish government backed educational developments. In 1616 the Scottish Privy Council required every parish to establish a school 'where convenient means may be had', and in 1633 the Scottish Parliament made provision to tax the landowners (heritors) to raise the necessary funding, tightening loopholes in 1646. Consequently the availability of parish schools improved greatly. By 1660 all the parishes in Dunfermline presbytery had a schoolmaster, thirteen out of fourteen in Kirkcaldy, seventeen out of nineteen in each of St Andrews and Cupar, half or more of the parishes in Ayr presbytery, and six out of eight in Ellon, Aberdeenshire.[1] However, the North and North-West Highlands may have had no parish schools, though there were schools in Inverary and Dingwall. Further activity took place in the next thirty years, and the lowland parish normally had a school by 1689. In 1696 it was formally enacted that there should be a school erected in every parish in the kingdom, with the teacher's salary met by a local tax on landholders and tenants. In the burghs the schoolmasters' salaries were met mostly from municipal funds. Around 1700 sixty-one of the sixty-five parishes in the three Lothian counties had a school, fifty-seven out of sixty in Fife and forty-two out of forty-four in Angus, and the situation was similar in the presbyteries of Aberdeen, Ellon and Turriff. However, possibly only half the parishes in Stirlingshire and Ayrshire were so equipped, and Middlebie presbytery in Dumfreisshire had no settled schoolmaster in seven of eleven parishes in 1696; Lochmaben and Paisley presbyteries were also ill provided. Virtually complete coverage had been achieved in the lowlands by 1760.[2]

Burghs, meanwhile, were legally obliged only to provide one school and one schoolmaster per parish, like rural parishes. The medieval grammar-school pattern existing in towns such as Edinburgh and Aberdeen at the start of the period provided a model and in the fifteenth and sixteenth centuries such schools fell under council funding and control. The small burgh grammar schools taught reading, writing and arithmetic, like the rural parish schools, but took more boys on to Latin (and indeed admitted boys from local parish schools to take them further). In the eighteenth century the curriculum expanded to include geography, Greek and bookkeeping, for example at Dunbar. The bigger burghs, however, put quality above quantity, vying to maintain good reputations for their grammar schools at the price of leaving large numbers of poorer inhabitants illiterate. Edinburgh is the obvious example. An investigation of elementary teaching in 1758 revealed twenty-four English schools there, two being charity and twenty-two private ('adventure') schools, the cheapest charging fees of 5s per quarter, double the rural parish school rate. The total being taught to read was 800 out of some 3000 'fit to go to school' – Smout suggests this may only mean those between six and nine years old.[3] The council, which supported the grammar school, opened four more schools, but at fees which deterred poorer parents, and this soon discouraged the Scottish SPCK from working in the city at all. Thus Edinburgh missed out on the scale of charity schooling enjoyed by early eighteenth-century London and Westminster. Smout describes the failure to provide means for making town councils provide good cheap schools like those in the countryside the 'Achilles heel' of the national system of education.[4]

However, for the middle and upper classes the burgh grammar schools offered the traditional Latin education for would-be clergy and lawyers and landed gentry, with the development of commercial subjects – mathematics, bookkeeping and modern languages – either in the curriculum or as extras, or pupils enrolled privately for tutorship in these subjects out of school. In 1746 Ayr grammar school offered three streams, classical, English and scientific. Academies modelled on the English dissenting academies were set up in some towns towards the end of the eighteenth century, the first at Perth. These ignored the classics and taught mathematics, natural science, astronomy, physics, history, chemistry, drawing, painting, geography and French.

What did all this mean? Even in the Lowlands parishes could be large, in Stirlingshire averaging three or four miles by two or three, but as much as ten by five-and-a-half at St Ninians. In a large parish it could be impossible to site a school where younger children could walk to it from every part of the parish. Moreover, large parishes had school-age populations too large for the one parish schoolmaster alone in the single parish school which the law required. (Their average pupillage was fifty to sixty.) St Ninians by 1750 had an estimated school-age population of over 1000.[5] One outcome of the numbers pressure was that there was little encouragement for children learning for more than about four years, and for girls even so long (or at all), nor was there insistence on regular attendance. Just looking at literacy, it seems unlikely therefore that the rosy belief in a Lowlands where almost everyone could read and write in the vernacular by around 1750 can be substantiated. R. A. Houston estimates about 35 per cent male illiteracy in the lowlands in the mid-eighteenth century, comparable with 40 per cent in England nationally, but 36 per cent in the four northern counties. In his view Scotland's achievements in literacy were among the best in Europe, but far from unique.[6]

In the Highlands the picture was less promising. There were few schools before the last quarter of the seventeenth century and little enthusiasm for learning. Most inhabitants spoke Gaelic, a language in which few books were printed. A Gaelic translation of the Psalms was published in 1670, but there was no New Testament translation until 1767 and no whole Bible until 1801. The parishes were huge: Glenorchy sixty miles by twenty four, Killmalie sixty by thirty, though some were only the size of large lowland parishes, for example, Drymen, Stirlingshire, nine miles by seven. In these unwieldy parishes the population was scattered fairly evenly, creating no major village focal point to site the one legally requisite parish school. By the mid-eighteenth century, however, four out of five highland parishes had some school financed by taxing landowners, and by the end of the century virtually all parishes benefited. A few had the practical sense and ability to keep several schools rather than one, perhaps each open only part of the year. The Scottish SPCK, founded in 1709, aimed to found schools to teach reading, writing, arithmetic and religious instruction. Gaelic was banned from these schools until 1766, and even thereafter not much used, as learning English was seen as one of the benefits offered to highlanders since it could open up opportunity for employment mobility. The Scottish SPCK had erected five schools by 1711, twenty-five by 1715, 176 by 1758, teaching nearly 6500, not all in the Highlands. From 1738 the Scottish SPCK also ran spinning schools (mainly for girls) which also taught reading (note the priority); there were nearly a hundred of these by the end of the century.[7] It is thought the charity schools failed to do more than keep abreast of the population increase in the later eighteenth century, and results fell far below the lowland parish system in effective literacy distribution.

In the seventeenth century Scottish children began schooling at the age of five to seven and were meant to stick at it for five years and then move to a burgh school or even directly to university, but few children of the poor stayed beyond the age of eight. The parish schoolchildren learned reading, writing and arithmetic but the main emphasis was on piety: 'godliness and good manners'. Older children learned Latin, even at some parish schools, but the Bible in English was the only reading text. There was no compulsion to attend school, though the reformers had intended it, with necessary funding for the poor, and by the end of the seventeenth century it was simply hoped ministers and kirk sessions could exert sufficient moral pressure on resisting parents to achieve full attendance. Education was not free, but it could be relatively inexpensive because of the taxing of landlords and municipal subventions. According to Smout fees rose little between 1690 and 1803, and he cites 1790s Aberdeenshire fees as typical: 1s 6d per quarter for reading and writing, 2s per quarter for Latin and arithmetic.[8] Contemporaries in the eighteenth and early nineteenth centuries boasted of the Scots' 'system' of national education and its statutorily required schools and salaried masters, which were seen as superior to England's more haphazardly provided facilities. From this superior 'system' Scottish apologists claimed a ladder of opportunity for the talented and a love of learning across social classes, easy class mixing and a literate and intelligent working class. However, provision was not sufficient to render private profit-making schools, usually of lower educational quality, unnecessary and their existence shows a demand for education in excess of the national 'system'. Robert Burns learned his literacy at John Murdoch's adventure school in Alloway, opened in 1765.

Girls' education remains more obscure. As everywhere, girls took second place. Sometimes they were sent to parish schools only because there were not enough boys for the teacher to make a living without them. When boys and girls were taught together at parish schools, they often had different lessons and the boys predominated in numbers and importance. Houston comments that the burgh school in late sixteenth-century Ayr was unusual in teaching girls to read and write. He accepts that every town of any size had a girls' academy by the mid-seventeenth century. But estimates of female literacy suggest facilities for girls only scratched at the surface. Houston's study of Scottish High Court of Justiciary depositions exposes an illiteracy rate of 81 per cent for women between 1650 and 1770, the same level as pertained in the English northern circuit assize depositions between 1640 and 1760. The percentages vary between social classes of course, professional and gentry women being well ahead of farming, labouring and servant women; even in craft and trade classes women were over 70 per cent illiterate.[9]

At the pinnacle of the Scottish education system stood its five universities, which modernised themselves over the period rather more effectively than their English equivalents. At Glasgow Andrew Melville's principalship of 1574–80 saw an advancing curriculum set up, with humanities in the first year, mathematics, cosmography and astronomy in the second, moral and political science in the third and natural philosophy and history in the fourth. Largely Aristotelian philosophy was replaced in Scotland in the eighteenth century by the more radical thinking of Francis Hutcheson, David Hume and Adam Smith. Isaac Newton's friend David Gregory and his successor as professor of mathematics at Edinburgh, Colin MacLaurin, were teaching Newtonian science long before Cambridge accepted it. Joseph Black, who became chemistry lecturer at Glasgow in 1756, and professor at Edinburgh in 1766, discovered carbon dioxide. In the eighteenth century Edinburgh acquired four chairs in law, a faculty of medicine, a chair in rhetoric and four chairs in science – chemistry, natural history, astronomy and agriculture. Even Oxford's authoritative history has to admit that eighteenth-century Oxford could not rival Leiden or Göttingen, Edinburgh or Glasgow, as a centre of intellectual dynamism.[10] Instruction by regents who took each class through all subjects over its four years was abandoned at Edinburgh in 1708 and everywhere except King's College Aberdeen by 1753. Latin lectures were first replaced by English by the philosophy professor at Glasgow in 1729. Edinburgh expanded from about 400 students in the late seventeenth century to about 1300 at the end of the eighteenth, but Glasgow only had 250 in 1696. Students began university study younger than in England, aged about fourteen. There was considerable student recruitment from England after the Union of 1707, especially from the dissenting academies, some of whose tutors were Scottish university graduates. Despite the vaunted ladders of opportunity, 'lads o' pairts' at university were often ill prepared and failed to graduate, but the lower middle-class students seem to have benefited in a way their peers in England did not.

Overall, even with its legendary reputation exposed, Scotland emerges extremely creditably for its educational activities over the period. Its universities showed greater willingness to be up-to-date than England's, Edinburgh looking to Leiden as a model, and some alumni moved, obviously adequately prepared, to studies on the Continent; its middle classes benefited from grammar schools with wider opportunities to reach outwards into commercial subjects and upwards into the universities, and its poorer classes also benefited, initially in the Lowlands from the parish school system, later in the educationally challenging Highlands with the Scottish SPCK's charitable provision. The institutional achievement is obvious, and the cultural achievements of individuals demonstrable in the high peaks of philosophers (David Hume, Adam Smith), architects (Robert Adam and his brother John), scientists (John Napier, Joseph Black) and writers (Robert Burns), middle-ranking men applying new technological processes, and the much commented-upon enthusiasm of mere peasants for literacy.

Wales

Wales had been part of the Roman Empire, but as with Scotland and England it was the Latin Christian church, not imperial government, which had the lasting influence on education there. Impressively, Latin scholarship was kept alive by the British church in Wales when it was lost in England during the Anglo-Saxon invasions from c.450. Like Scotland, Wales was affected by the Vikings, and like lowland Scotland it was penetrated by the Norman conquerors of England. Unlike Scotland, however, it was never a single self-governing kingdom; only under Llywelyn ap Gruffydd was there a single recognised Welsh ruler, but even his power was strongest in his Gwynedd base, and his principality an unstable federation which Edward I succeeded in toppling in 1282. From this date Wales was bound more closely to England, and while some resistance was offered when opportunities arose, a Welsh squirearchy salvaged the local administration for itself by co-operation with Westminster. Anglo-Welsh political relations adversely affected the Welsh educational situation because many top appointments in Welsh administration – justiciars, chamberlains and sheriffs – and in the church went to men of English birth and education, speakers and writers of English and Latin. So Welsh natives had fewer opportunities of advancement to inspire them to undertake, or provide, education. Moreover, unlike the lowlanders of Scotland but in common with the highlanders and native Irish, the Welsh had a non-Germanic language of their own, but the Act of Union of 1536 imposed English as the language of courts and administration.

The basic substructure of European education existed in medieval Wales in the church's grammar schools, mainly found at cathedrals, for example St David's, and St Asaph's, and other leading churches, for training clergy, in monasteries for the novitiate, and in elementary and song schools often associated with chantries. The fifteenth century seems to have been a poor time for Latin learning and culture in Wales, and while Scotland acquired three universities in that century, Wales had none. Consequently, and right through the early modern period, Wales lacked that crowning tier of institutional education. Not only were its most academically ambitious natives forced to go to universities elsewhere, and perhaps tempted not to return, but they were also attracted to the London inns of court for legal education – some ninety were admitted there between 1570 and 1610.[11] Oxford was the nearest university, and had sufficient Welsh intake for Welshmen to be identified *en bloc* in medieval student riots; in 1571 Hugh Price, a clergyman from Brecon, founded Jesus College there for Welshmen. In Cambridge, specific scholarships for Welshmen were established at St John's College.

There was, however, a flourishing if inward-looking native culture in Wales, within which poetry, prose, genealogy, heraldry, history, Welsh law and music were handed down among cultured laymen. The Welsh language was never the tongue only of the comparatively uneducated, though it was their language too. This made for an additional complication to Welsh education.

In the sixteenth century the Tudor policy was to anglicise Wales by disregarding difference. Latin grammar schools were founded, for example at Brecon (1541), Carmarthen (Lloyd's 1543, Queen Elizabeth's 1576), Abergavenny (1543), Bangor (1557/61), Presteigne (1565) and Ruthin (1574/95). These schools taught Latin grammar and literature, and a little Greek. The founders were usually anglicised Welshmen, successful careerists, eager to open up ladders behind them for other local boys, exactly the motives of many successful provincially-born Englishmen at the same period. The schools paralleled English schools of the time. The statutes of Bangor were drawn up in 1568 with the advice of Alexander Nowell the catechist, Dean of St Paul's and formerly headmaster of Westminster School. Ruthin was founded by Gabriel Goodman, Dean of Westminster. Goodman, who regularly conducted the periodical examination of Merchant Taylors' pupils, modelled Ruthin on Westminster, giving it 120 pupils in six forms of progressive Latin, with Greek in the last three. Leading Welsh landowners sent sons to Shrewsbury, or further afield to Westminster or Eton: for the elite in both countries the educational aims and curricula were the same. Scholars at the Welsh grammar schools were deterred from speaking Welsh, as indeed English pupils were from using their vernacular. However, circumstances in Wales were more complicated as there were two vernaculars in contention. The Act of Union declared that all justices, commissioners, sheriffs, coroners, escheators, stewards and their lieutenants, and all other officers and ministers of the law should proclaim and keep their various sessions and courts in English. All oaths of officers, juries and inquests and all other affidavits, verdicts and wagers of law should be in English, and henceforth no persons using Welsh speech or language should have or enjoy any office or fees within the realm of England, Wales or other dominions of the king on pain of forfeiting them, unless they used English. So whereas the ambitious English could hold office at various levels with mastery of their native tongue and, for the elite, Latin, the native Welsh speaker had to learn English also in order to get on in society. The whole history of Welsh education is coloured by this problem, for at all times with the best of intentions, various Welsh educationists have disagreed, some defending the teaching and learning of English (citing the advantages of career mobility and access to a wider range of printed literature) and others Welsh (citing the impracticability of teaching children to read in a language they did not understand, and fearing a cutting-off from cultural heritage consequent upon allowing the language to lapse). Where the translation of Latin works into English could only be seen in England as opening them up to those literate in English, similar translation

into Welsh could be seen as, in making the works available to Welsh
language literates, discouraging such readers from learning to read
them in English, a more liberating enterprise in the long run, since so
much more was available in print in English than in Welsh. Furthermore, throughout our period, the language situation presented Welsh
educationists with the problem of children beginning schooling with
different starting points. In areas which were monoglot Welsh-speaking
the children needed teaching in Welsh, or, where English was prescribed for their 'improvement', they at least needed some explanation
in Welsh. Where English was already widespread in a district the children might arrive at school either English-speaking or bilingual. By the
time they reached grammar school they were expected to translate
Latin into and out of English, not Welsh.

Works had been translated into Welsh, and of course initially composed in it, in the Middle Ages and continued to be so throughout the
period. Dr William Morgan's Welsh Bible in 1588 was a folio edition for
parish churches rather than for private reading; the 1630 'small Bible'
was for personal reading. The Cambridge Calvinist William Perkins's
Foundation of Christian Religion (1590) was translated into Welsh by
Robert Holland around 1617 and again by Evan Roberts in 1649, and
Roberts, with Oliver Thomas, produced a Welsh catechism in 1640.
These are mere examples.

As in England and Scotland, the Reformation, and particularly Puritan influences, impelled an urgency into education in order to improve
popular faith. The Act for the better Propagation and Preaching of the
Gospel in Wales (1650) had immediate educational consequences. The
overthrown Church of England's property and emoluments in Wales
were vested in commissioners who were to appoint public preachers, at
£100 per annum, to parishes, and to recommend 'fit persons of
approved piety and learning' to be employed in educating children in
piety and good literature, on salaries of £40 per annum. Some sixty free
schools were organised. One at Wrexham taught Latin and Greek, one
at Lampeter Latin and English. There was support for founding a
Welsh university but it came to nothing, and the Restoration swept the
experiment away, but others followed. Thomas Gouge founded the
Welsh Trust in 1674, to teach poor children reading, writing and religion, and to furnish adults with the Bible and other books of piety and
devotion in their mother tongue. The work of the Trust illustrates
clearly the conflict over language in Welsh education, for its schools
taught poor children English, but its publications were in Welsh, giving

priority to the salvation of adult Welsh speakers through their own language. At the same period dissenting academies sprang up in Wales as in England, and some individuals moved freely between them. James Owen, a pupil of Queen Elizabeth's Grammar School Carmarthen before studying under Samuel Jones of Chirk, sometime fellow of Jesus, who taught young men at Brynllywarch after ejection in 1662 from his parish of Llangynwyd, was a tutor himself at Oswestry Academy and later at Shrewsbury; his brother Charles became a tutor at Warrington. The early dissenting academies, Welsh and English, used Latin, and when in the eighteenth century Latin was replaced by vernaculars as the medium of academic education, the Welsh academies, significantly, changed over to instruction in English, not Welsh.

English, not Welsh, was also the medium of the charity schools in south Wales, but schools in the north used Welsh, which, interestingly, was also used over the border in Herefordshire, in Ross-on-Wye and Weobley.[12] As in England the Charity School 'movement' was the work of the SPCK. Whereas Scotland waited till 1709 to set up its own society, Wales was from the start in the sphere of the London-based society, and indeed Welsh interests were prominent in its establishment. Four of the five founders were Welshmen or closely connected with Wales: Dr Thomas Bray, Sir Humphrey Mackworth, Mr Justice Hooke and Colonel Colchester. The SPCK's charity schools in Wales slide smoothly into place between the Welsh Trust schools (thirty of the first schools were set up in places which had had Welsh Trust schools) and the circulating schools set up from the 1730s by Griffith Jones of Llanddowror, rector of Laugharne c.1709–16, who had earlier been a curate and SPCK teacher. Sixty-eight SPCK schools had been founded in Wales by 1715; none was founded after 1727. The Society produced literature for its schools throughout Britain and was broadminded enough to reprint Welsh works first published by the Welsh Trust, new translations, and new works in Welsh. It appointed Moses Williams to edit the new Welsh Bible (1718) and its second edition (1727). Ten thousand copies of the 1718 edition were printed and sold, testimony to a sizeable Welsh-reading bible-buying public.

The circulating schools were a practical solution to the challenges of teaching literacy to a poor, largely agricultural clientele. The schools were held for three months, usually in winter in the 'off season' for farming. They taught using the local vernacular: Welsh in predominantly Welsh areas, English in predominantly English-speaking areas. It was reported that up to two-thirds of the scholars of the circulating schools were adult men and women, the masters teaching them for three to four hours in the evening after the day school, in which fewer scholars had been taught. The system had a brilliant flexibility. It wasted no money on building, adopting barns and outhouses and even churches for its short usage. The teaching was offered for one three-month course, take it or leave it, a concentration of opportunity which made people jump to the chance of taking it while it was there. The teachers were ill paid – in 1737 one received 2 guineas for the quarter, but some only had £3 a year (the SPCK paid £20–£30 per annum) and some were only recruited from the schools themselves, though Jones set up a college and hostel for training them at Llanddowror. There was no shortage of willing teachers, however. The schools only taught reading and learning the catechism in the restricted time available, and sensibly utilised the local Sunday sermon for comprehension testing. The Bible, New Testament, Catechism and Psalms were the main textbooks, with works Jones wrote for the purpose. According to *Welch Piety*, the annual report of the movement, there were thirty-seven schools in existence by 1731, with 2400 scholars in different villages; 150 by 1740, with 8767. When Jones died in 1761 *Welch Piety* credited him with the teaching of 158237 pupils in 3495 schools, night scholars not counted. Jones's friend and patron Mrs Bridget Bevan of Laugharne continued his good work and in 1764 there were 297 schools, the object of inquiry by Catherine the Great. Mrs Bevan died in 1779 and her own money, with the £7000 Jones had left her for the schools, was left for their continuation, but the will was disputed, the money frozen in chancery, and the schools came to an end. The next Welsh educational experiment was the Sunday school movement, but this is out of our period.

Welsh education over the period, as elsewhere, advanced on two fronts: in the increase of facilities for traditional grammar schooling (in Wales's case this being the top level of institutional facility in the absence of universities and until the arrival of dissenting academies) and in the increase of facilities for spreading literacy among the poor, a rich seam complicated by the existence of the Welsh language. Girls had no place in the grammar schools, and in the literacy schools generally an inferior curriculum adding needlework, knitting, weaving or spinning to the reading, possibly writing, and religious instruction to which the boys added mathematics. At least the restricted curriculum of the circulating schools could hardly have treated females worse than males.

Ireland

Political, social and religious conditions in Ireland throughout the early modern period were even less conducive towards the emergence of any widely available standard system of education than was the case in any other part of the British Isles. Unlike Scotland, Ireland did not enter the period as a separate kingdom with its own administrators and a tradition of self-government in its relations with the English Crown, which had effected some control by 1603. Like highland Scotland and Wales, however, it had a large non-English-speaking population throughout the period. Unlike Scotland, it did not espouse the Reformation from within, but rather had it in effect unsuccessfully imposed on it from without, creating yet another grievance against the English government. Uniquely in the British Isles it housed an explosive mixture of races and cultures: the native Irish, of Celtic origin, the Anglo-Irish or Old English, descendants of the Anglo-Norman invading settlers of the late twelfth century, and the new English, introduced by Tudor plantation and the English and Scottish settlement of early seventeenth-century Ulster, whose descendants dominated the eighteenth-century Irish parliamentary commons.

Ireland had not been colonised by the Romans, but had received Latin Christianity during the fifth century and rapidly achieved high standards in saintliness and scholarship, producing two outstanding Greek and Latin scholars in the ninth century; Sedulius Scotus, and Johannes Scotus Eriugena. Thereafter Irish scholarship declined, and was certainly not helped by the Anglo-Norman invasion of the late twelfth century. Alongside the Latin scholarship in the early Irish church, passed down through monastic training, there persisted in secular society the traditional Irish culture of the bards, handed down via a form of oral poetic, historical and legal apprenticeship, often hereditary, which lasted seven to twelve years. The descendants of the bardic schools were still functioning in the sixteenth century, but most died out in the seventeenth century with the collapse of the Gaelic social system which had provided their patrons.

Pushed back towards the west by the Anglo-Normans and successive English domination of the area round Dublin, Irish learning lost contact with the rest of Europe and became inward-looking, men of learning turning to their native language and becoming increasingly marginalised as a result. Moreover the attempt to impose English government exported to Ireland the panoply of English governmental institutions and offices, and English law, and English government clerks and laymen crossed the Irish Sea to fill administrative positions. All this influenced education because of the limited opportunities for the evolution of any governing elite of Irish born and educated persons. The native Irish were politically 'beyond the Pale', and the descendants of the Normans seemed, from the English government viewpoint, unreliably inclined towards going native and scarcely more trustworthy. In the Dublin Parliament of 1541 all the peers except one were of Norman or English descent, yet only the earl of Ormonde could understand English.[13] Administrators sent over from England had been educated there, and there was no university in medieval Ireland, so all graduates had to have acquired at least that part of their education abroad. From the thirteenth century there had been Irish students at Oxford and Cambridge and from the early days at the London inns of court, and in the fourteenth century Irish medical students appeared in France and Italy. None of this promoted the development of a three-tier educational provision – elementary, secondary and higher – in Ireland itself.

The Reformation increased divisiveness. The government was Protestant but the country remained predominantly Catholic. In the educational sphere, an act of 1537 provided for the setting-up of elementary schools in each parish, with an English schoolmaster paid for by the clergyman. This was reinforced in 1696 and remained the basis of English educational policy in Ireland until 1922. The purpose was to reinforce Anglicisation and Protestantism. However, only some 200 parish schools were operating at the end of the eighteenth century. The local parish provision was supplemented by Protestant enthusiasts setting up schools voluntarily, pushing the Bible and Catechism along with English and reading, writing and arithmetic.[14] Dublin's SPCK joined the providers of education to the poor, having a hundred schools and 2000 pupils by 1717, 163 and 3000 by 1725. After 1733 the Charter Schools came into being, to take poor Roman Catholic children under ten and raise them as Protestants, primed for apprenticeship. Between 1740 and 1750 twenty schools were erected by the Incorporated Society for Promoting English Protestant Schools in Ireland, the model being Castledermot (1735). Jones refers to the Charter Schools as 'Protestant manufactories' in popish areas. The pupils were practically slaves, the boys had to grow the food and the girls cook, clean and spin. These schools earned the condemnation of John Howard (the prison reformer) in the 1780s.

While few offspring of the majority defiantly Roman Catholic population attended the parish schools or indeed the Charter Schools, many of
them gained elementary (or better) education in the 'celebrated and
mythologised' hedge schools informally taught by unlicensed teachers
against the law under hedges, and later in the eighteenth century, as the
relaxation of penalties occurred, in barns and outhouses. The term is
particularly applied to schools set up after 1750, but there were earlier
examples. Their historian P. J. Dowling cites the case of the
Jesuit Stephen Gelosse teaching in the neighbourhood of New Ross:
'when Cromwell's tyranny ceased, Father Gelosse... taught a small
school... in a wretched hovel beside a deep ditch, and there educated
a few children furtively'.[15]

Hedge schools originally met out of doors under cover of hedges
because they were illegal, and harbouring such a school would
have brought penalties on any property owner. They were highly informal, having no permanence of site and few properties like school
furniture or stocks of textbooks. The masters, moving under cover to
escape prosecution, were often the product of such schooling themselves. Dowling calls the hedge schools the most vital force in popular
education in Ireland in the eighteenth century, but 'popular' must
not be equated with either exclusively rudimentary or mainly free
education. The hedge schools taught reading, writing and arithmetic,
but many of the teachers were capable of much more, and some taught
also Latin, even Greek, to pupils seeking it. Many taught in the Irish
language in Irish areas, and there emerged from them quite a few
scholars who had able Latin but no English. (Later the schools came to
teach English, by popular demand.) The school fees in the later eighteenth century were 1s 8d to 2s 2d a quarter for spelling, 2s a quarter
for reading, 4s 4d to 7s a quarter for arithmetic: a shilling represented
one to three days' agricultural wages.[16] Teachers were often paid in
kind, or boarded and lodged in the houses of better-off families.
Some acted as tutors in private families before and after their school
day; others interwove periods of private tutoring and hedge-school
teaching. Numbers were apt to drop in winter, with consequent fall
in income for the master. Some teachers had as many as a hundred
pupils, and an indigenous use of monitors grew up before Lancaster
and Bell invented their systems. Writing, mensuration and bookkeeping
seem to have been generally well taught. A pupil who outgrew his
master's capacity was encouraged to move in pursuit of a more distinguished master, and some of the students laid in these schools adequate

foundations for passing into continental colleges for the Irish, such as that at Salamanca.

The hedge-school phenomenon could only thrive, given its essential lack of endowment and facilities, in a society which valued the school-master's learning (supplementing his income by paying him to perform notarial duties), and generously befriended travelling poor scholars. There were no great quantities of printed textbooks in Irish available, and many of the teachers resorted to copying out texts and built up working manuscript libraries for themselves. Children were encouraged to bring the Irish equivalent of the English chapbooks and the French *bibliothèque bleue* books, the 'Burton books' (first printed in 1700) or 'sixpenny books', to practise reading, whatever the content.

The hedge schools seem unlikely to receive fair appraisal because the authorities before Catholic Emancipation viewed them as dangerous purveyors of popish religion and radical Anglophobe politics, and the authorities after 1829, as educational bureaucrats, viewed their non-standardised practices as unacceptable. Historians treat them warily. They defy generalisation. Information about them is of uneven reliability, more narrative description than archival record, and patchy in coverage. They are not classifiable by curriculum because they taught subjects to no standard syllabus; they had no clear institutional continuity, and the personality of the master had an enormous influence. This is not the sort of material a historian is trained to evaluate. On the other hand, the schools now seem praiseworthy for refreshing idiosyncrasy; they depended absolutely on forthcoming pupils, so presumably taught what people wanted, and must have conveyed a dauntless philosophy of educational determination in an environment of uncertainty, lack of facility and low material reward. At the time they attracted some Protestant children because of their educational quality, and though they did not dovetail with any system in Ireland or outside it, they started some children off on a schooling which eventually took them to continental seminaries and universities, and it is clear from this, and the interchangeability of hedge teaching with private tutoring, that the standards stood up in the outside world.

Post-Reformation secondary education in Ireland was the subject of Elizabethan legislation (1570) ordering one free school in the principal shire town of each diocese, salaries being levied from the clergy. However, only eighteen of the thirty-four dioceses had these schools, teaching only 324 pupils, in 1788.[17] James I ordered one free school in each of the counties of Armagh, Cavan, Derry, Donegal, Fermanagh and

Tyrone, the six Royal Schools, with landed endowment instead of dependence on clerical taxation. However, in 1788 all the Royal Schools were only educating a total of 211 pupils, a drop in the ocean. There were also some privately endowed grammar schools founded from the sixteenth century onwards, generally offering both classical and Protestant education. The 1788 royal commission reported 348 such schools; they included Kilkenny, a grammar school founded in 1538 and refounded in 1684 as Kilkenny College, where Swift and Congreve were educated. The Jesuits attempted both formal and informal schooling in defiance of the anti-Catholic penal laws, and an estimated 549 'popish schools' were reported in 1731.[18]

The third tier of education was installed in Ireland in 1592 with the foundation of Trinity College Dublin. In its early years some Roman Catholic students did attend, but from 1637 to 1793 both Catholics and Dissenters were banned from taking its degrees. Roman Catholics tended to go to the Continent; Dissenters to Scotland. Some twenty colleges for Irish Catholic students were founded abroad between 1582 and 1681 including Salamanca (1582, incorporated with the university in 1608), Lisbon (1595), Douai (1596), Antwerp (1600), Prague (1631), Toulouse (1660), Paris (1677) and at least four in Rome (1625, 1626, 1656 and 1677). Catholic priests in training went to the continental Irish colleges. Trinity College Dublin was modelled on Oxbridge and its classical studies compared favourably with Oxford's in the eighteenth century. Among its successful students in this period were James Ussher, the antiquarian and scholar and Archbishop of Armagh; Jonathan Swift the satirist, and Dean of St Patrick's Dublin; William Congreve the playwright, who was English-born and only educated in Ireland because his father held an army posting there; and Edmund Burke, the political philosopher. These men's careers illustrate well the equality of the best Irish education with any obtainable in the rest of the British Isles, and the mobility of career which could be enjoyed by those accepted as educated on either side of the Irish Sea. These are the levels which Lord Chesterfield doubtless had in mind in pronouncing in 1751: 'the Irish schools and university are indisputably better than ours'. Trinity men mainly entered Holy Orders but there were other career patterns. Trinity produced a medical graduate by 1616 and had a chair of medicine from 1637. In 1759 a wide range of courses was being taught – languages ancient, oriental and modern, sacred, profane and ecclesiastical history, civil and canon law, theology, mathematics theoretical and practical, botany and chemistry, logic, ethics and metaphysics, natural and experimental philosophy, Newtonian philosophy, Boyle's experimental philosophy, anatomy and oratory and criticism.[19] The library was one of the best in Europe, ultimately absorbing James Ussher's collection.

Overall, however, it must be concluded that education in Ireland in the early modern period was damagingly divisive, and more so than elsewhere. Everywhere in the British Isles we find the distinction of grammar schooling for the administrative elite and gentry, with no more than basic literacy for ordinary people and an element of 'corrective' instruction in the charity schooling of the poor. In Ireland it emerges from all the foregoing that the middle classes were rather less well-placed educationally than elsewhere in the British Isles. The best of Irish education may indeed have been good and able to hold its own in Europe, but achievement below this level was less distinguished. Then there were the complications of the Gaelic language and Roman Catholicism, much more of an educational problem when sizeable cultural groups were under assault from the state. It is estimated that two-thirds of the population were Catholic and over two million spoke only Irish at the end of the eighteenth century. Within the early modern period the antagonisms grew worse because more 'foreigners' were planted in the country, from the native Irish point of view, and the matter of religion was inextricable from both race and power. So persuading or indoctrinating Catholics with Anglican arguments was doomed because the Reformation was another aspect of the hated Tudor Irish policy, and the resentment of the plantations in Ulster was made worse because of sympathy for the earls who had fled in 1607. Relations between Catholics and Protestants were embittered by mutual suffering of massacres at each others' hands in 1641 and 1649, even before the century went on to bring William III to Ireland. So uniquely in Britain, the normal institutors of educational policy, state church and lay government were imposing a language and a religion unwelcome to most of the native inhabitants, and to many of the most ancient immigrant families, and the education they wanted had to be sought either abroad or underground. Again this was divisive, for the choice was restricted: only the comparatively wealthy could get children safely educated abroad in the face of the Act to Restrain Foreign Education (1695) and the comparatively poor were left to hedge schooling. Catholics in England suffered similar penal-code disempowerment, but they were only a very small minority. Scotland and Wales had a similar language problem to Ireland's in facing a different dominant culture and policy makers, and in all three countries we can see some of the native speakers taking the pragmatic line that the language of the globally larger culture should be learned in the interests of mobility and advancement. In all three countries any willingness to be anglicised linguistically was at the same time deplored by traditionalists who feared the loss of the whole national heritage if the tongue which had conveyed it was destroyed. The pastoral nature of the Irish economy, especially west of the Shannon, gave the inhabitants very little need of English, so much more reason for resisting it. Maybe we are exaggerating the harmony in England, Scotland and Wales, but the bitterness of division in Ireland does seem to stand much more immovably in obstruction of educational co-operation and advance.

Western Europe

Particular conditions in western European countries varied widely at the end of the Middle Ages and through early modern times. Everywhere there was cultural and social stratification, with very varied availability of opportunities for individuals to cross class boundaries. Our period covers both the Reformation and the Counter-Reformation, within which Europeans gave vent to the full range of religious inclinations, from traditional Catholicism through moderate reform to extreme Protestantism. In places territory changed hands between states. These conditions all affected educational developments, yet, although there are enormous differences to bear in mind, there was a great deal of common ground. The normal situation was an illiterate majority, with a minority able to read and write in the vernacular, and a still smaller minority from this group also capable of communicating across linguistic and national frontiers in the medium of Latin, the international language of scholarship. Legacy of the Christian Middle Ages, this role for Latin, everywhere a second language which had to be formally learned, not assimilated as a mother tongue, dictated the continuation of the particular education system which had been established in the Middle Ages to teach it. The distinctive pathway for the educated elite began with a Latin grammar schooling designed to be completed over some four to six years. Besides this common inheritance of a Latin curriculum and the grammar schools to teach it, the medieval education systems also passed down the higher educational institutions, the universities, and their traditions of scholastic philosophy and theology. In turn, and with different timing, early modern education was affected by renaissance humanism, the Reformation and Counter-Reformation, and later by revolutionary scientific developments, and reached in the eighteenth century varying degrees of enlightenment and rationality.

Across western Europe the top tier of education was the university, and this particular period in its history has recently been examined in the second volume of the four-part interdisciplinary *A History of the University in Europe* (1996), edited by Hilde de Ridder-Symoens. Early modern European universities did not, overall, enjoy a good reputation among educational historians as recently as the 1980s, but they have begun to be rehabilitated. No longer viewed as decaying in these centuries, they are now credited with adapting to social necessities and demands. The study cited covers 190 universities existing and coming into existence throughout Europe in the period, but their definition varies, for example only in England and France was degree-awarding critical to their definition. Their organisation also varied, the two basic patterns, *Modus Parisiensis* (a university of masters) and *Modus Bononiensis* (student controlled) derived from medieval Paris and Bologna. Colleges were a feature of the Paris pattern and those which followed it, including Oxford and Cambridge, and the universities in this mould vested more power in, and originally gave more place in teaching to, the Masters of Arts. The Bologna pattern established more student power, and evolved salaried lectureships earlier.

Universities across Europe, then as now, were organised into faculties, though a university might possess only two or three of the basic four. Certain universities had superior reputations in a particular field: in France Paris excelled in theology; Montpellier in medicine. With only two universities at Oxford and Cambridge, England did not appreciate the distinction between internationally reputed and merely locally satisfactory universities which other western European countries experienced. In France, Paris, Montpellier and Toulouse had national and even international recruiting pull, but other universities recruited more locally. (France had seven universities by 1400, fourteen by 1600, plus Avignon and Orange, and twenty-four by 1789, five of these being the result of territorial expansion.) Salamanca was possibly the largest university in Europe towards the end of the sixteenth century, with 5000–7000 students matriculating annually – comparative figures are under 1000 for sixteenth-century Leipzig, and 5000 for Naples in 1607. Because of the ubiquity of the Latin language and the similarity of the substructure students could pursue studies in other countries than their own if they could afford the costs or gain private patronage or institutional support.

The Arts faculty offered the preparatory qualifications for going on to further study: the Arts graduate was expected to have sufficient grasp of Latin and basic philosophy to cope with the learning of civil and canon law, theology and medicine, all taught in Latin and using philosophy's disputative methods. As the period progressed some vernacular instruction entered the teaching, and new experimental and demonstrative methods for sciences. These developments can be traced from prescribed curricula and evidence of contemporary teachers' and students' notebooks, and from the provision of physical facilities such as botanic gardens, experimental laboratories and theatres for dissections. Self-respecting states needed universities to keep up an output of high-flying governmental personnel, diplomats, lawyers and top-ranking administrators and to keep up the state's reputation in the culture race. L. W. B. Brockliss's *French Higher Education in the Seventeenth and Eighteenth Centuries: a Cultural History* (1987) examines exclusively the institutionalised education of what he terms 'the liberal professional élite', and much the same focus was taken in R. L. Kagan's *Students and Society in Early Modern Spain* (1974). One development on the Continent which was not paralleled in England in this period (because of the existence from the Middle Ages of the English common law and inns of court, hardly threatened by Blackstone's lecturing on English law at Oxford in 1753) was the introduction of vernacular (customary) law studies into legal faculties previously concentrating on Roman civil and canon law. This took place in France in 1679 and in Spain in the mid-eighteenth century.

To feed adequately prepared entrants into their universities, states needed some provision of grammar schooling. Generally boys were educated either in a single grammar school which took them through to capability to begin at university, or they passed through the preliminary language and Latin literature at a grammar school, and topped this off with a couple of years of more advanced study, including philosophy training. In the German states the pattern was grammar schooling at the Latin (or particular) school, with advanced secondary schooling at the gymnasium or paedagogium. Gymnasia could be attached to a university or to particular schools or be independent: G. Strauss cites respectively Marburg, Stuttgart and Gandersheim as examples.[20] In medieval France Latin was taught in municipal grammar and cathedral schools and philosophy in the university Faculty of Arts, but there evolved, first in Paris in the mid-fifteenth century, the *collège de plein exercice* which the humanists and later the Jesuits developed to teach Latin and Greek, and later elegant French and preliminary philosophy. There were 348 of these colleges by 1789. Students began studying there at ten to twelve years of age and completed eight years in college, six years of linguistic and humanistic study (four of these specialising in grammar, then one in humanism and the last in rhetoric) and then two years of philosophy to gain the conceptual tools for further study. At this point the status of the institution began to matter acutely, since students wanting an arts degree could only be examined for the university MA if they had studied the philosophy course at a college legally affiliated to the university, and these colleges were normally limited to the university towns. In France the philosophy course had once been evenly divided between logic and ethics in the first year and physics and metaphysics in the second, but by the end of the seventeenth century it was dominated by physics, which filled the second year. In Spain, too, many of the grammar schools taught theology and the liberal arts after the basic language work, but could not award degrees. However, until 1771 courses taken in religious colleges were valid towards university degrees.

So the terminology and status of schools and universities and the overlap between them varied between countries, but the syllabus and basic levels of attainment were similar. Compare the syllabus at Leicester Grammar School in 1574 (outlined in Chapter 2) with that in German Lutheran Latin schools in the sixteenth century, culled by Strauss from a score of Latin school curricula issued between 1530 and *c*.1600. The German schools had four or five grades of advancing difficulty. In the first, beginners and students of Donatus mixed together, and by the end of the year boys were supposed to be able to read simple texts and write legibly; their reading included Cato's *Distichs* and sundry religious texts such as gospel readings and psalms and the Catechism in Latin and German. In the second grade they went on with Cato, added Aesop (in Latin), dialogues of Mathurin Cordier (after 1564), or simple colloquies of Erasmus, some Terence, and a conduct book such as Erasmus's *De civilitate morum puerilium* or Joachim Camerarius's *Precepta morum*. In some schools they began Greek. By the third year they added Melanchthon's Latin grammar and syntax textbooks, epistles of Cicero, more Terence, and Ovid, and in Greek Isocrates and the Greek gospel, music and Latin dictation. The fourth year's Greek took in Plutarch and Theognis, the Latin Horace (*Odes*) and Virgil (*Eclogues*), more Cicero, some Livy, and Erasmus's *Copia verborum*. The final year, if there was a fifth, took up the Aeneid, Melanchthon's Dialectics and Greek grammar, Hesiod, the Iliad, practice in translating from one classical language to another, and as Strauss comments, 'at long last arithmetic'.[21] Catechism study was common to all grades. Naturally the slant of the religious instruction made for differences in the texts studied and in the interpretations put upon them, and indeed in the degree of in-built tolerance or intolerance of other Christians as European states adopted Catholic or Protestant stances, but there was nothing revolutionary in the grammar-school syllabus itself. In Catholic Castile at the end of the sixteenth century largely the same classical authors were read – Caesar, Cicero, Horace, Livy, Virgil and others – and Cicero was staple fare in the French colleges. The choice of texts brought the students to some understanding of classical history and the Mediterranean world, though by about 1760 the history of modern Europe was entering the college curriculum in France.

Unlike England, Catholic Europe had the seminary for training men for the Catholic priesthood, a creation of the Council of Trent. The Society of Jesus (1534) made education a key part of its work, and established colleges and seminaries over Catholic Europe. In Spain the Jesuits, invited to take over municipal teaching by some communities, developed many colleges and schools offering a basic four- to six-year curriculum of grammar and philosophy, with theology, mathematics, geography, history, astronomy and religion, and in many of these institutions the primary reading instruction went on under the same roof. The Jesuits' teaching was free, but where boys boarded they paid fees. The Spanish educational census of 1764–67, on the eve of the Jesuits' expulsion, which precipitated an educational crisis there, showed 45 per cent of scholars attending municipal schools, 20 per cent with independent teachers, and 33 per cent at religious schools, 80 per cent of these being Jesuit.[22] The Jesuits had been popular with Spanish parents for offering a better disciplined educational institution than the universities, and with Spanish students for rather more assiduous teaching. Indeed the universities in some cases virtually abandoned arts and theology teaching to the Jesuits until their expulsion in 1767. In France, where the Jesuits were expelled in 1762, their influence had been similar: of the 348 *collèges de plein exercice* existing in 1789, 105 had been Jesuit.[23]

All European countries had vernacular literates below their professional elites and recent studies have brought out many statistics of literacy rates in different countries, small regions, town and countryside.

In France, it appears from marriage register signatures that the literacy rate overall was 29 per cent for men and 14 per cent for women around 1690, and respectively 47 per cent and 27 per cent by 1790. Women were catching up on men, but not evenly. It took a few generations for literacy, always male-led, to percolate to the other sex.[24] In late sixteenth-century Narbonne 65 per cent of the craftsmen and 20 per cent of the peasants were literate. In Marseilles between 1700 and 1730 male literacy was 50 per cent, by 1790, 69 per cent. In 1630 the male literacy rate in Amsterdam was 57 per cent, in 1780, 85 per cent. The outstanding literacy rate is found in Sweden. In the parish of Möklinta 21 per cent of both sexes were literate in 1014, but 89 per cent by 1085–94. In the diocese of Härnösand the figures were 50 per cent in 1645 and 98 per cent by 1714. In Skellefteå in 1724, 43 per cent of the population born in or before 1644 (that is, those over eighty) were literate, but 98 per cent of those born in or since 1705 (those under twenty).[25] The Swedish statistics moreover appear to be very soundly based, being the result of Swedish clergy visiting houses and testing literacy, as part of annual catechistical examinations. This process produces a more total picture than that to be gained from marriage signatures and samples drawn from the witnessing of deeds or in court, or from subscriptions to oaths, or wills.

On the whole it is agreed that literacy was higher in north and west Europe than in the South and East. Political and economic environment and religion are all reflected in the varying distribution of literacy. The European population doubled between 1500 and 1800, with an increase in commercial capitalism and communications. People living in commercial communities had a utilitarian need for and appreciation of vernacular literacy and numeracy. Consequently, in general terms, everywhere one finds literacy higher in towns. In France in the eighteenth century, rural literacy dragged about a century behind urban. In Spain the peasantry remained overwhelmingly illiterate into the twentieth century. However, the distribution is not absolutely straightforward. Kagan suggests urbanisation worked against the rise of popular secondary schooling in Spain. Seville had 620 boys enrolled in Latin schools in 1764, 6 per cent of the available age group, but La Baneza, a town of 2000 inhabitants, had two municipal masters teaching 37.5 per cent of the local boys.[26] In early Reformation Germany worries arose over the fact that vernacular schools were tempting people who were capable of more demanding Latin education (and needed by the church and state to undergo it and move on into the necessary professions) to settle for the easier, cheaper and more obviously utilitarian alternative. This leads us to the controversial point of religion and education. It is often argued that Protestants, placing higher value on the Bible and its private reading, put a premium on vernacular literacy which Catholics, staying faithful to the idea of a priest as a necessary intermediary and guide, and Latin as the language of the church, did not. The comparative literacy figures for Sweden and Spain lend credence to this view. But the diocese of Seville ordered parish priests and sacristans to teach reading, writing and arithmetic in 1512, and the Council of Trent added elementary schooling to the pastoral work of parish priests generally, and set up seminaries in dioceses. The huge educational activities of the Jesuits weigh in on the Catholic side, while there is evidence of a wariness of learning and distrust of intellectual pride in some Protestant sects such as the Baptists. Strauss's study of the indoctrination of the young in the German Reformation shows significant movement of position within the reformers, and contrasts the impressive institutional and archival achievement – the growth of schools in number and quality, the mushrooming of teaching texts (especially catechisms) and the erection of machinery for recurrent and recorded investigative inspection – with the sorry failure to achieve changes in attitude in town or countryside. Reformers' early espousal of literacy for all dampened as two unforeseen effects unfolded: Latin learning being disadvantaged, and independent bible reading beginning to look dangerous. Reformers' efforts to drill populations by catechisms in which they were indoctrinated in religious and social behaviour met with sullen non-co-operation. Redoubling the same efforts with the state's enforcement could improve behaviour but seems to have had little effect on inner piety, and children who had learned their catechism forgot nearly everything as adults. However, the religious instruction was entangled with very basic literacy – sextons were pressed to teach reading and the Catechism, or reading and writing with it, towns were well equipped with vernacular schools in the sixteenth century, and village schools were common by the 1580s and 1590s, certainly in Saxony. ABC teaching moved from letters to syllables to words, then to sentences and thus to the German catechism. Maybe the secular learning stuck better in the mind. Strauss himself adopts an optimistic assessment of German vernacular literacy without, as he admits, being able to prove it. His indirect evidence is that sixteenth-century reformers and their governments seem to have assumed heads of households would be able to read in the vernacular. Mandates and visitation directives in Protestant states assume vernacular literacy as the norm, and illiteracy as the exception, and not only in cities. (They may have been deluded, of course.) In Catholic Bavaria, where visitation officials were looking for heretical works, they found outlawed books in the possession of 'the common man' in the 1560s, and 'many peasants' owned misleading and corrupting books.[27]

In France, the parish school run by a master hired by the community with the priest's blessing, funded by rates, fees and endowment, forms what Furet and Ozouf describe as 'the central image'. Reading was taught before writing, and both before arithmetic. The elementary schools taught the Catechism, and some taught elementary Latin to prepare boys for grammar schooling. *L'escole paroissiale ou la manière de bien instruire les enfants dans les petits écoles par un prestre d'une paroisse de Paris* (1654) begins with the alphabet, then syllables from a book with the Ave, Pater and Credo, then children begin spelling whole words from a book containing the Magnificat, Nunc Dimittis, Salve Regina and the Psalms: in other words they learned the letters by use of Latin words. Moving on to the technical skill of writing, *L'escole paroissiale* concerns itself with tables, seats, penknives, ink, paper, drying powder and the actual upstrokes and downstrokes. Relevant examples were used – bills, bonds, farming leases and the like, underlining that where reading was contextualised in religion and morality, writing was a practical utility. The French elementary curriculum ended with counting and sums on paper, unless the school included elementary Latin.

Generalisations are sweeping, but certain things need not remain fragmented in our treatment of them. Western Europe, despite much difference in detail, largely explicable in the local context, faced everywhere similar educational problems, and met them in essentially similar ways. Rural peasantry needed little formal education in literacy and numeracy to survive; they could benefit from vernacular reading for pious use, and if they had gone to the struggle of learning (and its cost, in terms of both fees paid and wages foregone), could enjoy the odd chapbook – the French equivalent of the English chapbook is the 2-sou blue paperback from the seventeenth and eighteenth centuries which gives rise to the term *bibliothèque bleue*. But whether peasants had access to education, and whether they bothered to take it up, depended on many factors such as whether authority, in state or church, was pushing schooling, or a benefactor providing it locally. Sweden was vastly ahead of Spain, northern France ahead of southern (the 'north–south divide' is a line from St Malo to Geneva), towns and their environs ahead of rural backwaters. In towns there were more opportunities, partly because there were viable numbers able to be gathered together to teach, both for elementary vernacular education and Latin grammar schooling.

One could get to certain levels even of the professions without the full elite schooling, as Brockliss made clear. No one could become *curé* of a walled town, bishop, cathedral canon or collegiate dignitary in France without studying theology or canon law, or be an *avocat* or royal, or from 1680 seignorial, judge without canon and civil law, nor join the physicians' corporation to practise without being trained in medicine (and all these had to be bachelors, licentiates or doctors of a French university). There were, however, lower levels in the legal profession staffed by men who had only been trained through apprenticeship; the village *curé* needed no institutional theology qualification, and surgeons and apothecaries only began to have to attend institutionalised training in the eighteenth century. In Spain Ferdinand and Isabel ruled in 1493 that no *letrado* could have 'any office or post of justice investigator or *relator* in our council tribunals or chancelleries nor in any city town or village in our kingdom' unless he had a notarised document certifying that he had studied canon or civil law for a minimum of ten years at a university in the kingdom or foreign lands. Kagan, citing this ruling, comments that it was unique in Renaissance Europe (except for Portugal), though the full ten years was apparently not enforced.[28] Most of the German state governments supported serious academic learning in Latin schools, gymnasia, seminaries and universities as a political investment, but there was less willing financial backing for the elementary level of education, whose benefit to the state was less obvious and indeed in some eyes questionable.

Standards had to be similar if countries were to participate in international diplomacy and scholarship. Elementary literacy has to mean reading, and if one can do it in one's native language, haltingly or fluently (and hopefully the second can grow out of the first with practice, without further professional supervision), there is a basic standard about the achievement. Similarly with writing: either one can do it, again haltingly or fluently or in between, or not at all. Here there is more of a difference obviously, between persons who can write their own names, spelling them by no means necessarily consistently, and those who can copy but not compose, or compose a bill or receipt but not a long narrative letter, or a letter but not a tract. Spelling was not yet a matter of standardisation in vernacular tongues, but men were working on orthography and pronunciation. Legibility was important, but is still an educational problem!

The teaching and learning of Latin, everywhere a second language, is easily standardised as an achievement, though the effort which has to be put into it may vary as the learner's language may be Romance-based or not, making it comparatively easier or harder. However the end-product is the same: either one can understand Cicero or one cannot. The cosmopolitan mobility of university students in the early modern period, relatively greater than recent Erasmus Programme achievements, proves they could follow courses in Latin in different universities in different countries, so there must have been fairly uniform preparation. Mobility of students and staff in the European universities shows a similar interchangeability of standards. Indeed, student migration, between and within countries, is quite significant in revealing which places of study were in contemporary good repute. In Spain Alcalá, Salamanca and Valladolid had the best records for recruitment to *letrado* positions, which attracted students to them sometimes after taking their first degree at a local university. Generally movement was towards the major institutions from the lesser, though there was some movement the other way, usually motivated by the attraction of lower fees. Politics, as well as religion, made for migration and its cessation. Brockliss noted that foreign attendance at Orléans and Bourges declined after the end of the Thirty Years War in 1648. It was at university level, not at grammar school, that the most cosmopolitan mixing of students occurred. The fact that it was worthwhile to travel far within the university system underlines at once both the general equality and the specific excellence of institutions within it. In the academic ladder of arts bachelors and masters, and bachelors, licentiates and doctors of law, medicine and theology, any qualifying at any university was normally accepted as its equivalent at another; thus far an international equality of standards of learning was respected. But the sensitivity of students to the existence of institutions of better repute, where they might get a better education and a more valuable degree than where they started, is also borne out. There were universities advanced in some developments and behind in others. There were also young men furthering their education in a less structured way on the Grand Tour, some of whom did interweave short periods of formal enrolment at an educational institution, including universities and academies. Modern languages of other countries were beginning to be learnt seriously over western Europe at this time, as a product of greater communications and aided by the printing of grammars, glossaries and dictionaries.

Younger boys were sent abroad to study in boarding schools (for example with the Jesuits in Spain), or at day schools lodging with other families, related or not, but there was not much point in leaving one's country young except in the search for schooling forbidden at home, the motive for English Catholic boys going to Douai and St Omer, for example.

In a necessarily cursory sampling, the achievement of education in early modern Europe presents itself inevitably on two separate, and rather ill-bridged fronts: its academic peaks and its slow spread of literacy. In the sixteenth century the universities produced humanists, active on a cosmopolitan stage. The Italian Renaissance had elevated humanist, Latin, literary training for the cultured elite, as distinct from the largely legal professional training for civil servants and churchmen (the latter alternatively specialising in theology). Erasmus and Vives urged the ruling castes to Latinity in the Low Countries, Budé in France, Colet and More in England, Melanchthon in Germany. Spanish universities flowered early but fell into decline as early as 1620, when the peak expansion of gentry in English higher education was just beginning. In France the liberal professional elite in the seventeenth and eighteenth centuries dominated politics and literature as well as providing administrators. Brockliss makes an impressive case for the French alertness to recognising scientific discoveries, which had the unintended effect of opening up minds to rationality and utility as tests for politics too.

States, as Strauss commented, saw higher education as a political investment and over the period the universities amply justified their existence in producing bureaucrats for the top echelons of church and state. Within the universities more abstract idealists espoused the idea of furthering knowledge, and in the long term this too was achieved, but there was always at this time an inherently subversive aspect in discovery. Middling education tends to get overlooked in educational history, but must in fact have touched far more, though less influential, people. At every level the elite programme was losing students: postgraduates who could not complete their studies owing to financial stringency, mental exhaustion or disinclination; undergraduates who dropped out for a variety of reasons before completing even the BA degree; grammar-school pupils who never went on to university at all, yet progressed a fair way through the course; grammar-school students who managed only one or two years. All these had experienced, as far as they went, the kind of education described by those who have concentrated on the elite. In numbers they must have been significant, and in the jobs they held, and the communities where they lived, must have been more competent for having some formal academic schooling. Less attention has been paid to their leavening qualities in the population than it may be suspected is deserved. Below this level of education came the elementary scholars, taught to read and write and perhaps count, along with their catechisms. These were distinct enough from their illiterate contemporaries, and it is the line between these which is traced by tests of marriage registration signatures, German visitation protocols, Swedish parish visitations, court witness signatures and subscription oaths. Everywhere, too, there is the indirect evidence from the printing presses, a technological breakthrough which had occurred before our period but is one of the contributory factors in making the times 'early modern' as distinct from medieval. Biblical translation into the vernacular, and its diffusion in print, both reflected and boosted vernacular reading. Luther translated the New Testament into German in 1522 and the full Bible was available in German by 1534; the Geneva Bible in French dates from 1540, Petri's Swedish Bible from 1542. The Swedish visitations reveal bibles in one house in twenty in the eighteenth century, but catechisms in one house in five or six. Floods of catechisms were printed in both Protestant and Catholic Europe, from single-page sheets to substantial books. One limiting aspect to the spread of the printed word was cost. Luther's New Testament cost half a guilder when this was the weekly wage of a journeyman carpenter. *Bibliothèque bleue* books cost one or two sous each at a time when bread was two sous per pound, and urban workers were paid fifteen to twenty sous a week. English chapbooks, broadsheets and almanacs sold at 1*d*–2*d*. In Sweden chapbooks cost one skilling, the smallest coin in circulation.[29] It was essential to have cheap reading material if people below professionals and landed gentry were to be encouraged to read, and the production of cheap material testifies to the recognition of this and meeting of the need. Creating this readership was a real achievement, involving anonymous teachers everywhere quietly pulling more and more pupils into the literacy fold. This level of teaching had little status and small reward. It had no professional training and in some cases was a spin-off for local clergy and in others only a part-time occupation. It was no doubt well and ill done, but its cumulative achievement was extremely important, because the difference between literate and illiterate societies is fundamental, and this period encompasses when that balance changed in western Europe.

North America

As a postscript to this survey, we should glance at how colonists in North America established and ran education in their new home. In little over five generations, from the incorporation of London's Virginia Company in 1606 to the issue of the charter for Georgia in 1732, the British developed colonies on the east coast of North America, by direct foundation and by acquisition after war. By the end of our period, events were moving towards the American War of Independence, 1775–83. The educational interest within this period lies principally with first-generation colonists, who faced the task of establishing educational practices which later generations merely inherited and amended. New England draws our particular attention since we know that 85 per cent of male testators there signed their wills by 1760.[30]

The Massachusetts Bay Company, from its early days, accepted responsibility to provide ministers to preach, catechise and teach the Company's servants and their children and to extend their mission to native Americans. The teaching responsibility seems to have rested initially with the ministers of religion and it is assumed that much took place informally in their houses. Very early on, however, the townships wanted schools and specifically dedicated teachers. The Massachusetts Bay General Court in 1642 approved compulsory education (though this could be in the home) and in 1647 ordered that townships of fifty and more householders had to set up a writing and reading school, and townships of a hundred and more households a grammar school. Though there was much reliance on voluntary contributions, bequests, rents from properties granted at the outset or subsequently, and scholars' fees, taxation on the township to meet costs such as renovations to the schoolhouse lay in reserve, as is clear from the 1645 rules and orders concerning the school at Dorchester. Thus there was the germ of a compulsory education system, at public expense. In comparison with the British Isles, this is most akin to the Scottish parish-school provision, which was a legal obligation.

The style of education established in New England was a close derivative of the English, with its two levels. The elementary or common school taught literacy, some numeracy and religion to many children, and the elite grammar school taught a few boys mainly for the ministry. It never occurred to the pioneers of education in the American colonies that the old syllabus with Latin, Greek and Hebrew should be questioned as inappropriate. Rather, they quickly recognised the need to replicate an education system which would equal the standards of the Old World. In *New England's First Fruits*, published in London in 1643 as part of the fund-raising mission of Thomas Weld, Hugh Peter and William Hibbens, the foundation of Harvard College, named after its first great benefactor, the Emmanuel MA John Harvard (d. 1638), was described in terms of motivation, rules and weekly timetable. The Massachusetts Bay General Court voted £400 in 1636 to establish a school, which was the origin of Harvard. By 1643 the college already boasted a spacious hall, a large library 'with some books to it', and chambers and studies and other necessary rooms, and beside the college 'a fair grammar schoole, for the training up of young scholars, and fitting them for Academical Learning', so that 'as they are judged ripe, they may be received into the College of this School'. The students were not admitted to the college until they could understand Cicero or similar classical authors *extempore*, make and speak true Latin verse and prose, and decline perfectly paradigms of nouns and verbs in Greek.[31] Once admitted, the students followed a classical syllabus in Latin – logic, physics, ethics and politics, arithmetic, geometry and astronomy, Greek etymology and syntax, prosody and dialects, Hebrew, Chaldee and Syriac, rhetoric and divinity in the mornings, with disputations, grammar practice and style in prose and verse and bible study in the afternoons, with history (in winter) and the nature of plants (in summer).

It is not surprising that the scheme was so ambitious, for the personnel of the first generation of colonial educationalists was much influenced by its own English education. Cambridge University provided many emigrants to New England: Morrison accounts for 100 from Cambridge before 1646 and thirty-two from Oxford, three being connected with both.[32] Emmanuel College Cambridge was the most prolific college in this emigrant field. What is more surprising is that the aims were defined and fulfilled so quickly, even if the numbers were small. Harvard College was founded in the renamed Cambridge Massachusetts before the colony was ten years old. Every printed book had to be carried across the Atlantic until the first press was brought over by Jose Glover, a former rector of Sutton in Surrey in 1638; he died on the voyage, but his widow married Harvard's first president, Henry Dunster. The nascent college built its library upon John Harvard's 400-volume library, but already had books solicited as gifts from local magistrates and church elders, and further gifts were sent from well-wishers in England. Sir Kenelm Digby sent seventeen works. Morrison estimates a library of 800–900 volumes by 1655, in size, character and content similar to smaller colleges of Britain. Building had to be financed and constructed, and there was no machinery for appointment of staff: the first professor, Nathaniel Eaton, proved a disastrous choice who beat the first students (whom his wife starved through a combination of unwillingness to provide adequate food and negligence in its preparation), physically assaulted his assistant and misappropriated much funding. Harvard survived this unpropitious start, and the year's gap which followed; nine students survived to graduate in 1642. Of these, Benjamin Woodbridge, then aged twenty, had only recently come from Magdalen Hall and returned there to take his MA in 1648; George Downing, aged nineteen, later returned to England to a New Model Army chaplaincy, membership of parliament, an embassy and a baronetcy; Henry Saltonstall went on to Padua to take his MD and became fellow of New College, and Samuel Bellingham studied later in Leiden and practised as a physician in London. No more striking testimony need be sought of the acceptance of this fledgling university's degrees as equal to their European equivalents. Oxford University expressed this unequivocally by admitting James Ward, AB 1645 to a BA by incorporation and an MA in 1648.[33] Of the modern prestigious American 'Ivy League' foundations, five have their origin in this period, besides Harvard: Yale (1701), Princeton (1746), Columbia (1754) and Dartmouth (1769). The College of William and Mary at Williamsburg dates from 1693. Trinity College Dublin is seen as something of a precedent for colonial university colleges.

At the secondary level, Harvard's feeder school was not the first Latin grammar school in New England, the honour claimed by Boston Latin School. A school was founded at Boston in 1635, and the appointment of the Emmanuel MA Daniel Maude in 1636 removes doubt that it might only have been an elementary school. Other grammar schools quickly followed, for example Dorchester (1639) and Roxbury (1645). These schools and the higher educational colleges were only for boys throughout our period. The common reading and writing schools took children of both sexes to thirteen or fourteen. Private elementary schools also existed, and Lockridge thinks it may have been private elementary education which began raising female literacy in the mid- and late eighteenth century.[34]

The basic teaching followed the contemporary English pattern, with primer, Psalter, Testament and Bible in use as early reading texts. The speller eventually drove out the primer, and through its varied contents furthered introductory understanding of arithmetic and geography. G. E. Littlefield's somewhat whimsical study of schoolbooks in New England underlines the close and enduring relationship with the mother country before Independence. While there were few presses on American soil, many textbooks had to be imported, but significantly the next step was to print editions of these in America, before texts by American-born authors began to be printed. Littlefield examines a wide range of schoolbooks, elementary and advanced, including some self-teaching manuals. In 1700 'Strongs spelling bookes' and 'Youngs spelling bookes' were listed in the inventory of the stock of the Boston bookseller Michael Perry, and are identifiable in a London catalogue of schoolbooks in general use in 1766.[35] Trusted books were published in many places. The Quaker George Fox's *Instructions for Right Spelling*... came out in London in 1673; subsequent editions followed there, and in Dublin, Boston and Newport. The emigrant publisher Benjamin Harris composed and issued *The New England Primer* in Boston in 1690, described by Littlefield as 'the most popular textbook of colonial or provincial times'. (Incidentally, a native language version of the primer was printed in Cambridge (Massachusetts) in 1669, translated by the Rev. John Eliot, a BA of Jesus College Cambridge, who emigrated in 1631.)[36]

All the arithmetic books used in colonial schools in the seventeenth century Littlefield believed imported from England. The first published arithmetic textbook by an American author is identified by Littlefield as Isaac Greenwood's *Arithmetick Vulgar and Decimal*... (Boston, 1729). The author was the first Hollisian professor of mathematics and natural and experimental philosophy at Harvard, 1727–37. Littlefield notes that a tenth edition copy of John Ward's *The Young Mathematician's Guide*..., including algebra, geometry and conic sections, published in London in 1758, survives with the inscription 'John Marrett's book 1763', Marrett being a Harvard graduate in the class of that year. It was an octavo volume of 495 pages published at £3 10s.[37]

English and Latin grammar texts crossed the Atlantic and works imported included Brinsley's *Latin Accidence* (1611), Hoole's edition of Corderius's *School Colloquies* (1652), *The Rudiments of the Latin Grammar*... (1659) and *The Common Accidence Examined and Explained*... (1695). Cheever's *Short Introduction to the Latin Tongue*... published in Boston in 1709, was popular for a century. The 'Famous Mr Ezekiel Cheever' of the title page had been born in London in 1614 and educated at Christ's Hospital. Emigrating to New England, he taught at New Haven, Ipswich, Charlestown and Boston's Latin School, where his grandson was appointed his assistant in 1699 at a salary of £40 per annum. He died in 1708. Possibly his son or grandson brought the work out; it went on being published until 1838. William Camden's Greek grammar, published originally in 1597, was only superseded at Harvard in 1800. Hebrew grammars from continental and London presses preceded the first one written in America, for Harvard use, by Judah Monis, an Italian, in 1735.

Latin, Greek and Hebrew held their own as the classical languages for scriptural textual study, but there was obviously less use for the French language among the English colonists of America, so that area of English upper-class education was much less developed. Many of the other schoolbooks discussed by Littlefield were of English origin as publications. They go to show that the colonists had no radical break to make with traditional educational patterns. For their new school buildings they built schoolhouses of similar proportions to English ones. The dimensions of Boston's Latin schoolhouse of 1704 were 40' by 25', which may be compared with Ashbourne's and Burnsall's. The colonists also kept much the same school hours, 7 a.m. to 5 p.m. or 8 a.m. to 4 p.m. according to season, with a break from 11 a.m. to 1 p.m. However these circumstances are only the cosmetic surface; the similarity of the curriculum is much more important, with consequent free movement of scholars with common level of attainment between the Old World and the New.

Just as we can compare the schooling, we can compare the literacy rates. Lockridge's study of literacy in colonial New England, based on will signatures, postulates a 60 per cent male literacy rate in 1660, 70 per cent by 1710 and 85 per cent by 1760. For women, a third of the will makers dying before 1670 could sign, rising up to 45 per cent thereafter. Lockridge believes that migration to New England brought there an unusually high proportion of artisans, merchants and professionals. The first-generation settlers were more literate than the overall English population from which they came, and Lockridge draws attention to Connecticut's particular attraction of well motivated re-emigrants from Massachusetts and 'highly commercialised Puritans from London'.[38] Connecticut and Massachusetts appear to have attracted more literate migrants than New Hampshire, and the early rank order of literacy of the colonies was still visible around 1710. The school laws should have increased at least the male literacy levels, but it appears they did not become noticeably influential until the initially dispersed population became more concentrated in the eighteenth century.

In his attempt to place New England literacy in comparative perspective, Lockridge displayed not dissimilar (two-thirds) male literacy in Pennsylvania and Virginia by the early eighteenth century, but this did not continue improving like New England's did. Partly their improvement came of other colonies attracting increasingly literate migration, and not only from England, while New England's immigration tailed off. Lockridge cites a 75 per cent male literacy rate in Dutch migrants to New York around the middle of the seventeenth century, and a 73 per cent male literacy rate in Germans arriving in Pennsylvania in the 1720s.[39] Believing Protestantism to be the key motivating variable behind New England's higher literacy, Lockridge naturally ends by looking at Calvinist Scotland and Lutheran Sweden (where uniquely both sexes achieved high literacy) for comparison. Thus we return to the need for an overview focus of western education, and the transatlantic situation makes a useful end point here, since it integrates, not surprisingly, with its European origins.

7

CONCLUSIONS

The educational situation towards the end of the early modern period in England seems much closer to us than that pertaining at its beginning, a sign of the degree of 'modernisation' occurring during the timespan. In 1500 the educational institutions we can trace were for the elite and dominated by Latin: endowed grammar schools and universities. Even great scholars, however, had to begin by learning individual letters, and we know that the elementary learning of letters and then word reading in the vernacular was quite as far as some children got, some obviously informally taught. Each level was in its own way utilitarian, the elite for professionals, the more basic for 'mechanical arts and worldly business'.

During the sixteenth and early seventeenth centuries there seems to have been a dilution of the utilitarian focus in elite education, as the concept of the liberally educated gentleman acquiring learning for its own sake, to display unnecessary but elevating elegance and style, blossomed. This resulted in men using the universities and inns of court as social finishing schools, but fell away in the later seventeenth century, leaving the universities again more professionally orientated. Simultaneously there was probably an unprovable increase in the utilitarian applicability of the more practical education: unprovable because it took place in unrecorded, often informal ways, but likely because there was clearly more demand for vernacular literacy (reading and writing) and numeracy, just to staff the expanding and increasingly complex and commercial world. We can use literacy estimates to 'prove' more people

192

could read and write, without being able to prove they learnt these skills for utilitarian purposes, but it is likely that they did so, though admittedly some of the pressure for them to learn came from churchmen more interested in saving souls than in training shopkeepers.

The period between the end of the Middle Ages and the eve of the Industrial Revolution was undoubtedly one of educational expansion. It was a period of population growth, so educational facilities would have had to expand just to stand still. That they did more is clear from the improved literacy rates of men and women. That basic literacy among ever more of the population was not all that was achieved is clear from the margins above basic literacy shown by the marketing of vernacular books of great variety, including purely entertainment reading such as novels and poetry. A reader might struggle with *The Merchant's Avizo* for career purposes, or a version of the Catechism out of piety, but reading 'penny merriments' must surely have been for enjoyment. Way above that level was the readership of such English masterpieces as the works of Milton, Dryden, Pope or Swift, and way above that the readership for Newton's *Principia* (in Latin).

Though Stone's educational revolution only admitted some 2.5 per cent of the male age group to higher education, and this tailed off in the eighteenth century, that level of education was indeed a splendid achievement and a galaxy of cultured men who could hold their own with the best of any age emerged. No such obvious cluster of women springs to mind, but recent work has revealed numerous post-Restoration women writing for publication. The point about them, however, is that no education 'system' can take credit for their achievements; each was taught in her own unique circumstances, by male relatives, brothers' tutors or generous employers, despite the lack of serious institutional facilities for girls (a deficiency recognised by some women, for which they urged remedies).

There is no need to judge English education on its elite institutions and then criticise their exclusiveness. Their achievements stand and we should remain in awe of them: the quality of modern English prose is crude by comparison, and today's students' modern language difficulties give rise to concern. At the other edge of the spectrum there is no need to focus on the limited teaching of basic literacy and express dismay at its lack of compulsion or universality. Religious fervour drove some states to attempt both features in this period, but it is hardly a matter for criticism that England was not one of them. The motives for such enforcement in this period were rarely liberating or democratic.

Overall, English education may be considered to have been in a fairly healthy state in this evolutionary period. It was modernising, most obviously in its use of the more widely communicative vernacular. It embraced elements of both tradition and novelty, a fair number being combined in the dissenting academies. Already founded on social division, it did not particularly aim to be socially divisive. There were ladders of opportunity, at least for boys, though perhaps less than in Scotland, myths notwithstanding. There was no precise system and categorising has to be general, for example, apprenticeship embraced a multitude of arrangements, from the trainee goldsmith to the parish apprentice drudge. Though we can see extension in the provision of facilities, there was no steady educational progress in England chronologically over the period, nor equality of opportunity across the country at any one moment, and both class and gender obstructed equality. There was obviously a lack of overseeing direction: English education seems to have developed largely unsupervised, with no dominant planners, though plenty of theorists, and comparatively little government intervention. This at least minimised the making of educational policy mistakes! At all times education had good and bad features, efficient and dreadful teachers, co-operative and unyielding pupils. On balance, despite the continuous stream of lamentations that the teaching 'profession' (if such it may then be called) was financially underpaid and socially undervalued, lamentations with which teachers in subsequent generations have been wryly able to identify, the willingness of teacher–authors to nail their credentials to their title pages suggests rather better contemporary repute than has often been assumed.

English education has interest viewed alone, but our understanding of it is much strengthened by wider comparison with other parts of the British Isles and with parts of Europe and North America. The openness of the top layer has long been apparent, through the existence of scholars who attended and taught at universities in different countries, aided by the common language of universally taught Latin. More recent work on the less glamorous levels of education has begun to make informed comparison of different societies possible. So, for example, we can begin to see how education in the Cambridgeshire countryside as displayed by Spufford corresponds and contrasts with French rural education. A most valuable input has come from Sweden, where literacy preceded institutional schooling, a healthy reminder that 'the school', which is so dominant in English education today, has not always been everywhere the only purveyor of education worth serious consideration. Since the temptation in reviewing early modern education is so often to look for aspects we can identify as shared with us, it is also essential that we pay attention to those features which make us realise this is not yet our world, though a good deal closer to us than the situation in 1500 was.

NOTES AND REFERENCES

1 Introduction

1. D. Cressy, *Literacy and the Social Order: Reading and Writing in Tudor and Stuart England* (Cambridge, 1980), pp. 62–103; M. Spufford, *Small Books and Pleasant Histories: Popular Fiction and its Readership in Seventeenth-Century England* (Cambridge, 1981), p. 27; K. Thomas, 'Numeracy in early modern England', *Transactions of the Royal Historical Society*, 5th ser., 37 (1987), 103–32.
2. E. Hughes, *North Country Life in the Eighteenth Century: The North-East 1700–1750* (London, 1952), pp. 106–7.
3. D. Cressy, *Education in Tudor and Stuart England* (London, 1975), p. 96.
4. J. Jacobs, ed., *Epistolae Ho-Elianae: The Familiar Letters of James Howell*, III (London, 1892), pp. 523–4; Spufford, *Small Books*, p. 27.
5. Spufford, *Small Books*, pp. 30–2.
6. B. Hill, ed., *The First English Feminist: Reflections upon Marriage and Other Writings by Mary Astell* (Aldershot, 1986), pp. 143, 162. (The quotations are from *A Serious Proposal to the Ladies for the Advancement of their True and Greatest Interest*, Part I, 3rd edn, London, 1696.)

2 Outline of Developments

1. D. Cressy, *Education in Tudor and Stuart England* (London, 1975), p. 29.
2. J. Lawson, *A Town Grammar School through Six Centuries* (London, 1963), p. 15.
3. D. R. Leader, *A History of the University of Cambridge, I, The University to 1546* (Cambridge, 1988), p. 290.
4. J. McConica, 'The Rise of the Undergraduate College' in McConica, ed., *The History of the University of Oxford, III, The Collegiate University* (Oxford, 1986), p. 21 n. 4.
5. J. H. Moran, *The Growth of English Schooling 1348–1548: Learning, Literacy and Laicization in pre-Reformation York Diocese* (Princeton, 1985).
6. A. D. Grounds, *A History of King Edward VI's Grammar School Retford* (Worksop, 1970), p. 13.
7. J. N. Miner, *The Grammar Schools of Medieval England: A. F. Leach in Historical Perspective* (Montréal/Kingston, 1990), pp. 4, 263; J. Lawson, *Medieval*

Education and the Reformation (London, 1967), p. 76; Moran, *Growth of English Schooling*, pp. 237–9.

8. J. E. Neale, *Elizabeth I and her Parliaments 1559–81* (London, 1953), p. 99.
9. Cressy, *Education*, p. 7.
10. F. Watson, *The English Grammar Schools to 1660: their Curriculum and Practice* (Cambridge, 1908), pp. 491–3; E. N. Jewels, *A History of Archbishop Holgate's Grammar School, York 1546–1946* (York, 1963), p. 13.
11. M. C. Cross, *The Free Grammar School of Leicester* (Leicester, 1953), pp. 15–20, 26–7.
12. The quotations in this and the following paragraph are all from L. Stone, 'The Educational Revolution in England, 1560–1640', *Past and Present*, 28 (1964), 41–80.
13. Cressy, *Education*, pp. 8, 10.
14. D. Cressy, *Literacy and the Social Order: Reading and Writing in Tudor and Stuart England* (Cambridge, 1980), pp. 86, 2.
15. W. G. Bittle and R. T. Lane, 'Inflation and Philanthropy in England: a Re-Assessment of W. K. Jordan's Data', *Economic History Review*, 2, 29 (1976), 203–10.
16. See, for example, a bequest of 1402 in J. Raine, ed., *Testamenta Eboracensia*, I (London, 1836), p. 296. See also E. Russell, 'The Influx of Commoners into the University of Oxford before 1581: an Optical Illusion?', *English Historical Review*, 92 (1977), 721–45.
17. Cressy, *Literacy*, p. 38.
18. McConica, 'Rise of the Undergraduate College', p. 50.
19. Cross, *Free Grammar School*, p. 49.
20. M. Spufford, *Contrasting Communities: English Villagers in the Sixteenth and Seventeenth Centuries* (London, 1974), p. 189.
21. Stone, 'Educational Revolution', p. 63; T. G. Barnes, *Somerset 1625–1640: a County's Government During the "Personal Rule"* (Cambridge, Mass., 1961), p. 31.
22. A. C. F. Beales, *Education under Penalty: English Catholic Education from the Reformation to the Fall of James II 1547–1689* (London, 1963), pp. 56, 72.
23. Cross, *Free Grammar School*, p. 21.
24. J. Morgan, *Godly Learning: Puritan Attitudes towards Reason, Learning and Education 1560–1640* (Cambridge, 1986), pp. 165–6.
25. Cressy, *Education*, p. 23.
26. *Ibid.*, pp. 101–2.
27. J. I. Cope and H. W. Jones, eds, *History of the Royal Society by T. Spratt* (St Louis/London, 1959), p. 53.
28. I. Roy and D. Reinhart, 'Oxford and the Civil Wars' in N. Tyacke, ed., *The History of the University of Oxford, IV, Seventeenth-Century Oxford* (Oxford, 1997), pp. 711, 730; B. Worden, 'Cromwellian Oxford' in *ibid.*, p. 759.
29. J. Simon, 'Post-Restoration Developments: Schools in the County 1660–1700' in B. Simon, ed., *Education in Leicestershire, 1540–1940: A Regional Study* (Leicester, 1968), pp. 27–8, 35–6, 38, 32–3.
30. Beales, *Education under Penalty*, p. 230.
31. Cressy, *Literacy*, pp. 172, 176.

32. D. Gardiner, *English Girlhood at School: a Study of Women's Education through Twelve Centuries* (London, 1929), p. 245.
33. Cross, *Free Grammar School*, pp. 38–9.
34. J. Simon, 'Was there a Charity School Movement? The Leicestershire Evidence', in Simon, ed., *Education in Leicestershire*, p. 66–7, 78.
35. M. G. Jones, *The Charity School Movement: a Study of Eighteenth-Century Puritanism in Action* (Cambridge, 1938), p. 61.
36. R. A. Houston, 'The Development of Literacy: Northern England 1568–1800', *Economic History Review*, 2nd ser., 35 (1982), 199–216.
37. I. Pinchbeck and M. Hewitt, *Children in English Society, I, From Tudor Times to the Eighteenth Century* (London, 1969), p. 242.
38. *Ibid.*, pp. 135–6, 245–6.

3 The Aims of Education

1. A. B. Cobban, *The Medieval English Universities: Oxford and Cambridge to c. 1500* (Aldershot, 1988), p. 399.
2. J. Raine, jun., ed., *Wills and Inventories from the Registry of the Archdeaconry of Richmond* (Durham/London/Edinburgh, 1853), p. 28.
3. A. F. Sutton and L. Visser-Fuchs, 'The Provenance of the Manuscript: the Lives and Archive of Sir Thomas Cook and his Man of Affairs John Vale' in M. L. Kekewich, C. Richmond, A. F. Sutton, L. Visser-Fuchs and J. L. Watts, eds, *The Politics of Fifteenth-Century England: John Vale's Book* (Stroud, 1995), p. 105.
4. A. F. Leach, ed., *Early Yorkshire Schools*, ii (Yorkshire Archaeological Society, Record Series, 33, 1903), p. 122.
5. B. Varley, *The History of Stockport Grammar School*, 2nd edn (Manchester, 1957), p. 24; A. F. Leach, *The Schools of Medieval England* (London, 1915), p. 245.
6. W. K. Jordan, *The Social Institutions of Lancashire: a Study of the Changing Patterns of Aspirations in Lancashire 1480–1660* (Manchester, 1962), p. 37.
7. A. R. Myers, ed., *The Black Book of the Household of King Edward IV* (Manchester, 1959), pp. 126–7.
8. Cited in F. Watson, *The English Grammar Schools to 1660: their Curriculum and Practice* (Cambridge, 1908), p. 199.
9. A. Fraser, *The Weaker Vessel: Women's Lot in Seventeenth-Century England* (London, 1989), p. 155.
10. Watson, *Grammar Schools*, pp. 263, 264.
11. E. Hughes, *North Country Life in the Eighteenth Century: the North-East 1700–1750* (London, 1952), pp. 342, 360–1, 364–5; *North Country Life in the Eighteenth Century, II: Cumberland & Westmorland, 1700–1830* (London, 1965), pp. 293–5, 311–14, 298.
12. H. M. Jewell, 'A Notion of True Learning', *National Register of Archives Annual Report and Bulletin of the West Riding Northern Section*, 6 (1963), 14–20.
13. W. R. Prest, *The Inns of Court under Elizabeth and the early Stuarts 1590–1640* (London, 1972), p. 39; Prest, 'The English Bar, 1550–1700' in Prest, ed.,

Lawyers in Early Modern Europe and America (London, 1981), p. 70; D. Duman, 'The English Bar in the Georgian Era' in *ibid.*, pp. 91–3.

14. E. W. Ives, 'The Common Lawyers' in C. H. Clough, ed., *Profession, Vocation and Culture in later Medieval England* (Liverpool, 1982), p. 210.
15. J. E. Neale, *Queen Elizabeth* (London, 1934), pp. 25–6.
16. *Ibid.*, p. 26; Fraser, *Weaker Vessel*, p. 33.
17. Fraser, *Weaker Vessel*, p. 503; O. Moscucci, *The Science of Women: Gynaecology and Gender in England 1800–1929* (Cambridge, 1990), p. 9.
18. R. O'Day, 'The Anatomy of a Profession: the Clergy of the Church of England' in W. Prest, ed., *The Professions in Early Modern England* (London, 1987), pp. 30–1; J. H. Pruett, *The Parish Clergy under the Later Stuarts: the Leicestershire Experience* (Urbana/Chicago/London, 1978), p. 23.
19. Pruett, *Parish Clergy*, pp. 42–3.
20. H. Kearney, *Scholars and Gentlemen: Universities and Society in pre-Industrial Britain 1500–1700* (London, 1970), p. 99.
21. P. Williams, 'From the Reformation to the Era of Reform, 1530–1850' in J. Buxton and P. Williams, eds, *New College Oxford 1379–1979* (Oxford, 1979), p. 64.
22. P. K. Orpen, 'Schoolmastering as a Profession in the Seventeenth Century: the Career Patterns of the Grammar Schoolmaster', *History of Education*, 6, 3 (1977), 193.
23. M. V. C. Alexander, *The Growth of English Education 1348–1648: a Social and Cultural History* (Philadelphia/London, 1990), pp. 193, 195.
24. R. Greaves, 'Religion in the University 1715–1800' in L. S. Sutherland and L. G. Mitchell, eds, *The History of the University of Oxford, V, The Eighteenth Century* (Oxford, 1986), p. 401.
25. Pruett, *Parish Clergy*, p. 40.
26. L. Stone, ed., *The University in Society, I, Oxford and Cambridge from the 14th to the Early 19th Century* (Princeton, 1975), p. 39; Pruett, *Parish Clergy*, p. 36.
27. B. P. Levack, 'The English Civilians, 1500–1750' in Prest, ed., *Lawyers*, p. 115.
28. Prest, 'Lawyers' in Prest, ed., *The Professions*, p. 69.
29. *Ibid.*, p. 10; Duman, 'The English Bar' in Prest, ed., *Lawyers*, p. 89.
30. Prest, *The Inns of Court*, p. 131. Prest's detailed account is the basis of the following paragraphs.
31. *Ibid.*, pp. 52, 10.
32. *Ibid.*, pp. 141–2.
33. *Ibid.*, p. 237.
34. B. P. Levack, *The Civil Lawyers in England 1603–1641: a Political Study* (Oxford, 1973), p. 3. For later developments see his 'English Civilians', pp. 108–25, his 'Law' in N. Tyacke, ed., *The History of the University of Oxford, IV, Seventeenth-Century Oxford* (Oxford, 1997), pp. 557–68, and J. L. Barton, 'Legal Studies' in Sutherland and Mitchell, eds, *The Eighteenth Century*, pp. 593–605.
35. C. Hill, *Intellectual Origins of the English Revolution* (Oxford, 1965), pp. 83–4.
36. J. Vanes, *Education and Apprenticeship in Sixteenth-Century Bristol* (Bristol, 1982), p. 24.

37. A. J. Willis, compiler, and A. L. Merson, ed., *A Calendar of Southampton Apprenticeship Registers 1609–1740* (Southampton, 1968), nos 44, 292, 397, 443.
38. Moscucci, *Science of Women*, pp. 8–9.
39. D. Cressy, *Birth Marriage and Death: Ritual and Religion and the Life Cycle in Tudor and Stuart England* (Oxford, 1997), p. 61.
40. R. T. Gunther, *Early Science in Cambridge* (Oxford, 1937), p. 251.
41. G. Lewis, 'The Faculty of Medicine' in J. McConica, ed., *The History of the University of Oxford, III, The Collegiate University* (Oxford, 1986), p. 250; R. G. Frank, jr, 'Medicine' in Tyacke, ed., *Seventeenth-Century Oxford*, pp. 506, 508, 510, 513; C. Webster, 'The Medical Faculty and the Physic Garden' in Sutherland and Mitchell, eds, *The Eighteenth Century*, p. 683.
42. Gunther, *Science*, p. 293.
43. *Ibid.*, pp. 223, 303.
44. *Ibid.*, p. 305.
45. M. Pelling, 'Medical Practice in Early Modern England: Trade or Profession?' in Prest, ed., *The Professions*, pp. 102–5.
46. M. Spufford, *Contrasting Communities: English Villagers in the Sixteenth and Seventeenth Centuries* (London, 1974), p. 189.
47. Quoted in D. Cressy, *Education in Tudor and Stuart England* (London, 1975), p. 72.
48. D. Cressy, 'A Drudgery of Schoolmasters: the Teaching Profession in Elizabethan and Stuart England' in Prest, ed., *The Professions*, p. 135.
49. *Ibid.*, p. 140.
50. Cressy, *Education*, p. 65.
51. *Ibid.*, pp. 67–8; M. G. Jones, *The Charity School Movement: a Study of Eighteenth-Century Puritanism in Action* (Cambridge, 1938), pp. 100–1.
52. J. W. A. Smith, *The Birth of Modern Education: the Contribution of the Dissenting Academies 1660–1800* (London, 1954), p. 54.
53. D. W. Sylvester, ed., *Educational Documents 800–1816* (London, 1970), pp. 246–7.
54. Willis and Merson, eds, *Southampton Apprenticeship*, nos 5, 179, 226.
55. *Ibid.*, nos 408, 433.
56. Hughes, *North Country Life 1700–1750*, p. 106.
57. Willis and Merson, eds., *Southampton Apprenticeship*, pp. xxxvi-viii, liii-iv.
58. *Ibid.*, nos 83, 164, 461, 464.
59. *Ibid.*, nos 196, 230.
60. *Ibid.*, nos 852, 860, 858, 918.
61. *Ibid.*, nos 903, 904.
62. *Ibid.*, nos 962, 757, 760, 761, 784, 785, 822, 855, 912, 941.

4 Educational Facilities

1. N. Orme, *English Schools in the Middle Ages* (London, 1973), p. 66.
2. I. Pinchbeck and M. Hewitt, *Children in English Society, I, From Tudor Times to the Eighteenth Century* (London, 1969), pp. 149–51, 153–4, 118–19.

3. I. K. Ben-Amos, *Adolescence and Youth in Early Modern England* (New Haven/London, 1994), pp. 55–6.
4. M. G. Jones, *The Charity School Movement: a Study of Eighteenth-Century Puritanism in Action* (Cambridge, 1938); J. Simon, 'Was there a Charity School Movement? The Leicestershire Evidence' in B. Simon, ed., *Education in Leicestershire, 1540–1940: A Regional Study* (Leicester, 1968), pp. 55–100.
5. J. L. Axtell, ed., *The Educational Writings of John Locke: a Critical Edition with Introduction and Notes* (Cambridge, 1968), p. 256.
6. *Ibid.*, pp. 259, 260, 262–4.
7. D. Cressy, 'A Drudgery of Schoolmasters: the Teaching Profession in Elizabethan and Stuart England' in W. Prest, ed., *The Professions in Early Modern England* (London, 1987), pp. 130–1.
8. M. Seaborne, *The English School: its Architecture and Organization 1370–1870* (London, 1971), pp. 17, 25, 42, 49, 68, 74; W. K. Jordan, *The Charities of Rural England 1460–1660: the Aspirations and the Achievements of the Rural Society* (London, 1961), pp. 314, 303, 322.
9. Seaborne, *English School*, p. 13; M. C. Cross, *The Free Grammar School of Leicester* (Leicester, 1953), p. 15; J. H. Brown, *Elizabethan Schooldays: an Account of the English Grammar Schools in the Second Half of the Sixteenth Century* (Oxford, 1933), pp. 99–100; Seaborne, *English School*, p. 81.
10. J. Lawson, *A Town Grammar School through Six Centuries* (London, 1963), p. 17; Orme, *English Schools*, p. 125; Seaborne, *English School*, pp. 19, 64, 100 n. 27.
11. Axtell, ed., *Educational Writings*, pp. 269, 276–8, 281–4.
12. Brown, *Schooldays*, p. 107; E. J. Dobson, *English Pronunciation 1500–1700: I, Survey of the Sources* (Oxford, 1957), p. 125.
13. N. Orme, 'Schoolmasters 1307–1509' in C. H. Clough, ed., *Profession, Vocation and Culture in later Medieval England* (Liverpool, 1982), p. 224, and *English Schools*, p. 275; M. V. C. Alexander, *The Growth of English Education 1348–1648: a Social and Cultural History* (Philadelphia/London, 1990), pp. 196–7; R. O'Day, *Education and Society 1500–1800: the Social Foundations of Education in Early Modern Britain* (London, 1982), p. 172; Seaborne, *English School*, p. 89.
14. H. Blodgett, *Centuries of Female Days: Englishwomen's Private Diaries* (Gloucester, 1989), p. 184.
15. E. Gibbon, *Memoirs of my Life and Writings*, bicentenary edn, ed. A. O. J. Cockshut and S. Constantine (Keele, 1994), p. 69.
16. Axtell, ed., *Educational Writings*, pp. 289, 290.
17. D. Gardiner, *English Girlhood at School: a Study of Women's Education through Twelve Centuries* (London, 1929), p. 245.
18. T. Smith, ed., *English Gilds* (London, 1870), p. 209.
19. Ben-Amos, *Adolescence and Youth*, p. 112.
20. *Ibid.*, pp. 47, 44, 62, 84, 86–7, 88, 89–90.
21. A. J. Willis, compiler, and A. L. Merson, ed., *A Calendar of Southampton Apprenticeship Registers 1609–1740* (Southampton, 1968), nos 389, 390, 391, 400, 426.

22. G. Edelin, ed., *The Description of England by William Harrison* (Ithaca, 1968), pp. 70–1.
23. M. Feingold, 'The Humanities' in N. Tyacke, ed., *The History of the University of Oxford, IV, Seventeenth-Century Oxford* (Oxford, 1997), pp. 211–357.
24. L. Stone, 'The Size and Composition of the Oxford Student Body' in Stone, ed., *The University in Society, I, Oxford and Cambridge from the 14th to the Early 19th Century* (Princeton, 1975), p. 37.
25. V. H. Green, *A History of Oxford University* (London, 1974), pp. 118, 113.
26. V. H. H. Green, *The Commonwealth of Lincoln College 1427–1977* (Oxford, 1979), pp. 198, 389.
27. D.A. Winstanley, *The University of Cambridge in the Eighteenth Century* (Cambridge, 1922), p. 6.
28. I. G. Philip, 'Libraries and the University Press' in L. S. Sutherland and L. G. Mitchell, eds, *The History of the University of Oxford, V, The Eighteenth Century* (Oxford, 1986), p. 731.
29. H. McLachlan, *English Education under the Test Acts: being the History of the Nonconformist Academies 1662–1820* (Manchester, 1931), pp. 145, 177; J. W. A. Smith, *The Birth of Modern Education: the Contribution of the Dissenting Academies 1660–1800* (London, 1954), p. 172. These works are the source of the information in the following paragraphs.
30. Smith, *Birth of Modern Education*, p. 154.
31. *Ibid.*, p. 224.
32. D. W. Sylvester, ed., *Educational Documents 800–1816* (London, 1970), p. 241.
33. J. Stow, *Survey of London*, 1603 edn, ed. C. L. Kingsford (Oxford, 1908), pp. 76–7.
34. C. W. Brooks, 'The Common Lawyers in England *c.*1558–1642' in W. Prest, ed., *Lawyers in Early Modern Europe and America* (London, 1981), p. 53.
35. S. B. Chrimes, ed., *Sir John Fortescue: De Laudibus Legum Angliae* (Cambridge, 1949), p. 119.
36. W. Prest, *The Inns of Court under Elizabeth and the early Stuarts 1590–1640* (London, 1972), pp. 28–30, 45. This book is the principal source of information in this and the following paragraphs.
37. *Ibid.*, pp. 165–6, 205.
38. *Ibid.*, p. 168; D. Duman, 'The English Bar in the Georgian Era', in Prest, ed., *Lawyers*, p. 87.
39. Axtell, ed., *Educational Writings*, p. 324.
40. J. B. Black, *The British and the Grand Tour* (London, 1985), p. 155.
41. C. V. Wedgwood, *Thomas Wentworth first Earl of Strafford 1593–1641: a Revaluation* (London, 1961), pp. 24–6.
42. Black, *Grand Tour*, p. 228.
43. T. Kelly, *History of Adult Education in Great Britain*, 2nd edn (Liverpool, 1970), p. 21.
44. *Ibid.*, p. 55.
45. *Ibid.*, p. 45.

5   Educational Achievements

1. L. Stone, 'The Educational Revolution in England, 1560–1640', *Past and Present*, 28 (1964), p. 79.
2. R. T. Gunther, *Early Science in Cambridge* (Oxford, 1937), p. 313.
3. H. Kearney, *Origins of the Scientific Revolution* (London, 1964), pp. 69, 36.
4. J. Todd, *A Dictionary of British and American Women Writers 1660–1800* (London, 1987), p. 1.
5. Quoted in R. Perry, *The Celebrated Mary Astell: an Early English Feminist* (Chicago/London, 1986), p. 219.
6. Todd, *Dictionary*, p. 334.
7. Cited in J. Dover Wilson, *Life in Shakespeare's England* (Harmondsworth, 1959), pp. 77–8.
8. E. Gibbon, *Memoirs of my Life and Writings*, bicentenary edn, ed. A. O. J. Cockshut and S. Constantine (Keele, 1994), pp. 72–3.
9. J. L. Axtell, *The Educational Writings of John Locke: a Critical Edition with Introduction and Notes* (Cambridge, 1968), pp. 281–4.
10. Dover Wilson, *Shakespeare's England*, p. 93.
11. Gibbon, *Memoirs*, p. 78.
12. Axtell, ed., *Educational Writings*, p. 197.
13. *Ibid.*, pp. 268, 295.
14. Gibbon, *Memoirs*, pp. 184–5, 193, 85.
15. M. Feingold, 'The Humanities' in N. Tyacke, ed., *The History of the University of Oxford, IV, Seventeenth-Century Oxford* (Oxford, 1997), p.216.
16. Stone, 'Educational Revolution', pp. 60–1.
17. M. Spufford, *Contrasting Communities: English Villagers in the Sixteenth and Seventeenth Centuries* (London, 1974), pp. 177, 179.
18. Cited in H. Blodgett, *Centuries of Female Days: Englishwomen's Private Diaries* (Gloucester, 1989), p. 54.
19. Todd, *Dictionary*, p. 232.
20. H. S. Bennett, *English Books and Readers 1558 to 1603 being a Study in the History of the Book Trade in the Reign of Elizabeth I* (Cambridge, 1965), p. 148; *English Books and Readers 1603 to 1640 being a Study in the History of the Book Trade in the Reigns of James I and Charles I* (Cambridge, 1970), p. 108.
21. H. S. Bennett, *English Books and Readers 1457 to 1557 being a Study in the History of the Book Trade from Caxton to the Incorporation of the Stationers' Company*, 2nd edn (Cambridge, 1969), p. xiii.
22. Gibbon, *Memoirs*, pp. 122 3.
23. Axtell, ed., *Educational Writings*, Appendix 3.
24. Gibbon, *Memoirs*, p. 72.
25. Perry, *Celebrated Mary Astell*, Appendix B, pp. 339–54.
26. D. Cressy, *Literacy and the Social Order: Reading and Writing in Tudor and Stuart England* (Cambridge, 1980), pp. 176, 2.
27. *Ibid.*, pp. 131–5.
28. P. Burke, *Popular Culture in Early Modern Europe* (London, 1978), p. 263.
29. Spufford, *Contrasting Communities*, pp. 208–9.

30. M. Spufford, *Small Books and Pleasant Histories: Popular Fiction and its Read-ership in Seventeenth-Century England* (London, 1981), pp. 93, 101, 122, 129–47, xviii, 12, 15.
31. A. Hughes, *Seventeenth-Century England: a Changing Culture, I, Primary Sources* (London, 1980), pp. 6–7.
32. Spufford, *Small Books*, p. 21.
33. R. A. Houston, 'The Development of Literacy: Northern England 1640–1750', *Economic History Review* 2, 35 (1982), 205; Cressy, *Literacy*, p. 124.
34. Hughes, *Seventeenth-Century England*, p. 2.
35. Spufford, *Contrasting Communities*, pp. 173–4, 191, 193–200, 209, 211.

6   The Broader Perspective: the British Isles, Western Europe and North America

1.   T. C. Smout, *A History of the Scottish People 1560–1830* (London, 1987), p. 82.
2.   *Ibid.*, pp. 424–5.
3.   *Ibid.*, p. 440.
4.   *Ibid.*, p. 443.
5.   *Ibid.*, p. 425.
6.   R. A. Houston, *Scottish Literacy and the Scottish Identity: Illiteracy and Society in Scotland and Northern England, 1600–1800* (Cambridge, 1985), pp. 56, 22.
7.   M. G. Jones, *The Charity School Movement: a Study of Eighteenth-Century Puritanism in Action* (Cambridge, 1938), p. 179; Smout, *Scottish People*, pp. 434–5.
8.   Smout, *Scottish People*, p. 430.
9.   Houston, *Scottish Literacy*, pp. 65, 57.
10. L. G. Mitchell, 'Introduction', in L. S. Sutherland and L. G. Mitchell, eds, *The History of the University of Oxford, V, The Eighteenth Century* (Oxford, 1986), p. 1.
11. J. L. Williams and G. R. Hughes, eds, *The History of Education in Wales*, I (Swansea, 1978), p. 26.
12. *Ibid.*, p. 48.
13. J. J. Auchmuty, *Irish Education: a Historical Survey* (Dublin/London, 1937), p. 37.
14. Jones, *Charity School Movement*, pp. 224–6.
15. R. F. Foster, *Modern Ireland 1600–1972* (London, 1988), p. 208; P. J. Dow-ling, *The Hedge Schools of Ireland* (London, 1935), p. 18.
16. Dowling, *Hedge Schools*, p. 77.
17. Auchmuty, *Irish Education*, p. 59.
18. *Ibid.*, p. 66.
19. *Ibid.*, p. 133.
20. G. Strauss, *Luther's House of Learning: Indoctrination of the Young in the Ger-man Reformation* (Baltimore/London, 1978), p. 315 n. 81.
21. *Ibid.*, pp. 188–9.

22. R. L. Kagan, *Students and Society in Early Modern Spain* (Baltimore/London, 1974), pp. 56–7.
23. L. W. B. Brockliss, *French Higher Education in the Seventeenth and Eighteenth Centuries: a Cultural History* (Oxford, 1987), p. 22.
24. F. Furet and J. Ozouf, *Reading and Writing: Literacy in France from Calvin to Jules Ferry* (Cambridge, 1982), pp. 24, 26.
25. P. Burke, *Popular Culture in early modern Europe* (London, 1978), pp. 251–2; J. Boli, *New Citizens for a New Society: the Institutional Origins of Mass Schooling in Sweden* (Oxford, 1989), p. 130.
26. Kagan, *Students and Society*, p. 48.
27. Strauss, *Luther's House of Learning*, p. 128.
28. Kagan, *Students and Society*, p. 71.
29. Burke, *Popular Culture*, pp. 223–6; 254.
30. K. A. Lockridge, *Literacy in Colonial New England: an Inquiry into the Social Context of Literacy in the Early Modern West* (New York, 1974), p. 13.
31. S. E. Morrison, *The Founding of Harvard College* (Cambridge, Mass./London, 1935), pp. 432, 433.
32. *Ibid.*, Appendix B, pp. 357–410.
33. *Ibid.*, pp. 261–2, 349.
34. Lockridge, *Colonial New England*, p. 58.
35. G. E. Littlefield, *Early Schools and Schoolbooks of New England* (New York, 1904), p. 121.
36. *Ibid.*, pp. 147–52.
37. *Ibid.*, pp. 204–5.
38. Lockridge, *Colonial New England*, p. 47.
39. *Ibid.*, p. 74.

FURTHER READING

This further reading section comprises a wide selection of works, old (but still classic, or once significantly seminal) and new. Some works cited in the endnotes have not been listed here because they are of limited use, or only a small part of them is relevant to the topic. Some important works appear under more than one heading, but in general they are only listed where most appropriate.

Introductory and General Works

Alexander, M. V. C., *The Growth of English Education 1348–1648: a Social and Cultural History* (Philadelphia/London, 1990).

Charlton, K., *Education in Renaissance England* (London, 1965).

Cressy, D., *Education in Tudor and Stuart England* (London, 1975).

Cressy, D., *Literacy and the Social Order: Reading and Writing in Tudor and Stuart England* (Cambridge, 1980).

Fraser, A., *The Weaker Vessel: Women's Lot in Seventeenth- Century England* (London, 1989).

Gardiner, D., *English Girlhood at School: a Study of Women's Education through Twelve Centuries* (London, 1929).

Hill, B., ed., *The First English Feminist: Reflections upon Marriage and Other Writings by Mary Astell* (Aldershot, 1986).

Jewell, H. M., '"The Bringing up of Children in Good Learning and Manners": a Survey of Secular Educational Provision in the North of England, c.1350–1550', *Northern History*, 18 (1982), 1–25.

Jones, M. G., *The Charity School Movement: a Study of Eighteenth-Century Puritanism in Action* (Cambridge, 1938).

Kamm, J., *Hope Deferred: Girls' Education in English History* (London, 1965).

Lawson, J., *Medieval Education and the Reformation* (London, 1967).

Lawson, J. and Silver, H. eds, *A Social History of Education in England* (London, 1973).

Leach, A. F., *English Schools at the Reformation, 1546–8* (London, 1896).

Leach, A. F., *Educational Charters and Documents 598–1909* (Cambridge, 1911).

Moran, J. H., *The Growth of English Schooling 1348–1548: Learning, Literacy and Laicization in pre-Reformation York Diocese* (Princeton, 1985).

O'Day, R., *Education and Society 1500–1800: the Social Foundations of Education in Early Modern Britain* (London, 1982).

Orme, N., *English Schools in the Middle Ages* (London, 1973).

Orme, N., *Education in the West of England 1066–1548* (Exeter, 1976).

Orme, N., *Education and Society in Medieval and Renaissance England* (London, 1989).

Pinchbeck, I. and Hewitt, M., *Children in English Society, I, From Tudor Times to the Eighteenth Century* (London, 1969).

Simon, J., *Education and Society in Tudor England* (Cambridge, 1966).

Spufford, M., *Small Books and Pleasant Histories: Popular Fiction and its Readership in Seventeenth-Century England* (London, 1981).

Stephens, W. B., *Education, Literacy and Society 1830–70: the Geography of Diversity in Provincial England* (Manchester, 1987).

Sylvester, D. W., ed., *Educational Documents 800–1816* (London, 1970).

Outline and Developments

Barnes, T. G., *Somerset 1625–1640: a County's Government during the "Personal Rule"* (Cambridge, Mass., 1961).

Beales, A. C. F., *Education under Penalty: English Catholic Education from the Reformation to the Fall of James II 1547–1689* (London, 1963).

Charlton, K., *Education in Renaissance England* (London, 1965).

Cressy, D., *Education in Tudor and Stuart England* (London, 1975).

Cressy, D., *Literacy and the Social Order: Reading and Writing in Tudor and Stuart England* (Cambridge, 1980).

Cross, M. C., *The Free Grammar School of Leicester* (Leicester, 1953).

Curtis, M., *Oxford and Cambridge in Transition 1558–1642* (Oxford, 1959).

Gardiner, D., *English Girlhood at School: a Study of Women's Education through Twelve Centuries* (London, 1929).

Houston, R. A., 'The Development of Literacy: Northern England 1640–1750', *Economic History Review*, 2nd ser., 35 (1982), 199–216.

Howell, R. jun., *Puritans and Radicals in North England: Essays on the English Revolution* (Lanham, 1984).

Jewell, H. M., ' "The Bringing up of Children in Good Learning and Manners": a Survey of Secular Educational Provision in the North of England, c.1350–1550', *Northern History*, 18 (1982), 1–25.

Jordan, W. K., *Philanthropy in England 1480–1660: a Study of the Changing Pattern of English Social Aspirations* (London, 1959).

Jordan, W. K., *The Charities of London 1480–1660: the Aspirations and the Achievements of the Urban Society* (London, 1960).

Jordan, W. K., *The Forming of the Charitable Institutions of the West of England: a Study of the Changing Patterns of Social Aspirations in Bristol and Somerset 1480–1660* (Philadelphia, 1960).

Jordan, W. K., *The Charities of Rural England: the Aspirations and the Achievements of the Rural Society* (London, 1961).

Jordan, W. K., *The Social Institutions of Lancashire: a Study of the Changing Patterns of Aspirations in Lancashire 1480–1660* (Manchester, 1962).

Lawson, J., *A Town Grammar School through Six Centuries* (London, 1963).

Lawson, J., *Medieval Education and the Reformation* (London, 1967).

Leach, A. F., *English Schools at the Reformation, 1546–8* (London, 1896).

Leader, D. R., *A History of the University of Cambridge, I, The University to 1546* (Cambridge, 1988).

Leys, M. D. R., *Catholics in England 1559–1829: a Social History* (London, 1961).

Lloyd, A., *Quaker Social History 1669–1738* (London, 1950).

Loades, D., *The Reign of King Edward VI* (Bangor, 1994).

Lupton, J. H., *A Life of John Colet D. D. Dean of St Paul's and Founder of St Paul's School* (London, 1887).

McConica, J., ed., *The History of the University of Oxford, III, The Collegiate University* (Oxford, 1986).

Miner, J. N., *The Grammar Schools of Medieval England: A. F. Leach in Historiographical Perspective* (Montréal/ Kingston, 1990).

Moran, J. A. H., *Education and Learning in the City of York* (York, 1979).

Moran, J. H., *The Growth of English Schooling 1348–1548: Learning, Literacy and Laicization in pre-Reformation York Diocese* (Princeton, 1985).

Morgan, J. *Godly Learning: Puritan Attitudes towards Reason, Learning and Education 1560–1640* (Cambridge, 1986).

Orme, N., *English Schools in the Middle Ages* (London, 1973).

Orme, N., *Education in the West of England 1066–1548* (Exeter, 1976).

Orme, N., *Education and Society in Medieval and Renaissance England* (London, 1989).

Russell, E., 'The Influx of Commoners into the University of Oxford before 1581: an Optical Illusion?', *English Historical Review*, 92 (1977), 721–45.

Simon, J., *Education and Society in Tudor England* (Cambridge, 1966).

Simon, J., 'Post-Restoration Developments: Schools in the County 1660–1700' in Simon, B., ed., *Education in Leicestershire, 1540–1940: A Regional Study* (Leicester, 1968).

Simon, J., 'Town Estates and Schools in the Sixteenth and Early Seventeenth Centuries' in Simon, B., ed., *Education in Leicestershire, 1540–1940: A Regional Study* (Leicester, 1968).

Simon, J., 'Was there a Charity School Movement? The Leicestershire Evidence' in Simon, B., ed., *Education in Leicestershire, 1540–1940: A Regional Study* (Leicester, 1968).

Spufford, M., *Contrasting Communities: English Villagers in the Sixteenth and Seventeenth Centuries* (London, 1974).

Spufford, M., *Small Books and Pleasant Histories: Popular Fiction and its Readership in Seventeenth-Century England* (London, 1981).

Stephens, W. B., *Education, Literacy and Society 1830–70: the Geography of Diversity in Provincial England* (Manchester, 1987).

Stone, L., 'The Educational Revolution in England, 1560–1640', *Past and Present*, 28 (1964), 41–80.

Stone, L., 'Literacy and Education in England 1640–1900', *Past and Present*, 42 (1969), 69–139.

Stone, L., ed., *The University in Society, I, Oxford and Cambridge from the 14th to the Early 19th Century* (Princeton, 1975).

Sutherland, L. S. and Mitchell, L. G., eds, *The History of the University of Oxford, V, The Eighteenth Century* (Oxford, 1986).

Tyacke, N., ed., *The History of the University of Oxford, IV, Seventeenth-Century Oxford* (Oxford, 1997).

Vanes, J., *Education and Apprenticeship in Sixteenth-Century Bristol* (Bristol, 1982).

Vincent, W. A. L., *The State and School Education 1640–1660 in England and Wales: a Survey based on Printed Sources* (London, 1950).

Watson, F., *The English Grammar Schools to 1660: their Curriculum and Practice* (Cambridge, 1908).

Educational Aims

Alexander, M. V. C., *The Growth of English Education 1348–1648: a Social and Cultural History* (Philadelphia/London, 1990).

Axtell, J. L., ed., *The Educational Writings of John Locke: a Critical Edition with Introduction and Notes* (Cambridge, 1968).

Baker, J. H., 'The English Legal Profession, 1450–1550' in Prest, W., ed., *Lawyers in Early Modern Europe and America* (London, 1981).

Beales, A. C. F., *Education under Penalty: English Catholic Education from the Reformation to the Fall of James II 1547–1689* (London, 1963).

Ben-Amos, I. K., *Adolescence and Youth in Early Modern England* (New Haven/London, 1994).

Brooks, C. W., 'The Common Lawyers in England, c.1558–1642' in Prest, W., ed., *Lawyers in Early Modern Europe and America* (London, 1981).

Caspari, F., *Humanism and the Social Order in Tudor England* (Chicago, 1954).

Charlton, K., 'The Professions in Sixteenth-Century England', *University of Birmingham Historical Journal*, 12: 1 (1969), 20–41.

Charlton, K., 'The Education of the Professions in the Sixteenth Century' in Cook, T. G., ed., *Education and the Professions* (London, 1973).

Clarke, M. L., *Classical Education in Britain 1500–1910* (Cambridge, 1959).

Cliffe, J. T., *The Yorkshire Gentry from the Reformation to the Civil War* (London, 1969).

Clifford, D. J. H., ed., *The Diaries of Lady Anne Clifford* (Stroud, 1990).

Cobban, A. B., *The Medieval English Universities: Oxford and Cambridge to c.1500* (Aldershot, 1988).

Cressy, D., *Education in Tudor and Stuart England* (London, 1975).

Cressy, D., *Literacy and the Social Order: Reading and Writing in Tudor and Stuart England* (Cambridge, 1980).

Cressy, D., 'A Drudgery of Schoolmasters: the Teaching Profession in Elizabethan and Stuart England' in Prest, W., ed., *The Professions in Early Modern England* (London, 1987).

Curtis, M., 'The Alienated Intellectuals of Early Stuart England', *Past and Present*, 23 (1962), 25–43.

Duman, D., 'The English Bar in the Georgian Era' in Prest, W., ed., *Lawyers in Early Modern Europe and America* (London, 1981).

Fraser, A., *The Weaker Vessel: Women's Lot in Seventeenth- Century England* (London, 1989).

Fussner, F. S., *The Historical Revolution: English Historical Writing and Thought 1580–1640* (New York/London, 1962).

Gardiner, D., *English Girlhood at School: a Study of Women's Education through Twelve Centuries* (London, 1929).

Gunther, R. T., *Early Science in Cambridge* (Oxford, 1937).

Hanawalt, B. A., *Growing up in Medieval London: the Experience of Childhood in History* (Oxford, 1993).

Hexter, J. H., 'The Education of the Aristocracy in the Renaissance' in Hexter, *Reappraisals in History* (London, 1961).

Hill, C., *Intellectual Origins of the English Revolution* (Oxford, 1965).

Hughes, E., *North Country Life in the Eighteenth Century: the North-East 1700–1750* (London, 1952).

Hughes, E., *North County Life in the Eighteenth Century, II: Cumberland & Westmorland, 1700–1830* (London, 1965).

Ives, E., 'The Common Lawyers in Pre-Reformation England', *Transactions of the Royal Historical Society*, 5th series, 18 (1968), 145–73.

Ives, E. W., 'The Common Lawyers' in Clough, C. H., ed., *Profession, Vocation and Culture in later Medieval England* (Liverpool, 1982).

Jewell, H. M., 'A Notion of True Learning', *National Register of Archives Annual Report and Bulletin of the West Riding Northern Section*, 6 (1963), 14–20.

Jones, M. G., *The Charity School Movement: a Study of Eighteenth-Century Puritanism in Action* (Cambridge, 1938).

Kamm, J., *Hope Deferred: Girls' Education in English History* (London, 1965).

Kearney, H., *Origins of the Scientific Revolution* (London, 1964).

Kearney, H., *Scholars and Gentlemen: Universities and Society in pre-Industrial Britain 1500–1700* (London, 1970).

Levack, B. P., *The Civil Lawyers in England 1603–1641: a Political Study* (Oxford, 1973).

Levack, B. P., 'The English Civilians, 1500–1750' in Prest, W., ed., *Lawyers in Early Modern Europe and America* (London, 1981).

McConica, J., ed., *The History of the University of Oxford, III, The Collegiate University* (Oxford, 1986).

Morgan, J. *Godly Learning: Puritan Attitudes towards Reason, Learning and Education 1560–1640* (Cambridge, 1986).

Moscucci, O., *The Science of Women: Gynaecology and Gender in England 1800–1929* (Cambridge, 1990).

O'Day, R., *The English Clergy: the Emergence and Consolidation of a Profession, 1558–1642* (London, 1982).

O'Day, R., 'The Anatomy of a Profession: the Clergy of the Church of England' in Prest, W., ed., *The Professions in Early Modern England* (London, 1987).

Orme, N., *English Schools in the Middle Ages* (London, 1973).

Orme, N., *From Childhood to Chivalry: the Education of the English Kings and Aristocracy 1066–1530* (London, 1984).

Orpen, P. K., 'Schoolmastering as a Profession in the Seventeenth Century: the Career Patterns of the Grammar Schoolmaster', *History of Education*, 6: 3 (1977), 183–94.

Pelling, M., 'Medical Practice in Early Modern England: Trade or Profession?' in Prest, W., ed., *The Professions in Early Modern England* (London, 1987).

Pinchbeck, I. and Hewitt, M., *Children in English Society, I, From Tudor Times to the Eighteenth Century* (London, 1969).

Prest, W. R., *The Inns of Court under Elizabeth and the early Stuarts 1590–1640* (London, 1972).

Prest, W., ed., *Lawyers in Early Modern Europe and America* (London, 1981).

Prest, W., ed., *The Professions in Early Modern England* (London, 1987).

Pruett, J. H., *The Parish Clergy under the Later Stuarts: the Leicestershire Experience* (Urbana/Chicago/London, 1978).

Purvis, J. S., 'The Literacy of the late Tudor Clergy in Yorkshire' in Cuming, G. J., ed., *Studies in Church History*, 5 (Leiden, 1969), 147–65.

Robertson, J., *The Art of Letter Writing: an Essay on the Handbooks published in England during the Sixteenth and Seventeenth Centuries* (Liverpool, 1942).

Smith, J. W. A., *The Birth of Modern Education: the Contribution of the Dissenting Academies 1660–1800* (London, 1954).

Stone, L., 'The Educational Revolution in England, 1560–1640', *Past and Present*, 28 (1964), 41–80.

Stone, L., 'Literacy and Education in England 1640–1900', *Past and Present*, 42 (1969), 69–139.

Stone, L., ed., *The University in Society, I, Oxford and Cambridge from the 14th to the Early 19th Century* (Princeton, 1975).

Sutherland, L. S. and Mitchell, L. G., eds, *The History of the University of Oxford, V, The Eighteenth Century* (Oxford, 1986).

Sylvester, D. W., ed., *Educational Documents 800–1816* (London, 1970).

Tyacke, N., ed., *The History of the University of Oxford, IV, Seventeenth-Century Oxford* (Oxford, 1997).

Vanes, J., *Education and Apprenticeship in Sixteenth-Century Bristol* (Bristol, 1982).

Watson, F., *The English Grammar Schools to 1660: their Curriculum and Practice* (Cambridge, 1908).

Wide, S. M. and Morris, J. A., 'The Episcopal Licensing of Schoolmasters in the Diocese of London 1627–85', *Guildhall Miscellany* 2: 9 (1967), 392–406.

Williams, P., 'From the Reformation to the Era of Reform 1530–1850' in Buxton, J., and Williams, P., eds, *New College Oxford 1379–1979* (Oxford, 1979).

Willis, A. J. (compiler) and Merson, A. L., ed., *A Calendar of Southampton Apprenticeship Registers 1609–1740* (Southampton, 1968).

Educational Facilities

Alexander, M. V. C., *The Growth of English Education 1348–1648: a Social and Cultural History* (Philadelphia/London, 1990).

Axtell, J. L., ed., *The Educational Writings of John Locke: a Critical Edition with Introduction and Notes* (Cambridge, 1968).

Ben-Amos, I. K., *Adolescence and Youth in Early Modern England* (New Haven/London, 1994).

Black, J. B., *The British and the Grand Tour* (London, 1985).

Blodgett, H., *Centuries of Female Days: Englishwomen's Private Diaries* (Gloucester, 1989).

Brown, J. H., *Elizabethan Schooldays: an Account of the English Grammar Schools in the Second Half of the Sixteenth Century* (Oxford, 1933).

Cressy, D., 'A Drudgery of Schoolmasters: the Teaching Profession in Elizabethan and Stuart England' in Prest, W., ed., *The Professions in Early Modern England* (London, 1987).

Cross, M. C., *The Free Grammar School of Leicester* (Leicester, 1953).

Custance, R., ed., *Winchester College: Sixth-Centenary Essays* (Oxford, 1982).

Davies, W. J. F., *Teaching Reading in Early England* (London, 1973).

Dobson, E. J., *English Pronunciation 1500–1700: I, Survey of the Sources* (Oxford, 1957).

Fraser, A., *The Weaker Vessel: Women's Lot in Seventeenth- Century England* (London, 1989).

Gardiner, D., *English Girlhood at School: a Study of Women's Education through Twelve Centuries* (London, 1929).

Gibbon, E., *Memoirs of my Life and Writings*, bicentenary edn, ed. A. O. J. Cockshut and S. Constantine, using Lord Sheffield's second edition dated 1814 (Keele, 1994).

Green, V. H. H., *A History of Oxford University* (London, 1974).

Green, V. H. H., *The Commonwealth of Lincoln College 1427–1977* (Oxford, 1979).

Jones, M. G., *The Charity School Movement: a Study of Eighteenth-Century Puritanism in Action* (Cambridge, 1938).

Jordan, W. K., *Philanthropy in England 1480–1660: a Study of the Changing Pattern of English Social Aspirations* (London, 1959).

Jordan, W. K., *The Charities of London 1480–1660: the Aspirations and the Achievements of the Urban Society* (London, 1960).

Jordan, W. K., *The Forming of the Charitable Institutions of the West of England: A Study of the Changing Patterns of Social Aspirations in Bristol and Somerset 1480–1660* (Philadelphia, 1960)

Jordan, W. K., *The Charities of Rural England 1460–1660: the Aspirations and the Achievements of the Rural Society* (London, 1961).

Jordan, W. K., *The Social Institutions of Lancashire: a Study of the Changing Patterns of Aspirations in Lancashire 1480–1660* (Manchester, 1962).

Kearney, H., *Scholars and Gentlemen: Universities and Society in pre-Industrial Britain 1500–1700* (London, 1970).

Kelly, T., *A History of Adult Education in Great Britain*, 2nd edn (Liverpool, 1970).

McConica, J., ed., *The History of the University of Oxford, III, The Collegiate University* (Oxford, 1986).

MacKay, D. P. L., 'Dame schools: a Need for Review', *British Journal of Educational Studies*, 24: 1 (1976), 33–48.

McLachlan, H., *English Education under the Test Acts: being the History of the Nonconformist Academies 1662–1820* (Manchester, 1931).

Neuburg, V. E., *Popular Education in Eighteenth-Century England* (London, 1971).

O'Day, R., *Education and Society 1500–1800: the Social Foundations of Education in Early Modern Britain* (London, 1982).

Orme, N., 'Schoolmasters 1307–1509' in Clough, C. H., ed., *Profession, Vocation and Culture in later Medieval England* (Liverpool, 1982).

Pinchbeck, I. and Hewitt, M., *Children in English Society, I, From Tudor Times to the Eighteenth Century* (London, 1969).

Prest, W. R., *The Inns of Court under Elizabeth and the early Stuarts 1590–1640* (London, 1972).

Prest, W., ed., *Lawyers in Early Modern Europe and America* (London, 1981).

Prest, W., ed., *The Professions in Early Modern England* (London, 1987).

Seaborne, M., *The English School: its Architecture and Organization 1370–1870* (London, 1971).

Simon, J., 'Was there a Charity School Movement? The Leicestershire Evidence' in Simon, B., ed., *Education in Leicestershire, 1540–1940: A Regional Study* (Leicester, 1968).

Smith, J. W. A., *The Birth of Modern Education: the Contribution of the Dissenting Academies 1660–1800* (London, 1954).

Stoye, J. W., *English Travellers Abroad 1604–1667: their influence in English Society and Politics* (London, 1952).

Sutherland, L. S. and Mitchell, L. G., eds, *The History of the University of Oxford, V, The Eighteenth Century* (Oxford, 1986).

Sylvester, D. W., ed., *Educational Documents 800–1816* (London, 1970).

Tyacke, N., ed., *The History of the University of Oxford, IV, Seventeenth-Century Oxford* (Oxford, 1997).

Varley, B., *The History of Stockport Grammar School*, 2nd edn (Manchester, 1957).

Watson, F., *The English Grammar Schools to 1660: their Curriculum and Practice* (Cambridge, 1908).

White, B., ed., *The Vulgaria of John Stanbridge and the Vulgaria of Robert Whittinton* (London, 1932).

Wide, S. M. and Morris, J. A., 'The Episcopal Licensing of Schoolmasters in the Diocese of London 1627–85', *Guildhall Miscellany* 2: 9 (1967), 392–406.

Willis, A. J. (compiler) and Merson, A. L., ed., *A Calendar of Southampton Apprenticeship Registers 1609–1740* (Southampton, 1968).

Winstanley, D. A., *The University of Cambridge in the Eighteenth Century* (Cambridge, 1922).

Educational Achievements

Axtell, J. L., ed., *The Educational Writings of John Locke: a Critical Edition with Introduction and Notes* (Cambridge, 1968).

Bennett, H. S., *English Books and Readers 1558 to 1603 being a Study in the History of the Book Trade in the Reign of Eizabeth I* (Cambridge, 1965).

Bennett, H. S., *English Books and Readers 1457 to 1557 being a Study in the History of the Book Trade from Caxton to the Incorporation of the Stationers' Company*, 2nd edn (Cambridge, 1969).

Bennett, H. S., *English Books and Readers 1603 to 1640 being a Study in the History of the Book Trade in the Reigns of James I and Charles I* (Cambridge, 1970).

Burke, P., *Popular Culture in Early Modern Europe* (London, 1978).

Cressy, D., *Literacy and the Social Order: Reading and Writing in Tudor and Stuart England* (Cambridge, 1980).

Gibbon, E., *Memoirs of my Life and Writings*, bicentenary edn, ed. A. O. J. Cockshut and S. Constantine, using Lord Sheffield's second edition dated 1814 (Keele, 1994).

Gleason, J. H., *The Justices of the Peace in England 1558 to 1640: a later Eirenarcha* (Oxford, 1969).

Gunther, R. T., *Early Science in Cambridge* (Oxford, 1937).

Hill, B., ed., *The First English Feminist: Reflections upon Marriage and Other Writings by Mary Astell* (Aldershot, 1986).

Hill, C., *Intellectual Origins of the English Revolution* (Oxford, 1965).

Houston, R. A., 'The Development of Literacy: Northern England 1640–1750', *Economic History Review*, 2nd ser., 35 (1982), 199–216.

Kearney, H., *Origins of the Scientific Revolution* (London, 1964).

Perry, R., *The Celebrated Mary Astell: an Early English Feminist* (Chicago/London, 1986).

Rose, M. B., 'Gender, Genre and History: Seventeenth-Century Englishwomen and the Art of Autobiography' in Rose, ed., *Women in the Middle Ages and Renaissance* (Syracuse, 1986).

Schofield, R. S., 'The Measurement of Literacy in Pre-Industrial England' in Goody, J., ed., *Literacy in Traditional Societies* (Cambridge, 1968).

Simon, J., 'Post-Restoration Developments: Schools in the County 1660–1700' in Simon, B., ed., *Education in Leicestershire, 1540–1940: A Regional Study* (Leicester, 1968).

Spence, R. T., *Lady Anne Clifford, Countess of Pembroke, Dorset and Montgomery 1590–1676* (Stroud, 1997).

Spufford, M., *Contrasting Communities: English Villagers in the Sixteenth and Seventeenth Centuries* (London, 1974).

Spufford, M., *Small Books and Pleasant Histories: Popular Fiction and its Readership in Seventeenth-Century England* (London, 1981).

Stone, L., 'The Educational Revolution in England, 1560–1640', *Past and Present*, 28 (1964), 41–80.

Stone, L., 'Literacy and Education in England 1640–1900', *Past and Present*, 42 (1969), 69–139.

Todd, J., ed., *A Dictionary of British and American Women Writers 1660–1800* (London, 1987).

The Broader Perspective: the British Isles, Western Europe and North America

Ariès, P., *Centuries of Childhood* (Harmondsworth, 1973).

Atkinson, N., *Irish Education: a History of Educational Institutions* (Dublin, 1969).

Auchmuty, J. J., *Irish Education: a Historical Survey* (Dublin/London, 1937).

Boli, J., *New Citizens for a New Society: the Institutional Origins of Mass Schooling in Sweden* (Oxford, 1989).

Brockliss, L. W. B., *French Higher Education in the Seventeenth and Eighteenth Centuries: a Cultural History* (Oxford, 1987).

Burke, P., *Popular Culture in Early Modern Europe* (London, 1978).

Butterfield, H., *The Origins of Modern Science* (London, 1962).

Cannay, N., 'The Formation of the Irish Mind: Religion, Politics and Gaelic Irish Literature 1580–1750', *Past and Present*, 95 (1982), 90–116.

Dowling, P. J., *The Hedge Schools of Ireland* (London, 1935).

Foster, R. F., *Modern Ireland 1600–1972* (London, 1988).

Friedrichs, C. R., 'Whose House of Learning? Some thoughts on German Schools in post-Reformation Germany', *History of Education Quarterly*, 22 (1982), 371–7.

Furet, F. and Ozouf, J., *Reading and Writing: Literacy in France from Calvin to Jules Ferry* (Cambridge, 1982).

Galenson, D. 'Literacy and the Social Origins of Some Early Americans', *Historical Journal*, 22: 1 (1979), 75–91.

Gawthrop, R. and Strauss, G., 'Protestantism and Literacy in Early Modern Germany', *Past and Present*, 104 (1984), 31–55.

Goody, J., ed., *Literacy in Traditional Societies* (Cambridge, 1968).

Green, L., 'The Education of Women in the Reformation', *History of Education Quarterly*, 19 (1979), 93–116.

Grendler, P. F., *Schooling in Renaissance Italy: Literacy and Learning 1300–1600* (Baltimore/London, 1989).

Houston, R. A., *Scottish Literacy and the Scottish Identity: Illiteracy and Society in Scotland and Northern England, 1600–1800* (Cambridge, 1985).

Houston, R. A., *Literacy in Modern Europe: Culture and Education 1500–1800* (London/New York, 1988).

Huppert, G., *Public Schools in Renaissance France* (Urbana/Chicago, 1984).

Jones, M. G., *The Charity School Movement: a Study of Eighteenth-Century Puritanism in Action* (Cambridge, 1938).

Kagan, R. L., *Students and Society in Early Modern Spain* (Baltimore/London, 1974).

Knight, L. S., *Welsh Independent Grammar Schools to 1600* (Newtown, 1926).

Littlefield, G. E., *Early Schools and Schoolbooks of New England* (New York, 1904).

Lockridge, K. A., *Literacy in Colonial New England: an Inquiry into the Social Context of Literacy in the Early Modern West* (New York, 1974).

Morrison, S. E., *The Founding of Harvard College* (Cambridge, Mass./London, 1935).

Prest, W., ed., *Lawyers in Early Modern Europe and America* (London, 1981).

Ridder-Symoens, H. de, ed., *A History of the University in Europe I: Universities in the Middle Ages* (Cambridge, 1992).

Ridder-Symoens, H. de, ed., *A History of the University in Europe II: Universities in Early Modern Europe 1500–1800* (Cambridge, 1996).

Smout, T. C., *A History of the Scottish People 1560–1830* (London, 1987).

Strauss, G., *Luther's House of Learning: Indoctrination of the Young in the German Reformation* (Baltimore/London, 1978).

Sylvester, D. W., ed., *Educational Documents 800–1816* (London, 1970).

Williams, G., *Recovery, Re-orientation and Reformation: Wales c.1415–1642* (Oxford, 1987).

Williams, J. L. and Hughes, G. R., eds, *The History of Education in Wales*, I (Swansea, 1978).

INDEX

217

Astell, Mary, vii, 12, 106, 133–4, 136
  Ralph, 106
astronomy, 20, 31, 55, 59, 62, 85,
  114, 132, 159, 161, 178, 187
Atterbury, Francis, 133
Augsburg, 57
Avignon, 175
Aylmer, John, 59
Ayr, 157, 161
  grammar school, 159
Ayrshire, 158

Bacon, Francis, 122, 131, 142
Baker, Humphrey, 86
Balkans, 125
Ballard, George, 97
Banbury, grammar school, 11
  hospital of St John, 3
Bangor, 164
Banister, John, 146
Banks, Caleb, 104
Baptists, and education, 38, 68, 117,
  180
bardic schools, 168
Barlow, Edward, 94, 108
Barrow, 38
Bassett, Mary, 11
Bavaria, 181
Beaufort, Lady Margaret, 17
Bede, 4
Bedford, earl of, 11
Beetham, 47
Behn, Aphra, 133
Bellingham, Samuel, 188
benefactors, educational, 22, 29, 47,
  50–1, 52, 95, 112, 181, 187
Bentham, Thomas, 61
Berkhamsted, 100
Berners, Lord, 142
Besançon, 124
Bevan, Bridget, 167
Bible, 9, 15, 18, 26, 27, 34, 38, 45,
  59, 62, 68, 95, 101, 118, 126,
  128, 142, 145, 148, 149, 151,
  152, 159, 160, 165, 166, 167,
  169, 180, 185, 187, 188
  Authorised Version of, 30, 140, 145

bibliothèque bleue, 171, 181, 185
Birmingham, 102
Birstall, 100
Bishop Auckland, 36
Bishopsgate (workhouse), 95
Black Book of the Household, 53
Black, Joseph, 161, 162
Blackstone, William, 176
boarding schools, 7, 32, 41, 57, 93,
  94, 103–6, 136, 184
Bodley, Sir Thomas, 25, 114
Bolingbroke, Henry St John,
  Viscount, 40
Bologna, 175
bookkeeping, 85, 86, 158, 170
Boston, Lincs., 101
  Mass., 188, 190
  Viscount, 124
botany, 78, 115, 172, 176, 187
Boulton, Matthew, 127
Bourges, 183
Boyle, Robert, 35, 78, 131, 173
Bray, Dr Thomas, 128, 166
Brechin, 156
Brecon, 164
Brerewood, Edward, 31
Briggs, Henry, 31
Brinsley, John, 82, 95, 189
Bristol, 42, 44, 75, 84, 97, 108–9,
  117
  Red Maids' School, 95, 96
Britannia, see Camden
Bucer, Martin, 26
Buckrose, 61
Budé, Guillaume, 184
Bull, John, 31
Bullokar's Book at Large, 98
Bulmer, 61
Bunyan, John, 150
  his father, 150, 152, 153
Burke, Edmund, 172
Burns, Robert, 160, 162
Burnsall, 100, 190
Burton books, 177
Bury St Edmunds, 49
  Free School, 98, 100
business training, 49